PULATION PRESSURES:
MIGRATION AND GOVERNMENT
LATE NINETEENTH-CENTURY
ITAIN

eteenth-century English society was drastically and
idly "modernized" by the irresistible triad of population
wth, urbanization, and industrialization. This book fo-
es on a characteristically Victorian attempt to control
pace and nature of these social changes, not by birth
trol or direct state planning, but by the encouragement
a massive emigration to the British colonies. The author
chosen for his investigation the relatively neglected late
torian period, when "state emigration"—a panacea of the
ngry Forties—was revived in response to the economic
pression, new imperialism, and socialism of the times.
aat follows is the reconstruction of a major pressure
up largely forgotten because of the failure of its cam-
gn. State emigration brings together a number of aspects
Victorian society—labor unions and upper class social
science, Malthusianism and state socialism, imperialism
l democracy. Beginning with the surprising attempt by a
nbination of working class radicals and imperialists to
ure state assistance for emigration in the 1860s, the au-
or follows the lobby through two decades and concludes
th the major emigrationist campaign which closely fol-
ved the franchise reform and socialist riots of the mid-
80s. The struggle of the National Association for State
lonization illustrates the Victorian quandary over the
uses of poverty and unemployment, and the proper role
philanthropy and the state in social amelioration. This
dy is also of interest as a careful recreation of a typical
ctorian pressure group. The author's detailed examina-
n of the organization and tactics of the state emigration
bby expands our knowledge of the politics of class-
llaboration in a critical period of transition, while his
reful analysis of membership lists gives us insight into
e composition of late Victorian political and philan-
ropic elites.

sistant Professor of History at Tufts
ved degrees from Southern Metho-
nford University, and has held a
he University of Pittsburgh and a
at the University of London. Pro-
ured and published on emigration
roups. He is presently engaged in a
..es—parks, fountains, etc.—in Victo-
...., ... is compiling a directory of those who
devoted themselves to improving the quality of nineteenth-
century British life.

POPULATION PRESSURES:
EMIGRATION AND GOVERNMENT
IN LATE NINETEENTH-CENTURY BRITAIN

Assisted emigrants seen off to Canada by gentlemen of the East End Emigration Fund, 1870 (Source: *Illustrated London News,* May 7, 1870)

Population Pressures: Emigration and Government in Late Nineteenth-Century Britain

Howard L. Malchow

Department of History, Tufts University, Medford, Massachusetts

The Society for the Promotion of Science and Scholarship Inc.
(a nonprofit corporation)
SPOSS INC.
835 Page Mill Road, Palo Alto, California
94304 USA

The Society for the Promotion of Science and
Scholarship Inc. Palo Alto, California, USA

International Standard Book Number: 0-930664-02-7
Library of Congress Catalog Card Number: 79-64166

PRINTED AND BOUND IN THE UNITED STATES OF AMERICA

To the memory of my father,
Captain Howard LeRoy Malchow, U.S.A.F.

ACKNOWLEDGEMENTS

I have received much assistance from many people. My first thanks, however, must go to Peter Stansky, but for whose unflagging good spirits and encouragement I should never have finished. I must also thank Paul Seaver for his most helpful criticisms of an early draft, and for his apparently inexhaustible reservoir of patient kindness extended to me over many years. What merits this book may have are chiefly theirs.

I am deeply obligated to the Earl of Meath for his kind hospitality at Castle Killruddery and permission to consult the papers of his grandfather, the 12th Earl. And to Dr. John Springhall I owe considerable thanks for bringing the most important parts of that collection to my attention. Similar thanks must be extended to the Duke of Argyll, and J. T. Kennedy Short, Chamberlain of Argyll. Much kindness was shown to me by the archivist of the Huntingdonshire County Record Office, Mr. P. J. Locke, the librarians and staff of the Royal Commonwealth Society Library, the Lambeth Palace Library, and the Guildhall Library, and the many others in British public archives who preserve a legendary pleasantness in the face of the often unreasonable demands of rushed foreign researchers.

This research could not have been undertaken or completed without the generosity of the Leverhulme Trust Fund and the John Wetter Memorial Fund. I must also thank Mr. Timothy Toohey for his assistance in preparing the illustrations. Finally, a special debt is owed to Professor I. M. Cumpston, whose kindness several years ago helped a young graduate student new to England to find his feet.

H. L. MALCHOW

CONTENTS

ABBREVIATIONS LIST

B.C.E.S.	British and Colonial Emigration Society
Cab.	Cabinet Papers
C.E.S.	Central Emigration Society
C.O.	Colonial Office
D.N.B.	Dictionary of National Biography
E.I.O.	Emigrants' Information Office
E.E.E.F.	East End Emigration Fund
L.G.B.	Local Government Board
M.H.	Ministry of Health
N.E.A.S.	National Emigration Aid Society
N.E.L.	National Emigration League
P.P.	Parliamentary Papers
S.D.F.	Social Democratic Federation
S.P.C.K.	Society for Promoting Christian Knowledge
S.P.G.	Society for the Propagation of the Gospel
T.U.C.	Trades Union Congress
W.E.L.	Workmen's Emigration League

Chapter 1.   Introduction

each year some hundreds of thousands of Queen Victoria's subjects saw "the Last of England" from the decks of over-age sailing ships and cheap steamers. This unprecedented exodus naturally had a significant, if somewhat obscure, impact on the social, economic, and demographic structures of life in England, but the surprising thing, in retrospect, must be that a mass migration of this magnitude was accompanied by a near-consensus of approval from contemporaries. In the second half of the century the annual attrition of the most vigorous part of the nation reached a level quite comparable, in numbers at least, to that of the First World War.[1]

Of course, emigration was a continuous and generally undramatic dispersal. Englishmen were not driven from their homes by Cossacks, plague, famine, or religious fanaticism. Most left privately and quietly, without fanfare, as individuals bound for self-improvement rather than a new Jerusalem. And their hundreds of thousands were more than replaced each year by the remarkable nineteenth-century birthrate, which far exceeded not only the numbers of outward-bound, but also the grotesquely large infant mortality of Victorian England. Con-

1

sequently, many observers saw in the great migration not a fearful social malaise, but a providential mechanism saving the nation from Malthusian disaster. For them, the question of importance was whether the natural outflow was sufficient, or whether the health of the nation might not benefit from a larger and more rationally directed exodus.

This work is not a study of emigration *per se,* but the politics of state emigration. The time frame chosen is not that of the relatively well-known emigration schemes of the early-Victorian era, but rather the second half of the century when the urban-industrial economy assumed a more mature national integration and achieved at least the acceptance of familiarity. At this stage, in the context of a new imperialism and growing demands for social reform at home, the population "problem" had to be met, discussed, and resolved once again.

In the mid-Victorian era, liberalism had quieted debate with the comfortable promise of a naturally regulated system of emigration, finely adjusted by an invisible hand to changing economic necessity. In the late-Victorian period, however, the advocates of state-assisted emigration or colonization discovered new arguments in the relative economic decline of the "great depression." This gave renewed life and voice to an old panacea. While ultimately a failure, the reanimated state-emigration cause attracted a following which was large and diverse— though curiously weak in leverage. Beginning with considerable support from the radical Left, state emigration ironically ended up in this century as the fad of Tory press-lord imperialists. But the significant fact, perhaps, is not that state emigrationists of both the Right and the Left ultimately got trapped in the eddies and backwaters of politics, but that their cause was an issue which demanded to be faced and answered before "modern" collectivist politics, centered in the semi-autarchic corporate state of the twentieth century, could emerge. A logical corollary of the defeat of state emigration was the creation of barriers to casual immigration, a foundation stone of the closed welfare state that began to take shape in England in the decade before the First World War.

Public interest in state emigration is at least as old as Richard Hakluyt's advice of 1584 that, by settling paupers in America, Elizabethan England could solve its vagrancy problem, create colonial markets for its goods, and increase employment at home.[2] By the Industrial Revolution, settlements for trade and defense were still being encouraged in Nova Scotia and Canada. These were primarily military settlements which were intended to secure conquered territory while providing naval and other vital supplies to the mother country. A Royal Proclamation of 1763 offered free grants of American land to disbanded British officers and men. At the close of the American Revolution, loyalists and demobilized men were offered similar terms. The program was encouraged and expanded by Governor Simcoe, who feared aggression from the United States. The Canadian colonies provided valuable sources of supply during the Napoleonic wars, and government resorted again to military colonization in Canada and at the Cape after 1815.[3]

In the dawning liberalism of the early nineteenth century, however, colony-planting, for reasons of security and protected markets, fell out of favour, and the field of colonization was soon left to private enterprise. In 1826, the government sold two million acres of Canadian land to a commercial company. Military settlements did not

become a general topic of debate again until the imperialists of the 1880s and 1890s revived the concept and supported pensioner colonization in New Zealand and South
Africa.

Though settlements for reasons of defense and a controlled market lost favor, emigration to solve social problems at home gained ground during the bad times which
followed the war with France. In Scotland, clearances to
make room for sheep-raising and sport had already resulted in a considerable migration out of the Highlands.
The breakup of the clan system was encouraged by landowners, who themselves occasionally assisted their tenants to emigrate. A similar policy came to prevail in
Ireland, where landlords assisted tenants to leave in order
to consolidate holdings—especially after 1829, when dis-
enfranchisement of the Irish forty-shilling freeholders
ended their political value.

In England, concern over the dramatic growth of population, the grim predictions of Malthus, agrarian violence,
and the rising cost of poor-relief broke down the official
resistance to casual migration. In 1824, the repeal of the
Combination Acts made it legal for an artisan to leave the
country without special permission. In 1826–7, a select
committee to consider state emigration was dominated
by the Under-Secretary for War and the Colonies, Sir
Robert Wilmot-Horton, whose energetic advocacy of a
large emigration of paupers to British colonies set the
tenor of much of the public agitation.

The Wilmot-Horton schemes and the Wakefield movement, which was both an outgrowth from and a reaction
to them, excited much attention at the time.[4] When the
emigration lobby re-emerged later in the century, it owed
much of its rhetoric and program to the campaigns waged
by Wilmot-Horton and Wakefield in the 1820s, 1830s and
1840s.

Wilmot-Horton succeeded Henry Goulburn as Under-Secretary at a time, 1821, when economic distress widely thought to have resulted from the increase in population, had provoked social disruption, radicalism, and violence. Shortly after joining the Colonial Office, he drew up a plan for colonization, the basis for which was the use of the poor-rates to finance the emigration and settlement of paupers in Canada. Emigration on a large scale would reduce the rates, or local property taxes, in the long run and push up wage levels. Two experiments, planned by Wilmot-Horton, were carried out in 1823 and 1825, at a cost of about £22 a head. These were followed by a select committee which the Under-Secretary chaired and which reported favorably. Wilmot-Horton got the support of Malthus and the political economist Nassau Senior, and prepared to introduce an Emigration Bill. He was, however, unable to get the government to move farther than the inclusion of emigration-assistance clauses in the new Poor Law of 1834. This Act, extended to Ireland in 1838, enabled ratepayers of any parish to use up to one-half the average yearly rate to aid the emigration of the poor. Though the central theme of Wilmot-Horton's proposals was adopted, it was not mandated, and local authorities refused, by and large, to use their emigration powers.

Meanwhile, Wilmot-Horton became involved in a heated controversy over colonization methods with Edward Gibbon Wakefield and members of the National Colonization Society, organized in 1830 to agitate his scheme. Wakefield had published anonymously in 1829 *A Letter from Sydney.* This analysis of the economic problems besetting Australian settlements, and his subsequent study *The Art of Colonization,* enjoyed a wide popularity. Wakefield blamed the failure of the Australian colonies to develop, on the government's policy of selling Crown lands too cheaply. Colonial prosperity, he claimed, depended on an adequate concentration of labour to encourage capital investment necessary for development. At the same time, England suffered from a lack of capital markets, and needed to discover investment fields abroad to prevent falling interest rates. A "sufficient price" for colonial land would prevent labour from dispersing too quickly, and the land revenues could be used to assist immigration from England.

Eventually attracting strong support from a number of political economists, Wakefield and his friends launched a public campaign to urge the government to adopt his proposals for a "systematic colonization." At first his relations with Wilmot-Horton, who joined the National Colonization Society in 1830, were friendly. Differences, however, soon developed. Wilmot-Horton proposed only such emigration as would relieve the pressure of able-bodied paupers on the rates in England—the cost to be borne by English parishes. Wakefield advocated a scheme in which the colonies regulated emigration to suit their own economies, and paid for such assistance themselves. Meeting stiff resistance from the Colonial Office, and especially from the Permanent Under-Secretary James Stephen, Wakefield came to advocate colonial self-rule and control of Crown lands in order to achieve his system, while Wilmot-Horton's scheme demanded a strong imperial connection and the retention of Crown lands by the British government.

Wakefield, with his strong extra-parliamentary organization, his colonial contacts, and a working relationship with Radicals close to government, succeeded in gaining ministerial support. In 1831, he procured the discontinuance of free land-grants in New South Wales. In 1834, he and his supporters organized a South Australian Association which, two years later, secured the adoption of elements of his scheme in that colony. Dissatisfied with the South Australian experiment, however, the Wakefield group then turned their eyes to New Zealand, where a New Zealand Land Company established settlements along the lines of Wakefield's suggestions from 1839 to 1846. This resulted in a vitriolic debate with evangelical missionaries and Stephen, who were determined to protect the Maori. The Colonial Reform Association, which grew out of Wakefield's battle with "Mr. Mothercountry," lobbied throughout the next decade for responsible government for British colonies, including colonial control of Crown lands.

In 1836, the government had created a select committee on colonial land. This committee supported Wakefield's views, and the next year, Lord Glenelg appointed T. F. Elliot Agent General for Emigration. Elliot, under the stimulus of Wakefield's South Australian experiment, encouraged the government to try his scheme in New South Wales and Van Diemen's Land. In 1840, Lord John Russell replaced the office of Agent General with a Colonial Land and Emigration Commission, which functioned in the two following decades to assist emigration with colonial land revenues, and to oversee emigration traffic in accordance with the Passenger Acts. Deeply influenced by Wakefield, the Commissioners subsidized emigration but did not advocate a large transplantation of paupers. By 1865, the Commission's assistance all but ceased, as colonies secured control of their own lands and appointed their own emigration agents in London.[5]

The 1840s had been a period of colonization mania: "Plans, schemes, proposals filled the printing shops, flooded the Colonial Office, and washed over into Parliament."[6] Organized pressure was brought to bear on government by emigration philanthropists, colonial land speculators,[7] and humanitarians concerned about the conditions of emigrant passage—the overcrowding, lack of sanitation, sexual promiscuity, sharp practices, and careless management which marked emigrant traffic before steam reduced passage-time dramatically. Humanitarians were successful in securing legislation and the appointment of an inspectorate with wide discretionary power.[8] Those interested in state-financed emigration, especially as the "hungry forties" yielded to a palmier decade, were less successful. Lord Shaftesbury was able to get only limited support for his Ragged Schools emigration scheme. The dominant ideology of *laissez faire,* reinforced by mid-century economic prosperity and social peace, created a formidable opposition.

Prospects of success for the state-emigration lobby throughout the century naturally rested to a large extent on the severity and duration of economic crisis in Great Britain, and on the size and nature of unassisted emigration. The relevant statistics for the second half of the century provide a context for the narrative of the emigration lobby. In the chart below are represented together unemployment and emigration fluctuations (see Figure 1).[9]

It is at once apparent that emigration lags behind decline in trade and employment, and occurs in greatest volume after, rather than during, the periods of greatest distress. A number of reasons have been adduced to explain this well-known phenomenon.[10] What is significant here is that agitation for state emigration, which was set in motion during the worst periods of depression, frequently faced a difficult situation. Before it got properly under way, critics could claim that trade and employment were improving and that unassisted emigration was in-

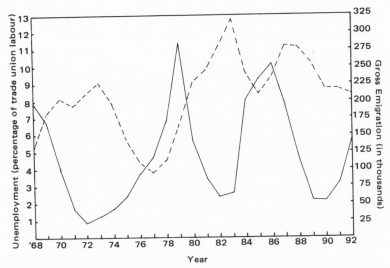

Figure 1 British unemployment (*solid line*) and emigration (*dashed line*), 1868 to 1892

creasing as well—without government assistance. Thus, the National Emigration League, born out of the sharp crisis of 1868, began its campaign in 1870, only to find the ground cut from under its feet by rapidly falling unemployment and rising voluntary emigration. Similarly, the National Association for Promoting State Colonization, which began its most serious campaign in 1886 in a trough of depression, did not succeed in getting a Select Committee appointed until 1889, by which time unemployment was down to 2.1 percent and emigration had risen to over 250,000 a year.

The emigration lobby of the late-Victorian period required a more sustained economic crisis to push its scheme home. But if its campaign was vitiated by the cyclical nature of economic woes, it nevertheless achieved a deep appeal among some sections of the community. It found strong support among organized labour, metropolitan clergy, middle-class professionals, and the landed aristocracy.

The late-Victorian agitation for state emigration and colonization is not as well-known as the movements for imperial federation or tariff reform, with with which it had much in common, but it was long-lived and did achieve a response, albeit modest, from government. Reconstruction of the lobby promised to be of interest on a number of levels. It is an example of "cause lobbying" in an important transitional period for the British political system, and discloses something of the characteristic style of approach to government by each of the major interests which were involved. Further, the Reform Acts of 1867 and 1885 transformed politics by creating a mass electorate. Lobbying, with its origins in an earlier era, had to adapt to a new world of party politics which tended to reduce the leverage of the independent amateur. Perhaps partly in response to these changes, the movement also reflects a strong characteristic of much late-Victorian pressure-group activity: its campaign was grounded in class collaboration rather than a sectional approach to politics. The story of its struggle reflects the ambiguities of leadership and objectives begged by such an approach.

In the realm of ideas, the movement casts some light on the nature of the neo-Malthusianism of the 1870s and 1880s. State emigration as a solution to population pressure was not Malthusianism pure and simple, but a kind of late-Victorian heresy which assumed—on the basis of increasing demographic evidence—that rising standards would not automatically produce a rising birth rate. It also illustrates a connection between the new imperialism of the period and collectivist social reform. For some, state emigration was an obvious "social imperialist" solution to racially degrading urban conditions at home, a means of undercutting socialist radicals by alleviating social distress, an alternative to reforms of a more radical nature (like land reform), and a boon to imperial defense by populating thinly settled colonial areas with potential conscripts. But, paradoxically, state emigration could also appeal to some liberals. Aid to help British labour migrate to jobs in the colonies can be compared with other Radical-Liberal programs, like the Parliamentary train, intended to rationalize and smooth out labour adjustments to the fluctuating demands of the world market. It might be considered, as the president of the National Association for Promoting State Colonization pointed out, merely the oiling by the government of the economic timepiece which naturally regulated the relationship between labour and capital.

In the following pages an attempt is made, not only to describe the politics of the emigration movement in some detail, but also to unravel, as far as possible, the complex tangle of motives and interests which were involved in this major effort to persuade the state to "build a bridge to the colonies."

Notes to Chapter 1

1. Emigration from British ports for the period 1880 to 1884 averaged over 260,000 a year, with a peak in 1883 of 320,118 (just under 1 percent of the total population). These figures, however, are only approximate; official statistics ignore return passages and, therefore, somewhat exaggerate actual emigration. See N. H. Carrier and J. R. Jeffrey, *External Migration, A Study of the Available Statistics, 1815–1950* (London, 1953).

2. Richard Hakluyt, *Discourse on Western Planting* ([1st edn., 1584] ed. Charles Dean, Cambridge, Mass., 1877), Chs. III-IV, pp. 19–44.
3. Stanley C. Johnson, *A History of Emigration* (London, 1914), 227–8 and Chapter 1; Helen I. Cowan, *British Emigration to British North America* (Toronto, 1961), Chapters 1–3.
4. R. C. Mills, *The Colonization of Australia (1829–42): The Wakefield Experiment in Empire Building* (London, 1915), and H. J. M. Johnston, *British Emigration Policy 1815–30* (Oxford, 1972).
5. Fred H. Hitchins, *The Colonial Land and Emigration Commission* (Philadelphia, 1931).
6. *Ibid.*, 290.
7. The most active of the spokesmen for this interest was probably Dr. Thomas Rolph, whose agitation in the 1840s prefigures, in many respects, that of J. H. Boyd and the National Association 40 years later. See W. S. Shepperson, *British Emigration to North America* (Minneapolis, 1957), 42, and Cowan, 123–6.
8. See Oliver MacDonagh, *A Pattern of Government Growth, 1800–60* (London, 1961).
9. B. R. Mitchell and Phyllis Deane, *Abstract of British Historical Statistics* (Cambridge, 1962), 50 and 64; A. F. Burns and W. C. Mitchell, *Measuring Business Cycles* (New York, 1946), 79. The unemployment line represents the figures from certain British trade unions, based on their expenditure for unemployment benefits. The emigration line represents gross outward movement from the United Kingdom. After the mid-1850s, Irish emigration began to fall, while that for England, Wales and Scotland rose.
10. See W. A. Carrothers, *Emigration from the British Isles* (London, 1929), 297–8, and R. T. Appleyard, *British Emigration to Australia* (Toronto, 1964), Chapter 6. Modern study seems to show that, while the "emigration threshold" may be crossed during bad times, most individuals require at least two years to follow up their decision with positive action.

Chapter 2. The National Emigration League

A significant movement for state emigration re-emerged in England on the heels of the economic difficulties of the 1860s and the Second Reform Act. While in some ways a continuation of the early Victorian "systematic colonization" agitation,[1] it was on the other side of the plateau of mid-century prosperity and, like the imperial federation movement, was a response to some waning of faith in inevitable social and economic progress. It testified to a growing imperialist sentiment in some quarters, but also to growing concern with the organization and effectiveness of urban philanthropy and to rising working-class hopes that partial enfranchisement in 1867 would lead to some expansion of state responsibility for the standard of life.

In the late 1860s, the tenor of the emigration movement was somewhat radical. There was a clear connection between the National Emigration League, organized in December, 1869, and the largely working-class Reform League of 1865 which fought for extension of the franchise to urban labour. Edmond Beales, president of the

Reform League, and George Potter, who helped organize it, were both active in the emigration movement. State emigration was a solution to the condition-of-England problem which was grounded in the idea of community responsibility and action rather than self-help.

The National Emigration League has been seen as "vaguely connected" with the "incipient Imperial movement" called into being during the furor over Granville's colonial policy.[2] But it was more than this implies. Emigration as a solution to social distress was not a monopoly of the new imperialists,[3] and the League's membership reflects the type of class collaboration which was typical of much of the moderate reformism of the time.

2.1 *The Cotton Famine*

The reappearance of the state-emigration movement in 1869 reflected concern over a steadily increasing birth rate and the migration of agricultural and Irish labour into English urban areas.[4] But the immediate impulse came from unemployment in the textile industry. Cotton spinning suffered in the 1860s from an uncertain market and, during the American Civil War, from a shortage of raw materials.[5] The result was a high level of unemployment in Lancashire which led labour to seek relief in appeals for public works and emigration assistance.

According to a contemporary observer, the question of emigration assistance was revived in 1863 when New Zealand, and later Queensland and Victoria, offered to grant funds for passages of distressed workers: "operatives' meetings suddenly became numerous, at which resolutions in favour of emigration were unanimously adopted."[6] The well-publicized plight of the cotton workers encouraged philanthropists from all over the country to advocate a large-scale assisted emigration. Charles Kingsley and William Ferrand, a Tory MP, called on government to assist those who wished to leave. Charles Villiers, president of the Poor-Law Board, however, refused to countenance such schemes, deferring to the requirements of "the large amount of capital in the country."[7] Instead, government relied on a reform of the Poor-Law system: the Union Relief Act of 1862 and the Union Chargeability Act of 1865, which allowed labourers to claim poor-relief outside their home parishes.

The Central Relief Committee, supported by the employers, and the Mansion House Relief Committee also refused to devote their funds to emigration. When the Blackburn operatives petitioned the Mansion House Committee it agreed that a sound case could be made for assisted emigration but refused to divert any of its resources for that purpose.[8] R. Arthur Arnold echoed the sentiments of most manufacturers and many economists when he wrote (in 1864) that a large emigration of skilled men would seriously damage the profitability of industry.[9] The secretary of the Cotton Supply Association claimed that the emigration of 50,000 workers could involve a loss to the trade of £ 4,000,000 a year.[10] In the face of this intransigence, a number of organizations were established to aid the operatives to emigrate: the Lancashire and Queensland Co-operative Emigration Society, the National Colonial Emigration Society, and the Emigrants' Aid Society among others. The Queensland and Victoria Agents General arranged for the emigration of several hundreds. In the first six months of 1863, over 2000 operatives were helped abroad through private efforts.[11]

Rioting at Stalybridge in March of 1863 was a spur to more generous public assistance and general interest in the "emigration question."[12] The Mansion House Committee now voted £ 5,000 "to establish the nucleus of an emigration fund" which was handed out mostly in capitation grants of one or two pounds per person.[13] The men themselves continued to press for help. In September, 1864, the Associated Cotton Spinners told the country that "it is only by emigration that the position of the working classes can be improved."[14] Nevertheless, the opposition of the employers, general doubts about the prospects of factory workers on the colonial frontier, and prevailing economic doctrine prevented a large national program.

It was during the Lancashire distress that George Potter, a labour leader well known for his part in the building-trades dispute of 1859 and editor of the radical newspaper *The Beehive,* began to put forward the idea of state emigration as a working-class right. He protested that Crown lands were turned over to colonial governments "for nothing" when they might be used to settle unemployed Englishmen. In part, his vision was a revival of the Torrens-Wakefield formula for a fresh combination of land, capital, and labour in the colonies through the "union of commercial principles with philanthropy" which would produce economic health all round. A small company might be formed to test the scheme if government would give the land.[15] There was little response to these ideas, and Potter transferred his attack to the reformation of Parliament which, if "fairly representing all classes ... would provide through our almost unlimited colonial lands homes for all who are able and willing to work."[16]

In fact the government did make at least a token effort to promote emigration during the period of greatest distress. In 1863, the Colonial Secretary, the Duke of Newcastle, sent a circular to colonial governments requesting their opinions on the possibility of increasing emigration assistance.[17] Replies were "unenthusiastic". Newly self-governing colonies with a broad suffrage were anxious not to antagonize organized labour, and colonial trade unions loudly protested dilution of the labour market with assisted emigrants. One response was for emigrationists to emphasize "colonization" as distinct from "mere emigration." The idea of placing the unemployed directly on the land, which was not a part of the earlier Wakefield scheme, was intended to allay colonial fears of a flooded labour market and soaring poor-rates. The distinction between emigration and colonization, however, appeared superficial to many. Since 1834 Poor-Law guardians had had considerable powers to assist emigration (with Board approval), but had always been reluctant to use them.[18] During the worst of the cotton famine, Villiers met with colonial agents to discuss a more extensive application of the rates to emigration assistance. This appeared to be pauper emigration in its crudest form, and the agents were opposed "to a man".[19]

The other public body with powers to assist emigration, the Colonial Land and Emigration Commission, had been created in 1840 to apply revenues from the sale of colonial lands to emigration assistance. By the 1860s, however, its function was largely bureaucratic and regulatory. The white settlement colonies gained control of most of their waste lands in the 1850s and 1860s, and the Commission continued its dwindling existence as a collector of statistics and colonial information, and as enforcer of the Passenger Acts. It was allowed to pass out of existence in 1878 through nonappointment of retiring members, and the last Commissioner, Clinton Murdoch, was strongly opposed to any form of systematic emigration to relieve English distress.[20]

On the other hand, the period was a lively one in the sphere of private activity. Within two years (1867–1868) four organizations for aiding emigration from distressed areas were established in London: the East End Emigration Fund Committee (E.E.E.F.), the British and Colonial Emigration Society (B.C.E.S.), the East London Family Emigration Society, and the Clerkenwell Emigration Club.[21] The latter two are typical of many of the Victorian self-help societies which had sprung up since the 1830s.[22] They were generally local and possessed very limited funds. The E.E.E.F. and the B.C.E.S., however, form something of a departure. They were large, permanent institutions created to find and organize some of the vast charitable resources available in the country at large. The B.C.E.S., with strong evangelical support, was a creation of a Mansion House conference in 1867 which met to consider the relief of unemployed shipwrights in the London area. The E.E.E.F., which later worked in conjunction with the Charity Organization Society, was more independent of City officialdom, though it, too, benefited from Mansion House charity drives. Together the two organizations managed to assist several thousands annually.[23]

2.2 *Philanthropic Emigration and a League of Societies*

The National Emigration League, a coalition of members of several of these private societies, was born out of a brief period of energetic agitation in 1869. It drew support from a cross section of society, less perhaps due to a sharp increase in real distress than to a public psychology of uncertainty—the result of the slow and spasmodic recovery from the financial crisis of 1866, and a general feeling that the exceptional boom years were past. Philanthropists, trade unionists, imperial federationists, and the promoters of commercial colonization companies came together to advocate government support in the spring of 1869.

The government itself drew attention to the possible relief of distress by means of state emigration when, during April, May, and June, it gave discharged workers from its dockyards and the arsenal at Woolwich free passages to America in troop ships. In all, 1704 of those laid off were so assisted, with the B.C.E.S. paying for their provisions and emigrant tax at port of arrival.[24] The same year, the very wealthy Angela Burdett-Coutts lent "a very large sum" to enable a group of Ayrshire weavers to emigrate to Canada (she had been assisting Irish emigration since 1863).[25] The season also saw the inauguration of the child-emigration efforts of Maria Rye and Annie Macpherson, and the assistance of over 4000 Londoners by the B.C.E.S.[26]

S.C. Johnson viewed this year as a turning point in the history of migration assistance, believing it to mark the "commencement of an era of private enterprise which had, at its basis, charitable as distinct from commercial motives."[27] But even philanthropic emigration, some believed, could be made to return interest on capital invested if some means were found to ensure repayment of loans. Profits might support a self-sustaining emigration fund. The same hope of "philanthropy at 5%" motivated other social campaigns of the period, notably that for improved working-class housing. The securing of repayment, however, was a complicated and, at best, uncertain thing, as many private emigrationists had reason to know.

Nevertheless, the prospect of an emigration fund which was to some extent self-sustaining became an important part of state-emigrationist propaganda.

The state-emigration front of 1869 derived in large part from the parallel activities of at least four groups: George Potter's Workmen's Emigration League (W.E.L.), the E.E.E.F., the B.C.E.S., and the National Emigration Aid Society (N.E.A.S.). The W.E.L. and the N.E.A.S., led by the Duke of Manchester, were the chief instruments in the creation of the National Emigration League, but all the groups advocated some form of organized large-scale emigration.

The W.E.L., probably based on the London Working Men's Association which Potter controlled,[27a] was organized sometime after February 22, 1868, when Potter led a deputation to Gladstone from London trade societies to air a variety of subjects including legal restrictions on trade-union activities, a minimum wage, and state regulation of piecework and overtime. However, he also drew Gladstone's attention to the need for an organized system of emigration.[28] Sometime in the following year, Potter and some of his radical associates in the labour movement attempted to work up a public agitation for state emigration. The W.E.L., with Potter as secretary, was created to lobby for government action, though it also gave direct financial assistance to men who applied to it for emigration aid.[29] This combination of political pressure with direct aid was a hallmark of many organizations, and a source of some weakness and confusion. Resources were spread very thin.

By summer, Potter was involved in a campaign to extend W.E.L. membership throughout the east and south of London. A series of "unusually crowded" meetings were held in working-class areas, and branch organiza-

tions were established. The Lord Mayor presided at a
meeting at Horne's Tavern on June 8, Sir George Grey[30]
at Borough Road Congregational Chapel on December
18. Potter was able to get the emigration question on the
agenda of the 1869 Trades Union Congress (T.U.C.), and
by January of 1870 the W.E.L. claimed a membership of
2000, distributed among 12 London branches.[31] Though
the working-class radicalism of the W.E.L. embarrassed
some of its potential upper-class collaborators, its campaign was to some extent coordinated with those of the
other philanthropic organizations.

The precise origins of the N.E.A.S. are unclear. It was
"a Revival and Reconstruction" of the National Colonial
Emigration Society, which had been in charge of selecting
and embarking many of the emigrants assisted during the
cotton famine.[32] In 1868 it reappeared under the presidency of the Duke of Manchester who was at this time
also involved, much to his regret, in the shakey and somewhat scandalous fortunes of the Chartered Venezuelan
Trading Company which sought to send British colonists
to Venezuela for profit.[33] The same year, he also played
a role in the establishment of the Royal Colonial Institute,
as did Frederick Young, another important activist in the
N.E.A.S.[34]

Other N.E.A.S. members included several London
churchmen with working-class parishes, like the Rev.
Styleman Herring of Clerkenwell who had organized an
emigration "club" on a contributory Friendly Society basis.[35] Military men and members of Parliament figure
among the society's vice presidents, the most active being Maj. Gen. W. Denison, Col. F. C. Maude, Robert R.
Torrens, W. T. McCullagh Torrens, and Edward B. Eastwick.[36] R.R. Torrens, son of the famous political economist and the first premier of South Australia, published a

small pamphlet on *State Aid to Emigration* in 1869.[37]
With his cousin, W. T. McCullagh Torrens, he frequently
took part in discussions on emigration in and out of Parliament. Torrens believed that certain sections of the working class were probably permanently distressed (notably
agricultural labourers) and advocated state emigration as
a two-fold benefit. It would immediately reduce labour
competition and help raise working-class standards, and
eventually it would increase the demand for English
goods by expanding colonial purchasing power. This was
hardly a new point of view, but one which became more
attractive as European competitors began to break into
English markets. State aid was required because the colonies had destroyed the Wakefield mechanism by refusing
to use land revenues for immigration assistance. A logical
source of funds to replace colonial land revenues would
be loans with the poor-rates as security.[38]

Throughout the year, the N.E.A.S. held meetings in
working-class neighborhoods, and distributed cheap
propaganda. Its goals, as explained by its secretary John
Bate, were to promote emigration from areas of high unemployment, to assist emigrants with loans for passages
and kits "whenever the funds of the Society permit," to
give advice and information about emigration, and to ar-
range for proper reception of emigrants in the colonies.
However, the society also meant to urge the government,
"by various agencies," to consider a "National Emigration
Policy". This was its "special object".

The National Emigration Aid Society is using its best efforts to
promote the emigrant's interests and welfare. It is about to move
PARLIAMENT, in order to obtain STATE AID for that purpose,
on grounds as strong as justified the grant of £ 8,775,000 and
upwards for the rescue of a score and a half of ABYSSINIAN
CAPTIVES, and the expenditure of £ 20,000,000 to set the NE-

GRO free from slavery. Surely none will be found hardy enough to say that the hundreds of thousands of England's labourers—slavery, thank God, is unknown in this free country—now pinched by poverty and pining in misery, are not worthy and deserving of, and equally entitled to, like compensation and relief?[39]

As a first step, the society contacted the guardians in distressed areas and urged them, without much success, to make use of their statutory powers to assist emigration by use of the rates. At the same time, an effort was made at public meetings to overcome the assumed reluctance of the unemployed to leave so that "the working men of all classes" would "unite their efforts with those of the National Emigration Aid Society to obtain State Aid."[40] Emigrationists were, of course, anxious not to appear to advocate the involuntary transportation of the poor. Bate called upon working men to seek assistance to emigrate not only because their departure would improve their own fortunes and reduce "the competition for employment" in England, but because "it is the manifest intention of Providence."[41]

The other two major London emigration organizations, the E.E.E.F. and the B.C.E.S., were less interested in agitation than immediate charitable relief. The E.E.E.F. had been formed in 1867 to assist the "deserving unemployed" to migrate or emigrate, and had, by 1869, assisted 1772 persons—mostly to Canada. It had confined its operations to the Poplar union, an area distressed by lay-offs in shipbuilding, but now it sought to extend its activities. A special meeting was convened at Mansion House on February 10, 1869, to discuss "an organized and continued system of emigration."[42] The keynote of the meeting, sounded by the Lord Mayor, was the need to deal with "chronic distress" with something beyond *ad hoc* and uncoordinated philanthropy. Though suggestions were made for the amalgamation of all the societies into a single system, consensus was apparently confined to the realm of broad generality. Proposals of a concrete nature, the interjection of W.E.L. radicalism, and the petty jealousies and suspicions of the various societies made real unity difficult to achieve. There was some cause, however, for a guarded optimism. Letters of support were read from the Duke of Cambridge and George Goschen, President of the Poor Law Board, who also sent a £ 50 donation. Lord Northbrook claimed that Edward Cardwell, Secretary for War, and the Duke of Cambridge would head a new subscription list. In fact, about £ 4500 was collected by May to enable the E.E.E.F. and the B.C.E.S. to extend their activities.[43]

The B.C.E.S. met regularly throughout the year at Mansion House and, judging by the numbers it was able to assist, appears to have been the most generously funded of the organizations. It was the only society at the time to have entered into active cooperation with a government program of relief.[44] Its subscription membership was the most prominent, and its tone was always cautiously non-political. Though several of its members advocated state aid, as a body it remained aloof from the agitation.[45]

These groups kept the emigration question before the public eye throughout the spring of 1869.[46] The immediate fruit of their efforts was a debate in the House of Lords on April 16, initiated by Lord Houghton (Richard Monckton Milnes) who called for "parliamentary intervention" in the face of a perplexing 5 percent rise in pauperism despite growing national wealth. While not optimistic about "large systematic schemes", Houghton proposed either giving power to boards of guardians to borrow from the government on the security of the rates, or allowing the Exchequer to assist emigration directly. In this way, the threat of revolutionary violence would be diminished by "a process in itself moral, salutary, and beneficial", and he called on Granville and Goschen to prepare a plan involving the cooperation of Poor-Law authorities, the government, and the colonies. To the familiar objection that a governmental scheme would dry up philanthropic assistance, he opposed the argument that the societies themselves had shown of late "an intense desire to initiate action in this matter." He concluded with overtones of imperial federation:

> it deserves consideration whether we might not deal with that apparent calamity [pauperism] by such an extension, as it were, of the British Empire and its colonies as to combine them in one great whole for the purpose of productive employment, substituting the area of the world, which, taken together, is thinly populated, for this little island with all its difficulties and its dense population.[47]

There were at this time several reasons why Gladstone's government might be expected to show little sympathy for Houghton's suggestions. Granville was in the midst of a public debate over his refusal of a New Zealand loan guarantee and the pending recall of imperial troops. Houghton seemed to put forward his proposals as a part of the protest against the government's colonial policy. Also, talk of a solution based on grants from the Exchequer irritated many Liberals dedicated to fiscal economy and decentralization. Granville denied that a problem of permanent distress existed among the able-bodied, and doubted, even if it did, whether "wild emigration schemes" would be of any use. He also objected to Houghton's call for a Royal Commission as costly (and unpredictable). It was the duty of the government to solve problems, and "not to refer questions of this kind to irresponsible Commissions." Private emigration of small capitalists was far preferable to a state scheme which would require large bureaucratic machinery. Finally, Granville pointed to the delicate nature of colonial relations which pauper emigration would threaten as his "overriding concern.".[48]

The most extravagant denunciation of emigration came not from government but from the Liberal back benches. Lord Overstone, sometimes an embarrassment to Liberal ministers,[49] extolled Britain as a land of plenty, "the richest country in the world" where capital—and the wage fund—were accumulating "at a rate which was almost gigantic." Unemployment was a sign of a progressive economy in which adjustments to the opening of new labour fields lagged behind the closing of old. Periodically recurring commercial crises were "the seed of expanding prosperity in the future." There was simply no need for emigration because there was no need for any kind of able-bodied relief. An aged Earl Grey echoed these sentiments, and in a rambling recollection of the schemes of the Wilmot-Horton era noted that government did not, even then, in the midst of Swing riots and real distress, adopt any system of wholesale emigration.[50]

The first reaction to the government's dismissal of the emigrationist case came from Frederick Young of the N.E.A.S., who attacked its stand in a pamphlet published shortly after the debate. *Transplantation, the True System of Emigration* is couched in the language of the Wakefield movement, an earlier agitation in which Young himself had played a small role.[51] The pamphlet presented a picture of "terrible social difficulties" caused in part by overpopulation and constituting a great threat to the security of persons and property. The inability of the economy to absorb the excess of births over deaths and voluntary emigration was borne out by the increasing pauperism revealed in official figures. Behind these stood a vast number on the verge of poverty who lived in misery and constant danger of precipitation into despair by inevitable trade fluctuation.[52] Though not antagonistic to radical social measures at home, Young believed that these would "take years to accomplish". Lord Overstone was lacerated for his "inhuman doctrine" in terms that clearly illustrate how middle-class emigrationists were able to discover a common rhetorical ground with the radical labour movement.

> [Having a large reservoir of surplus labour] may seem correct, according to the harsh and cold ideas of so called political economists, but it is not the principle to find favour with human frames of flesh and blood, compelled to experience the consequence of their cruel conclusions.[53]

Young called for a special emigration department headed by a cabinet minister to direct a permanent system of "National Emigration".

Young's pamphlet secured support from rather diverse sources. One reviewer, a socialist, delighted in Young's exposure of the capitalist fallacies of Overstone. Another seized on the scheme as a solution to the burden of the poor-rates, while yet another saw in Young's statistics of overcrowding and poverty a proof of the need for extensive reform of land law and the meaninglessness of other Liberal legislative nostrums.[54] *Transplantation* became more or less the catechism of state emigrationists for the next 20 years. It quickly ran through two editions.

Publication of Young's propaganda piece coincided with the renewal of N.E.A.S. agitation throughout the country, culminating in Mansion House meetings in December to consider the formation of a league of emigration societies. On June 3, the Duke of Manchester led an N.E.A.S. deputation to the Home and Colonial Secretaries, H. A. Bruce and Granville, who were presented a memorial to the effect that economic depression, "chiefly due to population growth", could be relieved by the settlement of colonial lands. A long list of precedents for state assistance was produced.[55] Bruce, however, deplored the risk "to the independent character of Englishmen" which state aid involved.

At the end of June, there was another N.E.A.S. deputation, this time to Goschen at the Poor-Law Board, with equally disappointing results.[56] The unsatisfactory outcome of these approaches to government and an abortive attempt to mobilize the metropolitan guardians[57] must have had a chilling effect. The main question considered at a conference on June 22 was not state aid, but whether colonization or emigration might be made self-supporting "or even profitable". The report, written by William Freston, was published as a pamphlet. It despaired of government action and called for a joint stock company to purchase, colonize, and sell land in the colonies. If profitable, this commercial system could be expanded, and would ameliorate the condition of labour in England, direct emigration away from the United States, and curtail the danger of Fenianism. Manchester, who presided at this conference, and Lt. Gen. William Fielding shortly thereafter used these suggestions to establish a commercial company in New Zealand, but for the most part the other emigrationists were unprepared to abandon the struggle with the government.[58]

By the end of summer, the tide seemed to turn somewhat in their favour. In July, the metropolitan guardians responded more favourably to their advances, and sent a memorial to the Poor-Law Board recommending a "Metropolitan rating" for emigration purposes. At a meeting of the Poplar guardians a national emigration tax was called for. On August 14 the *Times,* in an editorial on the annual report of the Emigration Commissioners, seemed to swing behind state emigration. Noting that the colonies for the most part had ceased their emigration assistance, the reviewer advocated British aid which could be seen not as an increase in national expenditure but as a diversion from the costs of pauper maintenance.[59]

Throughout the autumn the N.E.A.S. and the W.E.L. continued their drive for public support, in resonance with at least some sections of labour.[60] On December 22, a "Preliminary Conference" was held at Mansion House to investigate the possible amalgamation of the N.E.A.S., the W.E.L., and the B.C.E.S. This was followed by a full meeting of the three societies the last day of the year. The amalgamation question was a perennial one. The arguments for such a move rested on the superior efficiency of a large central organization in terms of resources, selection methods, and lobbying. As a general rule, however, the societies were too jealous of their own resources and methods for much chance of success. The unification question in December of 1869 was further complicated by the state-aid issue. The B.C.E.S. was interested for the most part in strengthening charitable emigration, while the N.E.A.S. and the W.E.L. were looking to establish a broadly based pressure group.

The Lord Mayor, Robert Besley, presided at both meetings, which were well attended. Frederick Young appears to have been the primary force behind the move, and beforehand had distributed an "emigration Circular" among the representatives of the three societies. He called for the welding together of a single society with the

dual purpose of charitable emigration and political pressure, though the latter function was clearly uppermost.
The Anti-Corn-Law League and the National Education
League were the explicit models Young had in view.[61] He
did not, however, succeed in winning over the majority
of the B.C.E.S. At the New Year's Eve meeting, they
voted to remain outside the new organization, but to cooperate through periodic conversations. In part, this decision was due to a fear that close association with radicals
like Beales and Potter would cause their subscriptions to
decline.[62] The National Emigration League proceeded
without them. Manchester was elected president and a
membership fee was set at £ 5 for life or 5s. annually.

2.3   *The League in Action*

The League held its first public meeting at Exeter Hall on
January 5, 1870, to inaugurate a year of energetic, though
ultimately futile, activity. Its beginning was not propi-
tious. The gathering, crowded with "gentlemen well-
known in connection with social questions", was dis-
rupted by what the *Times* called "Irish persons" who
demanded a counterresolution that emigration was
wrong in principle and land reform the real remedy. A
general turmoil ensued amid cries of "Fenians". The police arrived "amid a great uproar", and eventually the
malcontents departed in a body. Those remaining then
passed their resolutions calling for state-aided emigration
and a deputation to the Prime Minister.[63]
    Shortly following this embarrassment, Manchester him-
self precipitated a crisis which threatened to destroy the
common front Young had laboured to create. Independent of his position as president of the League, Manchester set up a National Emigrants' Aid Corporation on the

commercial lines of the Freston report, and encouraged the League to cease agitation for state aid in favour of private enterprise. Young, as chairman of the executive committee, was thus driven to clarify the objects of the League in such a way as to leave no doubt that agitation for state aid was its *raison d'être*. On January 12, he wrote to Manchester, rejecting in strong terms

> your Grace's view, that the object [the League] had so public-ly and so clearly pledged itself to pursue is a "chimera"; or that the League will for one moment listen to any Recommendation (from whatever influential quarter it may come) to abandon its avowed object of soliciting State Aid, in the work of Emigration, and to identify itself, instead, with any private joint stock com-pany . . . .[64]

A week earlier, Col. Maude had strongly urged that the League needed to have a settled policy and could not afford to "listen to every mushroom society which sprang up in a night." He called for an unequivocal statement that "the aim of the League should be to agitate."[65] Man-chester retreated and did not press his scheme on the League. The rift was patched over in a conciliatory letter from Young.

> I perfectly understand the motives, which induced you to asso-ciate your name with the "Emigration Aid Corporation Com-pany." I have more than once expressed the opinion, that I was sure you did so entirely from philanthropic motives, and in order "to get something done"; feeling that the emergency was great, and that, while the "grass was growing," in other directions, "the steed was starving".[66]

Manchester remained dubious about being able to obtain state aid, but agreed to keep the two projects separate. Young, on the other hand, was now confident that "the time is not distant when the Government will take [emigration] up in earnest, in response to the irresistable voice of the people".[67]

The League opened its assault with a deputation to Gladstone, followed during the next two months by a campaign in the provinces led by Young, Potter, Grey, and Edward Jenkins, the League's honorary secretary.[68] A "monster petition" of over 104,000 signatures was gathered. Expressions of support came from Carlyle, Ruskin, Tennyson, John Stuart Mill, and Thomas Hughes.[69] There were two more deputations to ministers, and a debate in the House of Commons. Meanwhile, relations worsened with the B.C.E.S. which, after an unfavourable editorial in the *Times*, finally broke its ties and announced its opposition on the grounds that agitation for state aid "tended to retard subscriptions very materially."[70]

The *Times'* reversal was most likely prompted by the clear opposition of Liberal ministers and a sensitivity to some of the stridency of the demands of the League.

> The zealous persons who have been so busy of late in getting up Emigration Leagues and Emigration Societies do not ... stop [with voluntary efforts]. To judge from their language, Emigration is not only a way of alleviating the stringency of the labour market, but a panacea to be always trusted for a thorough working cure of its evils. More than this; they declare that ... it is the duty of the Government even if it be a costly duty, to find a sphere for the labour of the workmen.[71]

The only permanent remedy lay in "self-restraint and a higher morality" among the working classes. Edmond Beales' claim that it was the duty of government to find work for the unemployed would be seized upon "by communisitic persons who carry ideas to their logical conclusions." Philanthropists like Samuel Morley were "well-meaning and benevolent" but had an "innocent unconsciousness" of their own inadequacies. "The principle

of action of the [Jan. 26] meeting was a confused socialism."[72]

On the other hand, the League received support from
James Anthony Froude who, in January, began his well-
known seri s of articles on the colonies in *Fraser's Magazine.* The first installment contained hearty approval of
emigration as a solution to home distress. Emigration remained "the only practical remedy" not only for Ireland,
but for Scotland and England as well. He chastized politicians who claimed that "the direction of our emigration
is not of the slightest consequence to us." Emigration to
British colonies was desirable for reasons of national security and trade, but it was being hindered by "the very
wealthy manufacturing class" who wished to keep a pool
of cheap labour at hand. The same class, very powerful in

Samuel Jones Loyd, First Baron
Overstone (Source: *Ill. London
News,* Dec. 1, 1883)

James Anthony Froude (Source:
Ill. London News, July 22, 1871)

Parliament though not "a hundredth part" of the nation, was motivated by a "Liberal dream" which, when fulfilled, would leave England one great urban waste of bad air, bad water, and bad food, where children "dwindle as if blighted" and vice, disease, and drunkenness run rampant. "Every great city becomes a moral cesspool." Salvation lay in a "hardy and abundant peasantry" which would preserve national health and greatness, and could be had now only in the colonies—to which England ought to send "as many millions as we can send out."[73]

> We are told that Government has no business with emigration; that emigration, like wages, prices, and profits, must be left to settle itself, according to the laws of nature. Human things are as much governed by laws of nature as a farm or a garden, neither less nor more. If we cultivate a field it will yield us corn or green crops. The laws of nature will as assuredly overgrow it with docks and nettles if we leave it to govern itself. The settlement of Ulster under James I. was an act of government; yet it was the only measure which ever did good to Ireland.[74]

On February 3, a League deputation that included Samuel Wilberforce, the Bishop of Winchester, met Gladstone and Goschen to urge government to discharge its "Christian obligation" (while securing "a great political advantage") by adopting an emigration scheme. A memorial was presented, describing general distress and falling wages. W. T. M. Torrens said they wanted, in effect, "cheap third-class Parliamentary trains, and passages at cost price, so to speak, across the ocean." Gladstone promised to lay the proposals before the Cabinet, but spoke of "the great difficulties attaching to the whole subject."[75]

Gladstone's unenthusiastic response was hardly unexpected, and the deputation was but a part of a coordinated effort to achieve public exposure before anticipated parliamentary discussions. The giant petition circulated through the W.E.L. branches in the East and South of London was in the final stages of preparation. It was presented on February 15 to Bruce at the Home Office. Signed by 104,000 "London working men", it directed government's attention both to emigration aid and the necessity of retaining close ties with the colonies. It was presented by a committee chosen at a mass rally at Lambeth Baths on January 27.[76]

In the shadow of an anticipated parliamentary debate, Grey, Jenkins, and Potter then left London together for a month of hard campaigning in the provinces. Large evening meetings, which allowed the working class to attend, filled an exhausting schedule that included Leeds (February 7), Derby (February 8), Rochdale (February 9), Bristol (February 18), Leeds again (February 21), and Birmingham (March 1). The line reiterated on those occasions was that "Great social changes must be made at home, but that would be the work of time, and meanwhile people were starving."[77]

The same day (March 1) that an enthusiastic and crowded meeting in Birmingham approved state emigration "with acclamation," Robert Torrens moved in the House of Commons for a national emigration fund secured by the poor-rates. He also suggested that the government assist private benevolence by placing unused military transport ships at the disposal of the N.E.A.S. The debate which followed focused primarily on the principles involved, with government spokesmen emphasizing the supposed "socialistic" nature of state aid, while defenders of the motion[78] pointed to the Poor Law and the Irish Land Bill as sufficient precedent. Dilke, in a perceptive speech, went to the heart of the issue. First, the motion really involved a confusion of two questions, that of emigration as a cure for domestic ills, and that of the future of colonial relations. Secondly, he speculated that there were many issues closer to the heart of working men than emigration assistance, and the measure, if successful, might open the door to other "agitations here at home far more dangerous."[79]

Gladstone brought the debate to a close with a reply which concentrated on the lack of a consensus on a single detailed scheme. But, he claimed, "we are perfectly ready to entertain any proposal likely to be beneficial, if it be within the range of our power to carry it into effect." That range, however, was tightly circumscribed. As a precedent in establishing the principle of state aid, the Poor Law, which, "if you scrutinize it closely, presents the greatest difficulties to the philosophic mind," was "neutralized" in practice by the working of restraints involved in its local character—entailing a sense of self-respect and shame—which would not operate in a general scheme of emigration assistance. Nor would it be possible to exercise the kind of selection necessary to get the colonies to accept such a program, once the "right" to emigration assistance had been established. In conclusion, Gladstone disagreed with the emigrationist analysis of England's domestic condition:

> it happens as an incident of modern civilization that sores and sufferings which in ancient times were not generally known are now brought to light, for great vicissitudes mark the industrial condition of society; and we pass rapidly in a series of cycles from periods of great prosperity to periods of sharp distress. At these periods of sharp distress the minds of men, especially where a representative system prevails, are hard driven to find an immediate remedy, and from time to time it has always happened that this subject of emigration has been discussed . . . .[80]

The House then divided, and Torrens' motion lost decisively in a light vote (48 ayes, 153 noes). Clearly it was not taken very seriously in the House.

The immediate reaction of the League was to decide to pursue further organization in the provinces, where Potter and Grey felt there had been good progress, and to organize "a great demonstration" in London.[81] Jenkins reported to Manchester that the agitation would be kept up "to induce the Government to do something even this year. Mr. Gladstone seems to be wavering,"[82] — a curiously optimistic interpretation of the Prime Minister's speech which Granville, at least, assumed had "killed & buried State aid to Emigration."[83]

Finances now became the chief problem, if the League was to extend its activities into summer and autumn. Jenkins complained to Manchester on March 7:

> The only obstacle to progress is the deficiency of money. The whole expenses of the League from the beginning have been only between £ 350 & £ 400 as we who are its honorary officers have kept a strict surveillance over the paid officers of the association. I was obliged, however, to tell the Council that the parliamentary and public policy of the movement was as much as I could manage without having any anxiety about the League's finances—and it was resolved to endeavour to raise a subscription and guarantee fund of about £ 1000 or more for one year.[84]

The appeal for more money appears to have been relatively successful. Promises of over £ 800 were raised by April. It was, however, a hand-to-mouth existence. The League's offices, staff, and other expenses required a monthly expenditure of about £ 190.

Perhaps impelled by its financial problems, the League convened a conference in April to reappraise its goals. The result was a decision to remove direct charitable assistance for emigration from its charter and substitute the encouragement of "the formation of Workmen's Emigration Societies" and the provision of "gratuitous advice and information to intending Emigrants".[85] At the same time,

William E. Gladstone, Prime
Minister, disagreed with the
emigrationist analysis (Source:
Ill. London News, Feb. 7, 1874)

Edward Jenkins, the Secretary
of the National Emigration
League (Source: *Ill. London
News,* May 2, 1874)

the League's name was altered to the National Colonial
and Emigration League. This may indicate an increase in
the influence of the imperialists on the League council:
the imperial federationists, Labilliere and Macfie, assumed vice presidencies at this time.[86]

Responding to the emigration agitation, the Colonial
Office had despatched a circular on February 14 to colonial governments asking for their views.[87] The circular
was fairly, even sympathetically, worded—not always the
case when the government was forced to make gestures
of this nature. But the answers, as anticipated by the permanent staff and Granville, were very discouraging to the
hopes of the emigration lobby. By May, Tasmania and the
Cape had returned discouraging replies, and these were

presented to Parliament.[88] Ultimately, Queensland, New South Wales, and South Australia joined in expressions of "great distaste" for immigration assistance. Queensland did suggest that immigrants could be taken if the British government would guarantee a loan for public works or advance money for settling them on the land. To this, Clinton Murdoch, the senior Emigration Commissioner, appended: "It is superfluous to observe that, so far as the Imperial Treasury is concerned, neither of the expedients is admissible."[89]

In view of the negative results of Newcastle's circular of 1863, the colonial replies must have been anticipated by both government and the League. They were used by Murdoch to formulate the definitive, for 1870, answer to the emigrationist lobby: the annual *Report of the Colonial Land and Emigration Commission*. Statistics were marshalled to demonstrate the natural increase in emigration over the past several years, and the Commission argued that state aid would have the effect of reducing this flow. Because no one would pay out of his own pocket to emigrate if he had a chance of receiving state aid, Murdoch reasoned that the government would have to grant an average of £ 650,000 a year just to keep emigration at its present level. A substantial increase in emigration would require a considerable tax burden on the middle class. Colonization schemes depending on loans to settlers were impractical because of the proven difficulty of collecting repayments; for evidence he cited the fate of the Highland and Island Society (organized in 1852 with the patronage of Prince Albert) and Angela Burdett-Coutts' Ayrshire weavers, who "made no effort to repay the cost of their passages."[90]

The Commission's report reflects the power of a semi-autonomous civil servant with long years of experience to smother unorthodox ideas with the weight of precedent. The central argument, that state aid would check the flow of voluntary emigration substantially, rested on a simple and persuasive logic. But it was only supposition, not proven fact. In any event, the published report gave those opposing state aid useful ammunition, and was apparently fatal to the League's much-touted summer offensive. There was no sign of the provincial and London agitation which the conference of April 26 had promised. Jenkins resigned the secretaryship on May 19. Perhaps he was already nurturing the political ambitions which tempted him to stand, unsuccessfully, for Parliament for the constituency of Truro the next year.[91] It is likely that some of the upper-class support departed with Jenkins.[92] Many of these people re-emerged in the imperial federation movement, and it may be significant that their abandonment of state emigration came on the heels of Granville's reversal of his earlier decision to refuse the New Zealand loan.[93] This gesture to the imperialists may have had the effect of precipitating a dissolution of the emigrationist coalition, of splitting those whose chief interests lay in drawing the colonies closer to England from those—the labour leaders and social reformers—who were more interested in domestic distress.

Jenkins' successor as secretary, the Rev. Horrocks Cocks, has left little record of his activity other than occasional pleas for financial assistance. As late as May 4, 1871, he still claimed, rather pathetically, that "the league is now popular throughout the country", but there is no record of significant agitation from the spring of 1870.[94] It also appears that, having failed in its campaign for state aid, the League resumed by 1871 its direct assistance of emigrants.[95] Cocks offered one excuse for the inability of the League to sustain its momentum. The Franco-Prussian War Appeal, he claimed, had taken "all our resources away."[96] In any case, after four months of frenzied activity in London and the country, and very soon after reaching a decision backed by some financial support to expand activities further, the movement collapsed into obscurity.

2.4 *Post-mortem*

The defeat of the emigration front in 1870 stifled organized agitation for state aid for more than a decade. The League, in a short time and with rather modest resources, had made its issue a national question. But its failure to get the slightest encouragement from governments at home and in the colonies was fatal. Talk of expansion, as is occasionally the case in business enterprises, was actually a symptom of a moribund condition.

The campaigns after which the League was patterned —the Anti-Corn-Law League or the National Education League—were long-sustained agitations with sufficient internal cohesion and depth of commitment to withstand repeated frustration. The Earl of Wemyss once remarked, with reference to another pressure group, that he believed it generally took at least three years to gauge whether a movement was likely to succeed.[97] The National Emigration League's effective existence spanned less than a year. It then joined what must be an endless list of short-lived, aborted organizations.

The League was a nonpartisan attempt to promote a cause through argument, and the demonstration of cross-sectional or class collaborative support. It was, however, unable to achieve, either outside or within Parliament, the kind of enduring momentum necessary to trouble ministers very seriously. The 50 or so MPs of both parties who formed the emigrationist core in the House of Commons were unwilling to persist in the face of the government's refusal to take the issue seriously. The issue itself was one which challenged some of the most common assumptions of mid-Victorians, and many of the parliamentary sympathizers with some kind of emigration aid lacked a firm commitment to a large radical program. In any event, such efforts were likely to be sustained only if government itself opened a breach by admitting principle or necessity, thus giving independent MPs the chance of widening the opening without threatening a major anti-government confrontation. The only alternative was to try to "politicize" the issue—that is, to persuade the Opposition to take it up as part of a national program. This would be difficult to achieve, and would destroy bipartisan cohesion.

Part of the failure of the League to make headway may also be explained by its tactics in presenting only a general scheme which did not spell out the details of a state program. This was intended to leave the government room to devise whatever specific scheme it thought most suitable, and to make it difficult for opponents to pull the proposal apart. The League left itself plenty of room for maneuvering. But, as both Dilke and Gladstone were quick to point out, this was a weakness as well. It allowed the government to dismiss the proposals as unsubstantial, visionary, and incompetently and insufficiently thought out. This lesson was not forgotten. When the emigration lobby was resurrected again in the 1880s, it submitted the most tiresomely detailed proposals—much to the irritation of the overworked civil servants who were required to supply ministers with answers.

But there was also a confusion of goals within the League itself. Some saw state emigration as merely the occasional government subsidy to private institutions;

others, as a wholly rationalized state process. Some concentrated on the contribution emigration would make to imperial unity, while others spoke only of relieving economic distress at home.

Of course, the kind of hearing given to a pressure group owes much to the immediacy of the issue and the pace of events at the time. Unfortunately for the emigration lobby, 1869 and 1870 were years full of legislative activity. Government and Opposition were preoccupied with Irish reform, the Church, and Forster's Education Bill, which alone involved the government in a nightmarish tangle of conflicting interests. Any suggestion of further complicating the political situation with a new controversy must have been very badly received.

The lack of a detailed program, confusion over goals, and government preoccupation help explain the failure of the League to achieve immediate progress, while a trend to economic recovery that resulted in near full employment by 1872 damaged the movement's ability to recover from initial defeat. With the economic upswing, as is paradoxically generally the case, there came a large increase in voluntary emigration. At the same time, there was a flurry of activity among the philanthropic emigration societies, producing a record number of assisted emigrants for the year 1872. This considerably detracted from the urgency of the emigrationist case.[98]

The imperialist wing of the League emerged shortly in the midst of the movement for closer colonial relations. Jenkins himself launched this agitation in two articles in the *Contemporary Review* in 1871. At this time he was working closely with another League member, F. P. Labilliere, to popularize ideas of a colonial legislative union. Both men spoke on this subject at a conference at the Westminster Palace Hotel in July, and again at the

Davenport Social Science Congress in 1872.[99] The "Conference on Colonial Questions" at the Westminster Palace Hotel (Granville called it "an anti-Downing Street Colonial Conference")[100] was organized by members of the Royal Colonial Institute, colonials living in England, and Manchester and Jenkins. Of the 38 persons most involved, 27 can be identified as vice-presidents and council members of the National Emigration League.[101] Some of these men had simply moved on to another cause; others were casting about for another instrument with which to carry on the fight for state emigration. In Jenkins' opening address, and in many other papers, much importance was given to emigration as a part of an informal net of imperial connections which would facilitate social, political, and commercial amalgamation. The major emigrationist appeal was delivered by another member of the League, Edward Clarke, who sounded once again their call for a state program. He received the support of Young, Robert and William Torrens, and George Potter. Jenkins, however, demurred. Emigration, he said, was certainly desirable, but large governmental schemes had been made "impracticable" by the discouraging replies from the colonies to Granville's circular.[102]

This, then, is the rock upon which floundering state emigration broke apart. As it became apparent that further pursuit of a national emigration scheme would endanger colonial relations, those like Jenkins who saw imperial federation as a primary, overriding objective were prepared to drop the offending assistance program. The conference of 1871 was the end of the road for the League. Imperialists organized their own pressure group to pursue the phantom of Empire Federation. Manchester's speculative venture prospered in New Zealand. The many philanthropic emigration societies continued their separate ways, sending out through their subscriptions a few thousand of the deserving poor each year. George Potter continued to demand state emigration as a working man's right, but he was increasingly isolated and less influential within the labour movement. Applegarth and some of the other labour leaders who flirted with state emigration apparently dropped it as an unpromising and somewhat embarrassing issue.[103] Both William Torrens and Young held out hopes for a very modified program of government subsidies for the equalization of fares throughout the Empire. "Equalized passages", however, never really caught on, though it continued to be referred to by moderates throughout the following decade as the best hope for some kind of state action. Torrens himself despaired of being able to move the government for even so innocuous a program as this with the methods of persuasion available to a "respectable" pressure group. With the bitterness bred by frustration, he complained that the government seemed to think it was their duty to concede nothing to the people until "something like pulling down the Hyde Park railings" took place.[104]

Notes to Chapter 2

1. See R. C. Mills, *The Colonization of Australia (1829–42): The Wakefield Experiment in Empire Building* (London, 1915), and H. J. M. Johnston, *British Emigration Policy 1815–30* (Oxford, 1972).
2. C. A. Bodelsen, *Studies in Mid-Victorian Imperialism* (Copenhagen, 1924), 103–5.
3. For evidence of strong labour support for emigration as late as the 1880s see H. L. Malchow, "Trade Unions and Emigration in Late Victorian England: A National Lobby for State Aid," *Journal of British Studies,* Vol. 15, no. 2 (Spring, 1976), 92–116.

4. Population in England and Wales rose from 17,928,000 in 1851 to 22,712,000 in 1871. The rate of increase, after slowing to 11.9 percent of the previous census in 1861 rose to 14.7 percent in 1881. Urban population grew from 54.0 percent of the total population in 1851 to 58.7 percent in 1861, 65.2 percent in 1871, and 70.0 percent in 1881 (B. R. Mitchell and P. Deane, *Abstract of British Historical Statistics* [Cambridge, 1962], 64; Geoffrey Best, *Mid-Victorian Britain, 1851–75* [London, 1971], 6).

5. See William O. Henderson, *The Lancashire Cotton Famine, 1861–1865* (Manchester, 1934).

6. R. Arthur Arnold, *The History of the Cotton Famine* (London, 1864), 367.

7. *Ibid.*, 368; the *Times*, 31 March 1863, 6; *Hansard*, 3rd Ser., Vol. 170 (Commons, 27 April 1863), columns 814–5.

8. Arnold, 409.

9. *Ibid.*, 412.

10. Mr. Haywood, secretary of the (manufacturers') Cotton Supply Association; quoted by Arnold, 369.

11. Charlotte Erickson, "The Encouragement of Emigration by British Trade Unions, 1850–1900,' *Population Studies*, Vol. 3 (1949), 255.

12. Arnold, 408.

13. *Ibid.*

14. Henderson, 117–8.

15. *The Beehive*, 20 Dec. 1862, 4.

16. *Ibid.*, 10 Jan. 1863, 4.

17. P.P. 1864, *24th General Report of the Emigration Commissioners*, 17–18.

18. 4 & 5 William IV c. 76, s. 62, 1834 (and amendments in 1844, 48, 49, 50, and 66). A short survey of the Act and its many elaborations may be found in H. H. Phear, *Emigration* (London, 1886).

19. *Hansard*, Vol. 199 (Commons, 1 March 1870), 1047.

20. F. H. Hitchins, *The Colonial Land and Emigration Commission* (Philadelphia, 1931), *passim*.

21. *Low's Handbook of London Charities*, 1872; the *Times*, 11 Feb. 1869, 12.

22. R. B. Madgwick, *Immigrants into Eastern Australia, 1788–1851* (London, 1937), 98; W. S. Shepperson, *British Emigration to North America* (Minneapolis, 1957), treats many of the early Victorian societies organized on the basis of trade, religion, or region.

23. The *Times*, 8 Aug. 1868, 8; *Hansard*, Vol. 199 (Commons, 1 March 1870), 1042. Also see S. C. Johnson, *A History of Emigration* (New York, 1914), 65.

24. P. P. 1870 (C. 196), *30th General Report of the Emigration Commissioners*, 3.

25. P. P. 1889 (274), *Report from the Select Committee on Colonization*, 59.

26. Johnson, 278–9; *Hansard*, Vol. 199, 1042.

27. Johnson, 72.

27a. The London Working Men's Association continued to sponsor public meetings in support of state emigration long after the collapse of the League of 1870. See, for example, Potter to Brabazon, Sep. 8, 1886 (Meath Papers, Autograph Vol. I).

28. *The Beehive*, 22 Feb. 1868, 4–5.

29. The *Times*, 1 Jan. 1870, 8. Also actively supporting the campaign of the W.E.L. were Daniel Pratt, Alfred Houlder, R. M. Latham, Daniel Guile, and Edmond Beales.

30. Sir George Grey (1812–1898) was a vice-president of the N.E.A.S. and a member of the B.C.E.S. In 1870, he led a vigorous campaign in the provinces for the National Emigration League. He had been Governor of South Australia, New Zealand, and the Cape Colony, and was involved in frequent conflict with the Colonial Office. He returned to New Zealand after the failure of the League, and became Prime Minister (1877–9), successfully advocating a Radical program which included radical land reform.

31. B. C. Roberts, *The Trades Union Congress, 1868–1921* (London, 1958), 60; the *Times*, 3 Jan. 1870, 5.

32. John Bate, *Emigration. Free, Assisted, and Full-Paying Passages* (London, no date [1869]), 2; Erickson, 255.

33. Manchester Papers (Huntingdonshire Record Office): Box 20A, #3. Preparation for the reception of the immigrants in Venezuela was inadequate, and many suffered extreme hardship.

34. T. R. Reese, *The History of the Royal Commonwealth Society, 1868–1968* (London, 1968), 16, 19, 22.

35. The Revs. W. J. Caparn, R. A. Hancock, A. S. Herring, G. M. Murphy, and G. P. Ottey.

36. No complete membership list is extant, but the Society claimed the support of ten MPs, and I have seen nine mentioned in press accounts: Thomas Chambers (L.), E. B. Eastwick (C.), George

Hadfield (L.), Lord George Hamilton (C.), John Holms (L.), Alexander M'Arthur (?), Charles Reed (L.), R. R. Torrens (L.), W. T. M. Torrens (L.). The military men were: Capt. Blake, R. N., Capt. Bedford Pim, R. N., Capt. Parker Snow, R. N., Capt. Wake, R. N., Maj. Gen. W. Denison, and Col. F. C. Maude. Eastwick was, in 1870, private secretary to Lord Salisbury. William Torrens McCullagh Torrens (1813–1894) was an Irish barrister and biographer who sat as independent Liberal MP for the London constituency of Finsbury. His emigration interests stemmed in part from his concern for overcrowded working-class housing, and his legislative attempts to ameliorate slum conditions (the Torrens Act 1868). He was a vice-president of Herring's Clerkenwell Emigration Club, a member of the N.E.A.S., and vice president of the National Emigration League.

37. Catalogued at the Royal Commonwealth Society Library but destroyed in the Second World War. I have not been able to find another copy.
38. *Hansard*, Vol. 199, 1004–10.
39. John Bate, 3–4. Bate read a paper on emigration at the Birmingham T.U.C. in 1869.
40. *Ibid.*, 4, 14–5; the *Times*, 27 March 1869, 9, and 12 April 1869, 10.
41. John Bate, 14.
42. The *Times*, 11 Feb. 1869, 12. Present were most of the luminaries of the B.C.E.S. and the N.E.A.S.: Lord Northbrook, Baron Alfred de Rothschild, the Marquess of Townshend, Sir Thomas F. Buxton, R. R. Torrens, John Bate, the Rev. J. F. Kitto, and a large phalanx of London MPs and guardians.
43. *Ibid.*
44. The Marquess of Westminster alone gave £ 2,000 in July (the *Times*, 28 July 1869, 10); the B.C.E.S. worked with the government to assist the emigration of those who had been laid off at government dockyards and the Woolwich Arsenal (*30th Report, Emigration Commissioners*, 3).
45. The *Times*, 11 Feb. 1869, 12; 14 May 1869, 12; 13 Aug. 1869, 10. The B.C.E.S. Executive Committee included Grey, E. H. Currie (an East End employer who visited Canada for the society in 1869), the Hon. Reginald Capel, Sir T. F. Buxton, Joseph Gibbs, and the Rev. J. F. Kitto (chairman of the E.E.E.F. in 1883). Secretary of the society was J. Standish Haly, also of the E.E.E.F.

46. There was an N.E.A.S. deputation to Goschen at the Poor Law Board.

47. *Hansard*, Vol. 195 (Lords, 16 April 1869), 952.

48. *Ibid.*, 943–52.

49. Samuel Jones Loyd, first Baron Overstone (1796–1883) was an authority on banking and finance, the London and Westminster Bank being the family concern. Gladstone had a rather low opinion of "old O.".: "No man's judgments have really more exaggeration in them than his," Gladstone to Granville, 16 Sept. 1876, in Agatha Ramm, *The Political Correspondence of Mr. Gladstone and Lord Granville, 1876–1886* (Oxford, 1962), 8.

50. *Hansard*, Vol. 195, 958–69.

51. Frederick Young, *Transplantation, the True System of Emigration* (London, 1869). Sir Frederick Young (1817–1913) was a London merchant who had been a supporter of Wakefield (he accompanied the "Canterbury Pilgrims" to New Zealand in 1850) and of the Colonial Reform Movement. He was the guiding spirit of the N.E.A.S., chairman of the League, an outspoken empire federationist in the 1870s, and a vice-president and member of the Executive Committee of the National Association for the Promotion of State-directed Colonization in the 1880s.

52. The actual numbers on poor-relief increased steadily from 1864. 1869–71 were peak years with over three million each year. When seen as a percentage of the total population, however, those on relief remained fairly stable from 1853. Expenditure rose rather dramatically from £ 5.4 million in 1850 to £ 7.6 million in 1870. The numbers receiving relief are a poor guide to the dimensions of poverty. In this period those who claimed poor-relief were subjected to a rigorous new test aimed at cutting down the numbers (Best, 140–8).

53. Young, 5.

54. These reviews appeared in, respectively, *The Blackburn Times*, 31 July 1869; *Bells Weekly Messenger*, 16 Aug. 1869; and *Lloyds News*, 15 Aug. 1869 (from the collection of newspaper clippings in Young's "Speeches and Notices, 1872" at the Royal Commonwealth Society Library).

55. The *Times*, 4 June 1869, 5. The deputation included Lord George Hamilton, the Rev. A. S. Herring, John Bate, R. R. Torrens, and J. Holms. Precedents for state aid included government loans for drainage work and waste-land improvement, irrigation work in

India, relief grants during the Irish famine, compensation of West
Indian slave owners, and assistance given to enable Indians to
emigrate to Burma.

56. *Ibid.*, 22 June 1869, 6. This deputation included Young, Jenkins,
Bate, Charles Reed, E. B. Eastwick, and the Revs. Murphy and
Ottey.

57. *Ibid.*, 1 July 1869, 11. At a June 30 meeting at Session House,
Westminster, chaired by Lord Alfred Churchill with the support
of Manchester and Houghton. A. S. Ayrton (Liberal MP for Tower
Hamlets), speaking, it was believed, on behalf of the government,
had strongly stated at a meeting of emigrationists in Poplar that
aid ought to be obtained from the guardians as provided by law.

58. William Freston, *Report of the Conference Presided over by the
Duke of Manchester on the Question whether Colonization and
Emigration may be made Self-supporting or even Profitable for
those investing capital therein.* (London, 1869), 9–15. The National Emigrants' Aid Corporation's Fielding Settlement was established in New Zealand in 1874; Gen. Fielding made an
exploratory tour in 1870. See P. P. 1890 (354), *Report of the
Colonization Committee,* 90; W. Hazell and H. Hodgkin, *The
Australasian Colonies: Emigration and Colonization* (London,
1887), 70–4; and Johnson, 234–5.

59. The *Times,* 13 July, 1869, 9; 14 Aug. 1869, 4. The Poor Law Board
itself tried to discourage local guardians from pauper emigration.
In January, 1870, it circulated a warning to the English guardians
that "It is obvious that if any Board of Guardians should select for
emigration the idle, improvident, or worthless, they would be
only seeking to shift the burden of supporting . . . such persons
from themselves to the country to which they may send them."
M. H. 19/22, Correspondence and Papers (Poor-Law Board,
6539/70). The local guardians themselves were invariably opposed to much pauper emigration when the costs devolved upon
their union, but were usually favourable to any scheme based on
a wider distribution of costs.

60. For example, in September the secretary of the Dock Labourers'
Association, J. W. Richardson, called for the emigration by the
state of unskilled men (J.R. Taylor to Capt. R. F. Younger, 4 Sept.
1869, in the Manchester Papers, Box 20A, #3).

61. Frederick Young, "Emigration," dated 29 Dec. 1869, in "Speeches and Notices, 1870," 24.
62. The *Times*, 1 Jan. 1870, 8. The League committee included George Potter, Edmond Beales, Daniel Pratt, R. M. Latham, and Daniel Guile (for the W.E.L.), and Gen. Denison, E. B. Eastwick, the Revs. Herring and Ottey, Jenkins, Col. Maude, and Bate (for the N.E.A.S.).
63. *Ibid.*, 5 Jan. 1870, 10.
64. Frederick Young to the Duke of Manchester, 12 Jan. 1870, Manchester Papers, Box 51B, #4.
65. The *Times*, 7 Jan. 1870, 8.
66. Young to Manchester, 14 Jan. 1870.
67. *Ibid.*, and the *Times*, 15 Jan. 1870, 7.
68. Edward Jenkins (1838–1910), author of *Ginx's Baby*, was a London barrister who had grown up in the colonies. The son of a Presbyterian missionary, he was born in India and attended High School and McGill College in Montreal. A vocal Liberal-Imperialist, he was Agent-General for Canada in London, 1874–1875 (*Dods Parliamentary Register*, 1880).
69. The *Times*, 27 Jan. 1870, 6. Their letters of support were read at a mass meeting of 2000 at Lambeth Baths on Jan. 26. Carlyle had dreamed of an "emigration service" in *Past and Present*, John Stuart Mill supported Wakefield, and Tennyson was later to become involved in South African colonization.
70. The *Times*, 20 Jan. 1870, 9; 10 Feb. 1870, 6.
71. *Ibid.*, 28 Jan. 1870, 8.
72. This prompted a reply from the Rev. G. P. Ottey: "Sir, my socialism is not confused. It is founded in the belief that the Government is bound to take means for removing the sufferings of the people when private means are proved inadequate. I conceive that such a remedy may now be found in emigration to our colonies, which have room for the population of a score of Englands." The *Times*, 31 Jan. 1870, 10.
73. J. A. Froude, "England and her Colonies," *Fraser's Magazine*, Vol. 1, n.s. (1870), 1–16.
74. *Ibid.*, 3, 4.
75. The *Times*, 4 Feb. 1870, 8.
76. *Ibid.*, 27 Jan. 1870, 6; 16 Feb. 1870, 12. The presentation commit-

52   *Emigration in 19th-Century Britain*

tee included William and Robert Torrens, Grey, Col. Maude, J. E. Gorst, Froude, and C. W. Eddy.

77. The *Times,* 8 Feb. 1870, 10; 9 Feb. 1870, 9; 10 Feb. 1870, 5–6; 16 Feb. 1870, 12; 17 Feb. 1870, 13; 21 Feb. 1870, 9; 22 Feb. 1870, 10; 2 March 1870, 5.
78. "That, in order to arrest the increase of Pauperism, and to relieve the distressed condition of the working classes, it is expedient that measures be adopted for facilitating Emigration of poor families to British Colonies."
79. *Hansard,* Vol. 199 (Commons, 1 March 1870), 1004–10.
80. *Ibid.,* 1070–1.
81. The *Times,* 4 March 1870, 9.
82. Edward Jenkins to the Duke of Manchester, 7 March 1870, Manchester Papers, Box 51B, #4.
83. Granville to Gladstone, 2 March 1870, in Agatha Ramm, *The Political Correspondence of Mr. Gladstone and Lord Granville* (Camden Third Series, No. 81, 1952), Vol. 1, 9.
84. Jenkins to Manchester, 7 March 1870.
85. *Prospectus of the National Colonial and Emigration League* 1870), 2.
86. *Ibid.,* 1.
87. P.P. 1870 (179).
88. P.P. 1871 (c. 335); P.P. 1871 (c. 296).
89. P.P. 1871 (c. 296), 3. Sir Thomas William Clinton Murdoch (1809–1891) had been chairman of the Colonial Land and Emigration Commission since 1847.
90. *30th Report,* Emigration Commission, 5–11. These objections were made public before the report was published by Freston in a letter to the *Times,* 20 Jan. 1870, 9. The Commissioners had made similar objections to proposals to aid the Irish by state emigration in 1847. From its inception in 1840, the Commission had not been popular with emigrationists who saw it as a do-little device to take pressure off the Colonial Office. See, for example, E. G. Wakefield, *The Art of Colonization,* 397–8.
91. Jenkins went on to contest, successfully, Dundee in 1874 as a Liberal-Imperialist, but did not stand in 1880. Increasingly dissatisfied with Gladstonian foreign and colonial policies, he became a Conservative in 1885, but failed to regain a seat.
92. The *Times,* 19 May 1870, 7.
93. J. E. Tyler, *The Struggle for Imperial Unity* (London, 1938), 4.

94. The Rev. Horrocks Cocks to the Duke of Manchester, 4 May 1871, the Manchester Papers, Box 20A, #3.
95. Cocks to Manchester, 6 April 1871.
96. Cocks to Manchester, 4, May 1871.
97. Norbert C. Soldon, *Laissez-faire on the Defensive: the Story of the Liberty and Property Defense League, 1882–1914* (Unpublished Ph.D. thesis, University of Delaware, 1969), 140.
98. N. H. Carrier and J. R. Jeffrey, *External Migration. A Study of the Available Statistics, 1815–1950* (London, 1953), 22, 90, 92; Johnson, 65. Though the total number of emigrants rose only slightly, those from England and Wales increased sharply. 1873 was a high point (123,343 emigrants) and emigration did not surpass this figure until 1881.
99. J. E. Tyler, *The Struggle for Imperial Unity* (London, 1938), 100.
100. Trevor R. Reese, *The History of the Royal Commonwealth Society 1869–1968* (London, 1968), 33–38.
101. A printed advertisement for the Conference, in the Manchester Papers, Box 20A, #3, contains a list of vice presidents.
102. *Discussions on Colonial Questions* (London, 1872), 4–5, 93–116. In 1874, Jenkins became Agent-General for Canada.
103. There were rising complaints from colonial labour about immigration, and in England emigration proposals were roundly attacked by the Marxist Land and Labour League (Royden Harrison, *Before the Socialists* [London, 1965], 221–2, 244).
104. *Discussions,* 115.

Chapter 3. Other Directions, 1871–1882

F ailure in 1870 did not crush all life out of the emigration lobby; rather it knocked it into its constituent parts. In the decade that followed, these groups and individuals continued to promote private assistance and, occasionally, to call for government support of their sectional, limited interests. In the early 1880s, they coalesced once again into a national pressure group—more powerful and longer lived than the League of 1870.

3.1 *Juvenile Emigration: Saving the Children*

By far the most publicized emigration activity in the 1870s was the sending out of children, chiefly to Canada, by philanthropists working independently or in conjunction with Poor-Law authorities, reformatories, and industrial schools. In origin, this form of "relief" was closely related at the beginning of the century to child crime and vagrancy, and the problems which "juvenile delinquency" posed for urban social control and penal reform. Many humanitarians were persuaded that child offenders, in the absence of any kind of rehabilitation system in England, were better off in the colonies, away from the corrupting influence of the slum. This belief produced an alliance between philanthropy and judicial authorities which secured long terms of transportation for children for even minor kinds of crime. Even though transportation of criminals was stopped in the 1850s, the philanthropic emigration of pauper children never quite shook off its association with punishment and discipline.[1]

Nevertheless, the dispatch of poor children to homes in the colonies continued to have enthusiastic advocates, in spite of the obvious potentiality for abuse. Schemes to "rescue the children" from the urban slum attracted the best and worst in Victorian society—Shaftesburyite philanthropists and the most shameless profiteers, while debate over the proprietary rights of pauper or criminal parents versus the welfare of the children illuminates a Victorian moral dilemma.

Two women, Maria Susan Rye[2] and Annie Macpherson, were largely responsible for reviving in the late 1860s a type of assistance which had nearly died out in the previous decade due to the exposure of abuses, and to the Act of 1853 which prohibited the transportation of juvenile criminals. Poor-Law authorities had the power to transport pauper children from 1834 but, though the colonies were eager to receive children for adoption and for domestic and farm labour, few guardians actually used their authority. Emigration, except in the case of very young children, might be more expensive than keeping juveniles on relief for a couple of years until they could be pushed out into the able-bodied-labour market. It also posed a high risk of embarrassment for public officials. Parish authorities were ill-equipped to supervise emigration or see to proper follow-up investigation in the colonies. Therefore they ran the danger of enraging a tender public conscience over some sensational scandal of child abuse. Official procedures also grew more complicated. After 1844, Poor-Law authorities had to secure the consent of the Poor-Law Board before they could send pauper children abroad. In 1850 they were required to get the consent of the children. Finally, in 1851, the Poor-Law Board withdrew its permission entirely, pending investigation of a scandal over the St. Pancras Union's placing of children in the West Indies.[3]

Private emigration of children continued, however. An early attempt to organize this form of relief was that of the Society for the Suppression of Juvenile Vagrancy (afterwards the Children's Friendly Society) which in the 1830s established training homes in England for the children they apprenticed to colonial employers.[4] In the late 1840s, Lord Ashley's Ragged Schools began to recruit children for emigration from reformatories and the streets. In 1848, Ashley asked for state subsidies for Ragged School emigration.

> The Government should agree to take every year from these schools a number of children—say, 1,000—500 boys and the same number of girls—and transplant them at the public expense to her Majesty's colonies in South Australia [where they] will walk in all the dignity of honest men and Christian citizens.[5]

He received, in fact, a government grant of £1500, and a false sense of optimism: "This 'Ragged' motion has produced considerable effect; much is said everywhere. I received abundant letters, onymous [sic] and anonymous, in high terms of approbation."[6] Though "Lord Ashley's boys" were considered to be generally successful in the colonies, the grant was not renewed.[7] Much to his distress, he was thrown back on private charity.

So I am now to be disappointed, nay deceived! No emigration for my ragged children unless I raise a sum of money for that purpose. How is that to be done?[8]

Ashley, who became the seventh Earl of Shaftesbury in 1851, did, however, find private contributions, and Ragged School emigration continued into the 1860s.

Both Dr. Thomas Barnardo and Maria Rye were closely connected to Shaftesbury by ties of friendship and common purpose, and both took up child-emigration projects of their own in the metropolis. With Shaftesbury's patronage, Barnardo founded the East End Juvenile Mission in 1867, and opened his first Boy's Home in 1870. There was some emigration assistance from the beginning, though Barnardo did not become enthusiastic about this form of

A London School Board "Capture," 1871 (Source: *Ill. London News,* Sep. 9, 1871)

A "Distressed Gentlewoman" waits to embark, 1875 (Source: *Ill. London News,* July 3, 1875)

relief until the 1880s, when well organized and super-vised parties of boys were taken to Canada.

> I am now preparing to send 200 lads to Canada on March 17th. I shall probably leave myself in the end of March or the beginning of April to superintend the details of our new Colony in Manitoba. As your Lordship is perhaps aware, we have secured a little more than seven square miles of territory at Birtle, some 400 miles West and North of Winnipeg; I propose this season to start an Industrial Farm upon what I hope will prove to be a wise and financially successful basis.[8a]

Barnardo came to support a thorough government pro-gram.

> I regard with amazement . . . the unwillingness of a great adminis-trative department of the State to sanction a small expenditure for the maintenance of its child-clients in one of our Colonies *at half the annual cost that is already being incurred in maintaining the same children in England* . . . .[9]

Rye had been involved in emigration assistance from the beginning of her feminist efforts to secure work for women. In 1859, she raised, with Jane Lewin, a fund to assist girls to emigrate while, at the same time, helping them to find employment as clerks and journalists in En-gland. In the course of these efforts she came to despair of opening further employment for women in England, and was inclined "more and more towards the establish-ment of some scheme, by which educated women may with safety be introduced into the colonies" where social barriers to working women were far less onerous and entailed less loss of caste.[10]

In 1861, Rye founded the Female Middle-Class Emigra-tion Society (absorbed in 1884 into the United British Women's Emigration Association). After a tour of the colonies in 1867 to organize committees for the protec-

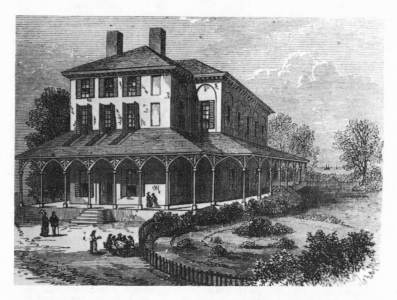

Miss Rye's Home for Emigrant Female Children at Niagara, Lake Ontario, 1877 (Source: *Ill. London News,* Sep. 29, 1877)

tion of her emigrants, she decided to concentrate all her efforts, with the help of Annie Macpherson and the Church of England Waifs and Strays Society, on the emigration of pauper children. Encouraged by Lord Shaftesbury, and with the financial support of William Rathbone, Liberal MP for Liverpool, she bought Avenue House, High Street, Peckham, in 1869—to which she took children from off the streets, in spite of some public opposition. These children were given courses in "useful skills" and sent to Homes in the colonies for dispersal to interested families. In the beginning, she personally accompanied each group to Canada and inspected their future homes.[11]

In the 1870s, Rye, who received a Civil List pension of £ 70 in 1871, worked in close cooperation with those

Poor-Law authorities in London who would have anything to do with child emigration. Poor-Law Board sanction was restored in 1870, and 451 workhouse children
were sent to Canada by Rye the following year.[12] These
efforts rapidly exceeded her personal capacity to inspect
results, and an unfavourable report by a Canadian Poor-
Law inspector in 1875 brought cooperation with the
unions to a temporary halt. It cited a lack of supervision,
examples of cruelty and exploitation in the foster homes,
and a calculation that Rye herself made a profit of £4 9s.
on each child. As a result, the English Poor-Law Board
prohibited further emigration pending a full Canadian
government report on the children already sent out.[13]
The withdrawal again of Board sanction raised a protest
from those unions which had used their powers to work
with Rye. On June 27, 1877, a deputation which included
W. H. Smith and Sir Charles Russell appealed for the
Board to continue emigration through Rye's organization.[14] Though child emigration was sanctioned again in
1883, it proved very difficult to get inspection in Canada,
and emigration proceeded only by bumps and jolts.[15]
However, the allegations of profit, like those made against
Shaftesbury in the 1840s, were almost certainly untrue.
The report grossly underestimated the cost to Rye of
training, passages, and reception. Rye and Macpherson
received testimony in support of their activities from the
Anglican Bishop of Toronto but were, like Barnardo,
strongly attacked by Roman Catholics.[16]

Rye's efforts attracted the attention of J. A. Froude, who
hoped for a large national program of child emigration to
other colonies, and particularly to southern Africa.

Thousands of boys and girls, 13 or 14 years old would be annually
leaving our National Schools. Rudimentally educated, but being

orphans and otherwise helpless they would have no prospect of finding useful occupations in town. If such boys & girls could be taken out under some system of apprenticeship and distributed among the farmers and established artisans in the Colonies, under indenture to remain with and work with their employers till they were 21 the Colonies themselves would be provided with the very best class of immigrants whom they would desire and the children themselves would humanly speaking be assured of a happy and prosperous future ... Expense would be no difficulty, for the cost of transport would be defrayed out of the wages which would accrue to the apprentices in their minority. And a handsome sum would be due to them to commence life with when their time was out. They would have received a training which would fit them to begin work on their own account with a certainty of success. Every care would be taken to assure their good treatment. They would be such valuable additions to the community that there was not the least fear that they would be neglected or ill used.[16a]

Fired with enthusiasm for this scheme, Froude interviewed the Cape Premier, John Molteno, in Africa in 1874. Molteno responded "warmly and eagerly", and Froude returned to England with high hopes. Board Schools might even offer free passages as prizes for good conduct. English authorities, however, quickly killed these dreams.

I myself thought that such an offer ought to be welcomed at home ... I regretted to find that it was not so regarded by the Home Authorities. I submitted what Mr. Molteno had said to the proper quarters. I found so cold a reception that I thought it useless to press the matter further.[17]

Child emigration was left to the private efforts of Rye and Macpherson and their many imitators.[18] On a somewhat larger scale, the Children's Emigration Homes at Birmingham (1872) and the Sheltering Homes at Liverpool (1875) began to assist juveniles to leave the country. An Act of 1872 enabled school authorities to finance emigration, and many private philanthropists established close relationships with local school officials. Many of the promoters of child emigration, however, were unsatisfied with these relatively modest and unorganized efforts. Barnardo, Rye, Macpherson, Cardinal Manning, Samuel Smith, Ellen Joyce, and J. A. Froude all became active members in the 1880s of the National Association for Promoting State-directed Colonization.

3.2 The "Great Depression"

The two decades from the mid-1870s are generally regarded as a period of at least relative economic decline, when Britain, as the first industrial nation, gradually lost her lead to the Continent and the United States. The "depression," however, was highly selective, affecting some sectors of the economy strongly while others flourished. Gradual, if hesitant, general improvement in real wages appears to have been accompanied by a high, though fluctuating, level of unemployment after 1878. The year 1879 was a particularly bad one, and a recovery boom which followed was disappointing in magnitude and short-lived. From 1884 to 1887 there was a singularly high level of unemployment. Though real wages rose steadily to 1876, fluctuated to 1882, and again rose markedly to 1900, money wages actually fell from 1873 to 1876 and remained very stable from 1876 to 1888.[19]

What gradual improvement there might have been, therefore was largely disguised from contemporary eyes by recurring crises, the increased threat of foreign competition, falling money wages, and nostalgia for the boom years of mid-century. Certainly the crisis years of 1879 and 1884–1887, with over 7 percent unemployed among the unionized trades, were serious times indeed for those whom General Booth called "the submerged tenth". According to the Webbs, the depression of 1879 produced a "universal feeling of despondency" and "crowds of unemployed."[20] There was a great increase in the number of strikes in all trades, with substantial losses for workmen in both hours and wages.

By the autumn of 1879, trade unions turned from industrial action back to the time-worn solution of emigration to relieve the labour market. In Sheffield, labourers in the iron and steel trades organized a Workmen's Emigration Association to assist laid-off members to emigrate. Another organization in the same district had been founded a month earlier to enable Sheffield workers to emigrate to the western United States.[21] A similar response occurred

Emigration agent lecturing striking Welsh miners, 1875 (Source: *Ill. London News*, Mar. 6, 1875)

in Oldham, where cotton workers inaugurated a scheme of emigration "in consequence of the depressed state of the trade" and applied, unsuccessfully, to the government for emigration assistance.[22] In some areas, agricultural labour as well turned to emigration, though Joseph Arch, founding father of the agricultural labour movement, was at the time not enthusiastic about it. The Kent and Sussex Labourer's Union, led by Alfred Simmons, arranged for 500 of its members to emigrate to New Zealand in 1879.[23]

By spring of 1880, emigration registered "an enormous increase" as labourers with the means reacted to the trade crisis and industrial confrontation.[24] The trade unions of Oldham, Sheffield, and Kent, which were most involved in the emigration of members during the crisis of 1879, formed the core of labour support for the National Association four years later. Union funds were seriously depleted by the 1879 crisis, which may account for their application, through the emigration lobby, for state aid.

Agricultural contribution to emigration increased significantly in the 1880s. It was in this decade that the full impact of American wheat was felt in Europe. After 1877, grain prices plunged in England, in spite of successive bad harvests, and were never to return to their previous level. In the 12 years from 1874 to 1886, the area under cultivation for wheat shrank by 1,344,000 acres.[25] Many tenant farmers and farm labourers emigrated, and many drifted to other occupations in England or swelled the ranks of "general labour". Of those who tried to alleviate distress by local movement, there were many who were dissatisfied and, though they could not afford to emigrate immediately, were ripe for emigration as a last resort.[26] This willingneess of rural labour to leave gave impetus to colonization plans which hinged upon the placing of English emigrants on colonial soil as peasant proprietors. Previously, objections to such plans had focused on the unfitness of urban emigrants for agricultural life. It could now be convincingly maintained that there was a pool of skilled farm labour willing to leave for the colonies. At the same time, many, especially urban trade unionists, expressed great concern that agricultural labour migrating into industrial towns at home competed unfairly with organized labour accustomed to higher standards. They saw in emigration a means of diverting this stream before it reached the cities.[27]

Inspired by the agricultural crisis, the wave of industrial strikes, and the threat of land reform which the agricultural labour movement seemed to presage, there was at this time a revival of middle-class interest in a "surplus labour" emigration panacea. Arch's movement, though doomed to a rapid decline, was supported by the Birmingham Radicals (Chamberlain, Dixon and Collings) and by the Land Tenure Reform Association. In the 1880s, Henry George's *Progress and Poverty,* his own speaking tours in England, increasing agricultural violence in Ireland and Scotland, and a general impression that the Liberal Party was being pushed inexorably by Chamberlain toward some kind of radical anti-landlord reform helped animate a large and varied group, bound together by the common threat of expropriation, and avidly searching for alternatives to land reform.

In 1877, J. F. Boyd, drawing attention to the impoverishment of English agriculture and continued population growth, submitted a "Scheme of State-directed Emigration and Colonization" to the Prime Minister, Benjamin Disraeli. Boyd quoted passages from *Endymion,* in which Disraeli himself had forecast serious changes in England due to the increase of a population not employed on the

"Last Day in Old England" for a
farm labourer, 1875 (Source: *Ill.
London News,* July 3, 1875)

Benjamin Disraeli, novelist and
Prime Minister (Source: *Ill.
London News,* Feb. 14, 1874)

soil. State emigration was a logical corollary to free trade.
If the government refused to protect labour with tariffs
the way other European countries protected their agricultural labour, it might at least give them the means to
remove to viable farms within the Empire.[28] There was
a number of similar efforts to interest the government in
state emigration in the years immediately following. For
instance, in 1879 a Mr. Duncan Campbell of Keighley
submitted an "Imperial scheme of emigration" to the Colonial Office, where it was quietly dismissed on the
grounds that it would interfere with colonial control of
their own waste lands.[29]

In the autumn of 1879, Stephen Bourne read a paper at
the Royal Colonial Institute (R.C.I.) on "Extended Coloni-

zation a Necessity to the Mother Country" before an approving audience which included W. E. Forster, Frederick Young (Secretary of the R.C.I. since 1874), and R. R. Torrens. Bourne gave a statistical demonstration of the decreasing percentage of food consumption which could be supplied by home farmers. Land reform would be of little use because farmers with small holdings would turn from wheat to the more profitable crops, further reducing the number fed per acre. Imports of grain produced a steadily worsening balance of trade. How long could the country live on its savings? " . . . on financial grounds alone there is a necessity for extended emigration. We have hitherto been parting with thousands; it must now be by hundreds of thousands, even if not by millions." Bourne threw aside the twin-Victorian idols of education and charity. Educating the working classes merely increased their sense of discontent. Charity simply palliated evils it was powerless to overcome. Salvation lay in finding an American West for England. No scheme for limiting population at home without emigration could promise a continuing expansion of wealth. This required the multiplication of life: "Colonial possessions will allow us to continue to expand our population—the real sources of riches."[30]

Bourne concluded with a plea for a "new colonization" rather than simple emigration, to be accomplished by the government's use of its power to dominate narrow colonial interests. The Colonial Secretary would become the most important minister of the Crown.[31] This scheme is of interest because it indicates a change in emphasis in emigration-thinking in the 1880s. "Colonization" was a step beyond the "systematic emigration" of the National Emigration League. It envisaged the wholesale planting of ordered communities by the state. Froude's praise of

James I's Irish settlements and his preference for an authoritarian Renaissance model of colony building had pointed the way. Colonization on these lines involved the state in the construction of a Utopian society abroad—encompassing the selection of land, erection of standardized prefabricated buildings, careful selection of emigrants for the right "mix", and state-held mortgages.

This call for state action as a guiding, creative force was alien to the mainstream of liberal thought, but was part of a general late-Victorian phenomenon. Rejection of *laissez faire* in favour of collectivism in one form or another was expressed philosophically by the neo-idealists at Oxford and politically by some of the new radicals. But colonization was also a logical result of the political situation emigrationists faced. Colonial electorates were firmly opposed to a large influx of labour, and these fears could only be allayed by a scheme which could promise the absorption of emigrants without serious economic dislocation. It was, as a program, constructed primarily for propaganda—though it conveniently dove-tailed with the new intellectual predisposition.

3.3 *Ireland and State Emigration*

The Liberal Party defeated "Beaconsfieldism" at the polls in April of 1880, and Gladstone formed his third government. Emigrationists, disappointed at Disraeli's lack of interest, hurried to submit their schemes. While in Opposition, the Liberals had given them little encouragement. Forster commented in November of 1879 that he did not feel any state emigration plan was feasible, though he did believe in the need for emigration. At that time he could only offer the hope that the colonies would imitate the United States' homestead legislation, accompanied perhaps by a more efficient system of emigration information in England.[32]

It came as a surprise, therefore, that the government was willing to entertain suggestions of assisted emigration from Ireland as a solution of the growing disaffection in that unhappy island. Emigrationists like Edward T. Wakefield, a London barrister, were quick to seize upon this as the thin edge, hoping that the government would not be able to refuse England that which it granted across the Irish Sea.

Liberals had last seriously considered a large scheme of state emigration from Ireland in the aftermath of the great famine of the 1840s. Massive aid to emigration was then seen as one possible solution to the land question—a Whiggish sort of measure to alleviate distress without tinkering with private property. The Earl of Clarendon, Chief Secretary at that time, urged Russell to adopt a large centralized system of government emigration assistance. Such a program would offer "permanent utility" in humanitarian relief, reduction of the poor-rates, and promotion of the transfer of land to persons with greater capital.[33]

In fact, both Grey and Russell proposed schemes for emigration assistance in the Cabinet in 1848. Russell's scheme, the only workable one of the two, was a comprehensive plan for the whole of the United Kingdom. Proceeds from a special property tax would be given to the emigration commissioners who would also be empowered to raise money by loans to a limit of £ 5 million a year. Whenever the rates reached 5s. in the pound, unions would be empowered to transport families of the able-bodied, the commissioners contributing as much as £ 2 per head.[34] As it happened, Grey and his cousin Sir Francis Baring, an advocate of strict economy, with Charles

Wood and Lord Lansdowne were able to obstruct Cabinet adoption. Russell, who "had the mortification to find that he could not carry his own proposal for emigration", toyed with the idea of resignation, but allowed Clarendon to persuade him to acquiesce. In place of action, the Cabinet agreed upon a weak statement that there was no objection to emigration assistance "in principle".[35]

There was no talk of emigration in the Irish proposals of Gladstone's first government. In 1879, however, the murder of the Earl of Leitrim, a notorious evicting landlord, ushered in a new phase of land war and acts of violence. Ireland became again the dominating issue in home politics. Though Forster was converted to coercion, the Cabinet placed its chief hopes in further land reform. The first measure, introduced April 7, 1881, contained the famous principles of fixity of tenure, fair rent, and free sale. A second Bill (the Arrears of Rent [Ireland] Act of 1882) included, along with government payment of one-half tenant arrears, sections enabling the Irish government to assist emigration.[36]

A memorandum forwarded to the Colonial Office by the Marquess of Lorne,[37] Governor General of Canada, from the Canadian Privy Council in November of 1880 appears to have been largely responsible for this emigration clause, though a Royal Commission on agriculture (1879–1882) and one on landlord-tenant relations in Ireland (1881) both recommended emigration from the West of Ireland.[38] Lorne's memorandum contained a proposal, drafted by the Canadian Minister of Agriculture at the suggestion of Sir A. T. Galt, High Commissioner in England, for the organization of Irish immigration to Manitoba and the Canadian Northwest. The Canadian government promised to cooperate "cheerfully" in "a well-considered measure of relief by means of a systematic immigration from Ireland." It was proposed that Canada make land available for the reception of Irish families, and maintain them on these prepared farms until the first crops came in.[39]

The resulting emigration clauses in the Arrears of Rent (Ireland) Bill, which allowed the Irish government to raise money for emigration without limitation, was "very much cut down and limited" at the insistence of Irish MPs. In the House of Lords, Carnarvon tried without success to restore these powers.[40] The final Act limited total expenditure to £ 100,000 and individual grants to not more than £ 5 per head. Unless supplemented by colonial governments or private organizations, the £ 5 limit effectively restricted the emigration to America. The Colonial Office sounded out the willingness of colonial governments to cooperate in state emigration of Irish peasants, but replies from the Cape, Natal, Queensland, and Victoria were decidedly negative. Though they stressed the tightness of the labour market and unavailability of open land, anti-Irish prejudice was clearly a large, if unstated, factor.[41] This was obviously the case in Natal, which, through its immigration agent Walter Peace, spent a great deal of effort attempting to secure English immigrants throughout the 1880s.

Canada, however, replied in the spirit of the memorandum of 1880, and claimed "employment can be found for any number of Mechanics, Farm and General Labourers, Navvies, and Domestic Servants in every part of Canada."[42] Behind this optimism lay the anticipated opening of the Canadian West by the Canadian Pacific Railway. An Irish Emigration Commission was set up in Dublin to coordinate emigration under the Act, and a number of Irish unions began making use of their powers in the autumn of 1882. The Act provided that these unions could obtain funds for emigration by borrowing on the rates or by direct grants from the Commission of Public Works, which was also empowered to make grants to any "other such body or persons and on such terms as the Lord Lieutenant may approve." The ceiling of £ 100,000 restricted the aid to a relatively small number of unions. The money came from the Irish Church Temporalities Fund.[43]

A private organization established in 1881 by the Quaker philanthropist J. H. Tuke[44] to raise and administer subscriptions for Irish relief sought and obtained qualification for the government emigration grants. Eventually, most of the actual work of emigrating from Ireland under the Act was carried out by the Tuke's Fund Committee. As early as 1880, Tuke himself had been in private communication with Canadian authorities, and in September a meeting was arranged by Forster with Sir John Macdonald, Canadian Prime Minister, and Galt. The result was an abortive Manitoba colonization scheme.[45] Forster, though not sharing direct responsibility for the Irish Land Bill of 1880–1881, urged Gladstone to include measures to prevent overcrowding.[46] In April, 1882, he wrote from Dublin Castle that "Emigration is the only hope for the western men."[47] In the three years of greatest activity, Tuke's Fund Committee spent about £ 20,000 of its subscriptions and £ 44,000 of government money (1882–1884).[48]

Tuke's Fund Committee sent 9482 Irish poor to Canada in three years. At the same time, the Irish unions extended their assistance from under 300 individuals a year to five times that number.[49] To advance these efforts, Tuke published an article on "Irish Emigration" in the *Nineteenth Century* in February of 1881, advocating "systematic emigration" as a joint Imperial and Canadian enterprise.[50] Systematic emigration did not, however, necessarily mean colonization. Tuke was, in fact, greatly disappointed in his Manitoba settlement efforts, and this led him to separate himself from the advocates of state-aided colonization by 1885. Instead, he believed that the simple emigration practiced by many philanthropic societies could be expanded and made more efficient by the amalgamation of resources and personnel into a single federated organization.[51]

Canadian interest in promoting emigration, state aid under the Arrears of Rent Act in Ireland, and indication that the program might be extended to at least the Highlands and Islands of Scotland[52] encouraged a spate of emigration and colonization schemes in the early 1880s. One of these is interesting from the clearness of its motivation and the Colonial Office response it engendered.

Edward Thomas Wakefield was a London barrister who had long been involved in metropolitan charity work. By 1881, he came to believe that systematic colonization was the only remedy which could bring about "the permanent pacification of Ireland."[53] He sensed a change in public opinion in favour of the state-aided emigration of families, and Lord Derby's arrival at the Colonial Office encouraged him to submit a detailed scheme to the Colonial Secretary in three letters. The program he proposed involved the acquisition of Australian land by the government, its division into homesteads based on the American model, the erection of prefabricated structures, free emigration to prepared and equipped homesites, government credit for seed, and no rent until the third year. At an average cost of £ 250 per family, the government could deal with the emigrants either directly or through the intermediary of a commercial company. Either way, the undertaking would be closely supervised and controlled by government even after the settlements had established themselves. He proposed an experiment of 1000 carefully selected Irish families.[54]

Wakefield's program was plainly socially conservative in its intent. "It is certain that a solid substratum of physical sufferings always underlies persistent sedition."[55] Emigration could promise civil peace in Ireland.

> I entertain no doubt that all the horrors of assassination, maiming, arson, and perjuries that have since been perpetrated, would have been averted, and their victims alive and well at the present hour [had an emigration scheme been adopted].[56]

In relieving revolution-breeding distress, the "real benefits" of emigration which would alleviate land competition and reduce rents, contrasted favourably with the "shadowy benefits" of Home Rule or land reform. Colonization was "capable of profoundly affecting the social condition of the people without touching any rights of person or property, and in this respect is in striking contrast with recent legislation."[57]

Derby was not, it appears, unsympathetic, and Wakefield's scheme was given due consideration by the Colonial Office staff. Assistant Under-Secretary Edward Wingfield, who had recommended rejection of Boyd's scheme in 1877, minuted favourably that "I am convinced that such a scheme, if well-worked, would even if it cost very much more than Mr. Wakefield estimates be a good investment for the United Kingdom and would also benefit the colonies." His superior, however, Permanent Under-Secretary Sir Robert Herbert, recommended a firm rejection of Wakefield's request for an interview in light of Australian disapproval of emigration schemes.[58]

Derby and his parliamentary Under-Secretary Evelyn Ashley (a son of Lord Shaftesbury) were, however, interested in the proposals, and Wakefield was not dismissed out of hand. Ashley believed

Departure of Irish Emigrants from Clifden, County Galway, 1883 (Source: *Ill. London News,* July 21, 1883)

Edward Henry Stanley, fifteenth Earl of Derby (Source: *Ill. London News,* Jan. 13, 1883)

> some such scheme as that sketched out by Mr. Wakefield would be a most beneficial measure—and Ireland at least will never be quiet until something of this sort is done. It ought not, however, to be confined to Ireland . . . .[59]

The unwillingness of colonies to receive emigrants was limited, he thought, to pauper emigration. Derby agreed to see Wakefield, over the objections of his permanent staff, which dusted off the Colonial Land and Emigration Commission Report of 1870 to refute Wakefield. Ashley replied that that Report was "out of date" and urged a cabinet-level decision.

> Mr. Wakefield's letter shows such a thorough knowledge of *Irish character, Irish views,* and the circumstances of Ireland & is so thoroughly instructive that I wish Lord Derby could somehow or other get it circulated to the Cabinet![60]

Derby did see Wakefield on April 6, 1883, and circulated the correspondence in the Cabinet, where in all likelihood it received a brief and uninterested reception. Wakefield's argument was tailored to appeal to those, like Derby, who were anxious to find some handhold on the Irish problem that did not involve either radical Chamberlainite interference with property, or Home Rule. The attractiveness which colonization schemes had for some landed aristocrats, and the refusal of Gladstone's government to consider these a part of a realistic solution to Irish distress, is one further indication of the divisions opening within the Liberal Party. The National Association for State-directed Colonization would show in its membership a strong Liberal-Unionist presence.

Notes on Chapter 3

1. See Alex. C. Scholes, *Education for Empire Settlement. A Study of Juvenile Migration* (London, 1932), Chs. 1–4.
2. Maria Susan Rye (1829–1903), daughter of a London solicitor, was inspired by Charles Kingsley's father to devote her life to social reform, particularly the condition of women. She was secretary (1852) of an Association for Promoting the Married Women's Property Bill and a founder of the Women's Employment Society. In 1859, she established a law stationer's business to give employment to middle-class girls, and in 1860 helped Emily Faithful to establish the Victoria Printing Press. In 1861, she founded the Female Middle Class Emigration Society with the support of Charles Kingsley, Shaftesbury, and Lord Brougham. In 1869, she turned to child emigration. The year before, Annie Macpherson, an evangelical social worker in the London slums, began her well-organized efforts to take children to homes in Canada. Her "Revival Homes" where emigrant children were prepared, her personal supervision

en route, and arrangements for reception provided a model for other emigrationists, and these principles were insisted upon by Canadian authorities in later years (Scholes, 41–43; D.N.B.).

3. Johnson, 274–8.

4. Johnson, 274–5.

5. Commons, 6 June 1848, quoted in Edwin Hodder, *The Life and Work of the Seventh Earl of Shaftesbury* (London, 1888), Vol. 2, 257–8.

6. Diary entry, 12 June 1848, quoted in Hodder, 258.

7. Schaftesbury's zeal in promoting Ragged School emigration led to rumors that the scheme was a disguised system of child slavery which produced a £ 10 profit for every child sent out. Similar allegations had earlier been made against the Children's Friendly Society. (See the *Ragged School Union Magazine*, Dec. 1849, p. 221; and the Pilgrim Edition of the *Letters of Charles Dickens*, III. 436–37n. I am indebted to Mr. Norris Pope for this information.)

8. *Ibid.*, 21 June 1848, 262.

8a. Barnardo to Brabazon, Jan. 20, 1887 (Meath Papers, Autograph Vol. II).

9. S. L. Barnardo and Sir J. Marchant, *Memoirs of the Late Dr. Barnardo* (London, 1907), 154.

10. Maria S. Rye, *Emigration of Educated Women* (London, n.d. [1861?]), 4.

11. Johnson, 278–9; W. A. Carrothers, *Emigration from the British Isles,* (London, 1929), 278; A. J. Hammerston, *A Study of Middle-Class Female Emigration from Great Britain, 1830–1914* (unpublished Ph.D. thesis: University of British Columbia, 1969), 240, 246.

12. Johnson, 279.

13. P. P. 1875 (275), *First Report of the Select Committee of the Parliament of Canada on Immigration and Colonization* included testimony in support of Rye and Macpherson and recommended a full investigation. Andrew Doyle's unfavourable report was published in 1877.

14. *The Times,* 2 July 1877, 12. Smith was a major contributor to the British and Colonial Emigration Society. In 1872, he visited Canada and the United States, prompted in part by his emigration interests. In 1882, he became chairman of Tuke's Fund Committee which helped organize Irish emigration.

15. Dilke, as President of the Board, gave his sanction in 1883; it was again refused by Chamberlain in 1886 (M.H. 19/7 [30243/83,

32771/83, 34413/83, 450203/83] and M. H. 19/8 [12501/86, 79859/86]).

16. On the grounds that the children, who were frequently Irish, received Protestant religious training at the homes, and were sent to Protestant foster parents. Both Rye and Barnardo were aggressively anti-Catholic.

16a. Froude to Brabazon, Dec. 25, 1886? (Autograph Vol. I).

17. *Ibid.*

18. Scholes, 41, 44.

19. S. B. Saul, *The Myth of the Great Depression, 1873–1896* (London, 1969), 31–4.

20. Sidney and Beatrice Webb, *The History of Trade Unionism* (London, 1926 [rev. edn.]), 345–7.

21. The *Times,* 4 Aug. 1879, 6; 2 Oct. 1879, 5.

22. *Ibid.,* 23 Sept. 1879, 8. Cotton operatives failed in a long strike in 1878 to prevent wage cuts (Webbs, 344).

23. P. P. 1889, *Report of the Colonization Committee,* 93–4. See Alfred Simmons' *Old England and New Zealand* (London, 1879) for a description of his trip out with the emigrants. The union received assistance from the New Zealand government, and the men were settled on the land. Arch later softened his attitude, perhaps due to the influence of Edward Jenkins who became a trustee of the National Agricultural Labourers' Union in 1873 (see Pamela Horn, *Joseph Arch (1826–1919), The Farm Workers' Leader* (Kineton, 1971), 88, and "Agricultural Trade Unionism and Emigration, 1872–1881," *Historical Journal,* Vol. 15 (1972).

24. The *Times,* 13 May 1880, 11.

25. Mitchell and Dean, 78.

26. Ross Duncan, "Case Studies in Emigration: Cornwall, Gloucestershire and New South Wales, 1877–1886," *Economic History Review,* Vol. 16 (1963), describes this kind of pattern in the southwest.

27. According to Gareth Stedman Jones, *Outcast London* (Oxford, 1971), Ch. 6, the widely held assumption that rural migration contributed directly and significantly to the pool of casual labour in London was mistaken. The farm labourers were drawn instead to less crowded areas where regular employment was to be found.

28. J. F. Boyd, *State-directed Emigration* (Manchester, 1883), 2, 17–8. *Endymion,* Ch. 82.

29. The *Times,* 17 Jan. 1879, 6.

30. Stephen Bourne, "Extended Colonization a Necessity to the Mother Country," *Royal Colonial Institute Proceedings*, Vol. 11 (1879/80), 28. The paper was read 25 Nov. 1879.

31. *Ibid.*, 31. See the *Times*, 26 Feb. 1880, 11, for another colonization scheme presented by William Forster (one-time Agent General for New South Wales) to the Society of the Arts.

32. Bourne, 46–54.

33. Clarendon to Wilson, 25 Dec. 1847, quoted by Emilie Barrington, *Servant of All* (London, 1927), Vol. 1, 129–32.

34. Spencer Walpole, *The Life of Lord John Russell* (London, 1891), Vol. 2, 76–7.

35. *Ibid.*, 76–9. Also see Donald Southgate, *The Passing of the Whigs* (London, 1962), 181–2.

36. 45 & 46 Vic., Ch. 47, Secs. 18–21. The volume of Irish emigration had diminished greatly since 1847 despite the philanthropic efforts of such as Vere Forster, who assisted 15,000 Irish women to leave in the 1870s.

37. John Douglas Sutherland Campbell, the ninth Duke of Argyll (Lord Lorne until 1900), was Governor General 1878 to 1883. The Princess Louise, whom he married in 1871, was a patroness of the Women's Emigration Society. Lorne himself was a supporter of the Central Emigration Society and a member of the 1885 committee to consider federation of emigration societies. In 1886, he was influential in inducing the government to establish an Emigrants' Information Office.

38. C.O. 384/146 (19000), 7 Nov. 1883.

39. P.P. 1881 (C. 2835): dispatch, with enclosures, from the Marquess of Lorne to the Earl of Kimberley, 9 Nov. 1880.

40. *Hansard,* Vol. 286 (Lords, 28 March 1884), 990.

41. C.O. 384/142 (5275, 6409, 16203, and 16333).

42. *Ibid.*, 16062.

43. Arrears of Rent (Ireland) Act, 1882 (45 & 46 Vic., Ch. 47, Secs. 18–21). The original unions were Belmullet, Newport, Swineford, Clifden, and Oughternard. By November, 26 unions had applied. See P.P. 1883 (C. 3581), *Annual Report of the Local Government Board (Ireland)*.

44. James Hack Tuke (1819–1896) was a Yorkshire Quaker who had helped organize relief in Ireland during the famine, and in Paris in 1871. He was a major contributor to the Self-Help Emigration

Society, and an active member of the Congested Districts Board of 1891. From 1886, he was a member of the executive committee of the government's Emigrants' Information Office.

45. T. W. Reid, *Life of Forster* (London, 1888), Vol. 2, 258, 274; J. H. Tuke, "Irish Emigration," *Nineteenth Century,* Vol. 9 (Feb., 1881), 358; Tuke, "State Aid to Emigrants," *Nineteenth Century,* Vol. 17 (Feb., 1885), 280.
46. Reid, Vol. 2, 304. In 1848, Forster had proposed reform of the Poor Law and colonization as solutions to pauperism. He was a close friend of Lord Houghton (Vol. 1, 205, 258).
47. Forster to Gladstone, 10 April 1882, quoted by Reid, Vol. 2, 422.
48. Johnson, 73.
49. P.P. 1883 (C. 3581). 13.
50. Tuke, "Irish Emigration," 358.
51. Tuke, "State Aid," 280, 285. It was notoriously difficult to keep Canadian settlements together in the face of the high wages offered for railway construction and the lure of friends and relations in the United States.
52. C.O. 384/146 (19000).
53. E. T. Wakefield, *Irish Disaffection, its Cause and Cure* (London, 1881).
54. Wakefield to Lord Derby, 28 Jan. 1883, in E. T. Wakefield, *State-aided Emigration made Self-Supporting* (London, 1883), 12–22.
55. Wakefield to Derby, 25 Feb. 1883.
56. Wakefield to Derby, 28 Jan. 1883.
57. Wakefield to Derby, 25 Feb. 1883.
58. C.O. 384/147 (1403).
59. *Ibid.*
60. *Ibid.,* 3581 (Ashley minute dated 6 March 1883).

Chapter 4.   The Making of a
National Association, 1881–1883

C onstruction of the Canadian Pacific Railway (C.P.R.)
finally got under way in 1880,[1] and was followed by
a Dominion Land Act (1883) designed to encourage
a rapid settlement of the vast tracts of wilderness along
the C.P.R. route. The Act provided free grant land in
160-acre sections in Manitoba and the Northwest, and
allowed its use as security for loans up to £ 100 per settler-
family. This made it possible to secure emigration advances.[2] Settling an agricultural population along the
railway route was thought vital to its success and profitability, and the president of the C.P.R., George Stephen,[3]
sent a colonization scheme of his own to the Colonial
Office in April, 1883. This proposal got the support of both
the Colonial Office and the Irish government. It involved
the colonization of land along the route of the C.P.R. by
Irish families, with money loaned by the British government to an intermediate private company. Negotiations
along these lines were well advanced when the Treasury
upset them by demanding a Canadian guarantee for the

£ 1,000,000 loan. This the Canadian government refused to grant, and the plans were suspended.[4]

The Stephen negotiations attracted much attention. In April and May, before the Treasury killed the project, it appeared that the Liberals were at last ready to embark on a large-scale emigration/colonization program. On April 10, there was discussion in the House of Commons in which Trevelyan asserted that the government had in fact established "the principle of Government aid to emigration".[5] The Dominion Land Act that made Stephen's scheme practicable also encouraged others—private speculators and philanthropists—to take advantage of the new degree of security.[6] The same year, Western Australia passed an Immigration Act providing for free passage and railway transport into the interior for immigrants nominated by an Immigration Board.[7] And in southern Africa the Boer victory at Majuba Hill and the subsequent peace settlement provided ammunition for state emigrationists who claimed that a larger British population there would discourage Boer aggressiveness. Natal, positioned uneasily between the recently-subdued Zulus and the triumphant Boer Republics, discovered a great interest in imperial colonization.[8] For the moment, it appeared that colonial opposition to state emigration was crumbling.[9]

In England, the storm over land reform prompted many to seek once again a safe solution to social problems in the state-emigration panacea. The year 1881 brought Land-League violence in Ireland, another Irish Land Act, an active if moderate Farmers' Alliance, Henry George's first popular tour, and the Democratic Federation—which from the beginning demanded land nationalization. In 1882, the T.U.C. adopted a land-nationalization resolution. English and Irish landed interests saw an attractive alternative in the concession of "three acres and a cow" to the farm labourer—in the colonies. On the other hand, emigration was seen by some to be a necessary prelude to successful land reform in England and Ireland. It would disperse impossible concentrations of impoverished tenants to make way for rational-sized freehold farms. Parnell himself was the chairman of an Irish Migration Company which, under the provisions of the Tramways and Public Companies Act (1883), sought to move Irish tenants out of areas of congestion—thus lowering rents and reducing evictions.[10] Migration or emigration was not simply a landlord's panacea by any means.

In London, slum conditions became the object of a popular press campaign in 1883, with Stead's publication of Andrew Mearns' "The Bitter Cry of Outcast London".[11] Earlier, analysis of urban misery had popularly rested on moral issues: drunkenness, idleness, the demoralizing effect of indiscriminant charity. In the 1880s, however, sensational journalism, demonstrations by crowds of unemployed, and "scientific" social investigation shifted the public view from the individual pauper to the residual class of poor at the bottom of the labour pool, concentrated in the slums of East London. "Overcrowding" and landlord greed were seen as the chief causes of this misery, without much understanding of the reasons why large numbers of casual (underemployed) labourers were tied to these areas. Popular solutions, dictated as much by fear of contamination and social disruption as humanitarianism, were found in the diversion of "healthy" labour to other areas, slum clearances and model housing, and migration of casual labour out of the center to "labour colonies" in England or the overseas Empire.[12]

Emigration, then, appealed to many of those who were interested in removing a residuum which threatened to contaminate the "respectable" working classes above it. But helpful as this is in understanding some upper-class motivation for state emigration, it is not the whole story. Many who cannot easily be called social conservatives favoured state emigration as a necessary concomitant to more radical schemes of urban social reform. For example, some municipal socialists, in the absence of nation-wide programs, required a controlled area for social experimentation. They feared that special relief in one city or union would attract a stream of paupers from others. Emigration might be a means of diverting this flood.

Colonial developments, fear of land reform, middle and upper-class apprehensive fascination with the urban slum, and technical improvements in steam transport and communications provided sufficient incentive for the revival of agitation for state emigration. The central figure in re-establishing a cohesive pressure group was J. H. Boyd—a person of uncertain antecedents and possibly interested motives. Through an offshoot of the Charity Organization Society, the Central Emigration Society, he secured a large and multifarious following in the spring and summer of 1883. Though he had a catalytic influence, the movement soon outgrew its founder.

4.1 *J. H. Boyd and a Colonization Program*

In the autumn of 1881, Boyd sent Gladstone the scheme with which he had lobbied Disraeli four years earlier.[13] This time, he was rewarded with a public attack on emigration schemes in general by John Bright, Chancellor of the Duchy of Lancaster and aging symbol of early-Victorian middle-class Radicalism. Bright had long opposed state emigration on the grounds that free trade brought adequate and cheap food to England's urban population, while land reform would eradicate what misery there was in the countryside. In November he reiterated these views to an audience of factory workers at Rochdale.[14]

Bright, however, was an increasingly isolated man, and his attacks were perhaps an advertisement for the movement. Boyd replied that the world had changed. Population growth, urban crowding, agricultural depression, and a worsening balance of trade undermined the platitudes of Bright's generation. Boyd's emigration proposals were published in pamphlet form with a short (and rather noncommittal) prefatory letter by the Earl of Dufferin. The "hopeless misery" of the old world chiefly arose from a disproportion between population and production: "The writer's matured conviction is that we are rapidly drifting towards an unexampled national catastrophe; a conviction based upon independent examination of published facts and figures."[15]

Unlike the League of 1870, Boyd claimed no influence from earlier movements. When Sir Alexander Galt brought Wakefield's *A View of the Art of Colonization* (1849) to his attention in 1881, Boyd replied that he was entirely unaware that state emigration had previously been an issue:

> There is a great deal of highly interesting elaborate argument in Mr. Wakefield's book, generally corroborating much I have advanced, but the ultimate outcome appears to reduce itself to recommendations that Government should sell colonial lands to capitalists, and assist unemployed labourers by paying their passage money out of the proceeds of such sales . . . my own project is original, practical and unique.[16]

Boyd saw his proposals riding on a new wave of public opinion. He attacked Bright as one of the "theorists who have been reared upon idle stale doctrines of self-help and non-interference."[17] If Boyd's scheme was socialist, however, it was a form of state socialism designed to promote and protect vested interests. He promised that an extensive program of state emigration would immediately profit financial corporations, bankers, railway shareholders, and steamship owners, while ultimately depriving

> the agitator, the social reconstructor, the dreamer who is bent on pulling everything down, of their professional stock-in-trade. Those friends of the working man find a hearing because times are bad.... Adopt this scheme quickly, execute it vigorously, courageously, and you shall find its bearing *vis a vis* of disturbing, menacing forces now urging a ruthless disruption of English society, will be that of an efficacious MESSAGE OF PEACE.[18]

The scheme itself involved a national system of emigration and colonization aimed primarily at Canada. Its objectives were the simultaneous relief of misery at home and creation of new markets for British goods within the Empire. The plan was "entirely a state one", adequate for the removal of 50,000 wage earners and their families (200,000 persons) a year to Canada, where they would be granted free land. A system of state inspection of applicants would require an authorized agent in every town in the United Kingdom. Government ships would provide transportation, and a corps of artisans would be permanently engaged to prepare colonial sites. Control would be vested in a board or commission of five members— including at least two Canadians. Passage, estimated at £ 5 a head, was not to be repaid.

Once in the colonies, the settlers would work at a fixed government wage to clear land and acquire skills. When an area was declared "ready to support life" by government inspectors, the immigrant would be given an 80-acre section to work, with a £ 100 mortgage to recoup all capital spent in setting up the immigrant. What the state lost through failures and deserters could be made up in the sale of reserved government land (80 acres out of every 160-acre section)—the value of which would rise due to proximate development. The largeness of the reserved area, which would also benefit the three private companies involved in the scheme—the C.P.R., Hudson's Bay, and the North-West Land Company—fed suspicions that Boyd was a tool of Canadian speculators.

An essential part of Boyd's scheme was the establishment of training homes in England, Scotland, and Ireland to which orphans, "street youths", and urban "refuse" could be sent to learn farm work—"the natural occupation of the great majority of mankind."[19] The initial cost of these training homes, passage, and establishing and maintaining settlers until first crops came in would be financed by floating a special "emigration stock" bearing an interest of 3 percent. About £ 5 million would be needed in the first two years. Parliamentary powers would have to be sought to enable the government to raise a maximum of £ 20 million, to be repaid in ten years.

The profitableness of the endeavour—and "there might be immense profits"—could not be calculated entirely in land sales and interest on loans. There would be the amount saved from the rates—perhaps as much as £ 2 million a year—and the purchase of British goods by "a new populous and wealthy society" in Canada. The unemployed who consumed wealth in England could, at a stroke, be made to produce it in the colonies. Such were the attractions of the state's establishment of a peasant

proprietorship. It could be done in England only by nationalization of the land, "a barbarian dream" that would
utterly ruin many.[20]

A large bureaucracy would be needed to oversee selection, training, passage, and settlement. "Most of these numerous officials would naturally be drawn from the ranks
of the middle-classes . . . ." Finding employment which
did not entail loss of caste for the educated sons and
daughters of a greatly expanded middle class was a common Victorian concern.

> It is impossible to catalogue with exactness all the positions that
> will be necessarily created, and must be filled—greatly to the
> advantage of the mother-country considered as one community,
> and to separate families whose heads are nowadays in so many
> instances thoroughly perplexed to know what is to be done with
> their young men.[21]

Advocacy, however, of an expanded state bureaucracy to
create positions for the educated unemployed, while familiar today in many developing countries, was hardly
likely to appeal to Gladstonian liberals.

Finally, Boyd offered state colonization as a solution to
another late-Victorian concern—falling profits from capital investment:

> a great settlement of Canadian territory will inevitably call for
> numerous public works (new railways among them) of great mag-
> nitude over there, for new banks, insurance companies, &c. The
> capital may, largely, be raised here, and fresh, sound openings for
> investors be created.[22]

This program was submitted to the Colonial Office in
the spring of 1883. Though Boyd approached government as an individual, he immediately set about mobiliz-
ing a show of support. He was able to find a significant
following, in part due to the simultaneous re-emergence

of the emigration issue among imperialists at the Royal
Colonial Institute and elsewhere. In 1881, W. M. Torrens
delivered a paper on "Imperial and Colonial Partnership
in Emigration" which received a wide distribution in
pamphlet form. Articles were published in the *Nineteenth Century* and letters appeared in the press.[23] By
1883, Tuke's emigration work in Ireland and the Canadian Pacific Railway negotiations were being widely discussed. Meanwhile, Dilke was investigating, under public
pressure, the possibility of lifting Local Government
Board refusal to sanction child emigration. Philanthropic
emigration became a subject for debate among London
charities, labour leaders, and within the Church of England.

On January 29, 1883, James Lowther, Conservative
MP for North Lincolnshire who had held office under Disraeli (as Under-Secretary for the Colonies 1874–1878
and Chief Secretary for Ireland 1878–1880), came out
in support of "a comprehensive and State-directed
scheme, which should enable whole families to be simultaneously but not compulsorily emigrated" from Ireland
to Canada.[24] It was left, however, to a back-bench Conservative MP, James H. Rankin, to introduce the subject into
parliamentary debate. From March 25, 1881, when he
first called upon Ministers to state their intentions regarding state emigration, to the demise of the National Association at the end of the decade, he was the chief
emigrationist gadfly in the Commons.

Rankin, first returned for Leominster in 1880, was the
son of a shipping magnate and a life-time member of the
Royal Colonial Institute.[25] At this time he was himself
organizing a private scheme to settle working-class English on the extensive lands in Canada which he had secured for that purpose. He personally bore all expenses

Canadian Pacific Railway: Sur-
prise Creek Bridge, Selkirk
Mountains (Source: *Ill. London
News,* July 24, 1886)

James Rankin, chief emigrationist gadfly in Commons, 1881–90
(Source: *Ill. London News,* July
3, 1880)

in settling, in 1885, 25 carefully selected famlies—about
£ 32,000 for the pilot experiment and for the vast tract of
land intended for future settlements. Though this project
proved a failure, he claimed to have saved his capital, and
even to have made 2 percent profit due to improvements
and land sales.[26] Rankin's motives were philanthropic,
and the rate of profit in this case was too small to justify
the abuse and suspicion to which some emigration critics
subjected him. Innuendos that he was a land speculator
trying to make good an unwise investment do not appear
to have had any real foundation.[27]

Boyd appears to have first made contact with Rankin
and other emigrationists like W. M. Torrens and Frederick Young through the Central Emigration Society. This

organization was established in the spring of 1883 largely through the efforts of James Stansfeld, the radical Liberal MP for Halifax who had been president of Gladstone's Poor-Law Board from 1871 to 1874. On March 19, he presided over a meeting of the Council of the Charity Organization Society to consider the formation of an emigration organization under the mantle of the Society. It was decided to convene a conference to discuss emigration and to send a deputation to Dilke on the subject of child emigration. A Central Emigration Association (later Society) emerged from the April 4 conference. Stansfeld was its president and Boyd its honorary secretary. The committee was largely composed of metropolitan clergy and philanthropists, many of whom were involved in other emigration organizations.[28]

A two-fold program was adopted, similar to that of the quasi-lobbies of 1869, advocating both state aid and immediate private assistance. Donations were requested for a preliminary fund of £ 5,000 for emigration assistance and lobby activities. Rankin, who shortly replaced Stansfeld as president of the Central Emigration Society, later claimed that, in spite of the ambiguity of its charter, "Our society was not formed for the purpose of actually doing the work; it was formed for the purpose of urging the Legislature to take up and assist some well-considered scheme."[29]

The first objective was to secure the sanction of the Local Government Board for child emigration by public authorities. The deputation to Dilke coincided with deputations from the metropolitan unions of St. George and St. Pancras, and was followed a few days later by a deputation from the Council of the Metropolitan Poor-Law Guardians Association.[30] Dilke agreed to review the subject of Miss Rye's activities in Canada. Rankin meanwhile pres-

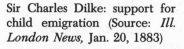

Sir Charles Dilke: support for child emigration (Source: *Ill. London News,* Jan. 20, 1883)

Joseph Chamberlain: a cold shoulder (Source: *Ill. London News,* Feb. 13, 1886)

sured Dilke in the House of Commons for an early decision. The result was the restoration (April 30) of the sanction, provided local unions followed a number of conditions.[31] The renewed powers were, however, rarely invoked. Only 481 children were sent to Canada in this way by 1886. Canadian inspection remained unsatisfactory.[32]

The emigration lobby probably saw the renewal of Board sanction as an encouraging victory. Dilke, apparently, was favourably disposed to some form of state emigration. In July he requested information from the Colonial Office on precedents for state schemes, and opened correspondence with Lord Lorne and Cardinal Manning on the subject.[33] The famous divorce scandal which overtook Dilke's career in 1885 cost the emigration lobby its most promising contact with government at the ministerial level. Chamberlain, who succeeded Dilke at the Local Government Board for the brief Liberal government of 1886, turned a distinctly cold shoulder.

In the spring of 1883 as well, George Potter and his Workmen's Emigration League (W.E.L.) again joined the campaign for state aid after twelve years of silence. In a long letter to the *Times,* Potter recommended the creation of an official commission to appoint emigration officers who would investigate applications for free passage and regulate the flow in accordance with colonial demand. "Disasterous consequences" threatened should increasing misery go unheeded.[34] In April, the Conservative *National Review* published an article by Potter on "Imperial Furtherance of Emigration", prefacing the paper with an apology for presenting work by a radical. This was allowable, the editor opined, when questions of a "national", non-party character were involved.[35]

Potter predicted that agitation against worsening social conditions in England would focus attention on solutions such as the emigration relief provided in recent Irish legislation. Whichever party introduced a scheme of state emigration for Great Britain could, at a stroke, prevent social disruption and win the political support of the working classes. In May, he moved to revive the lobbying activity of the W.E.L., and by August, large working-class meetings were again sending delegations to ministers to demand some form of state emigration. This activity apparently raised hopes among other emigrationists that their base could be extended beyond the middle-class "respectables" of the Charity Organization Society and allied philanthropic organizations.[36]

Meanwhile, Boyd's supporters proceeded to organize without attempting to join forces with the W.E.L. A precis of Boyd's scheme, however, was circulated among labour leaders for their approval on April 5.[37] A few trade-union men, such as H. W. Rowland, Secretary of the Amalgamated Cab Drivers, had already given their support. Replies to the circular varied from the flat refusal of John Burnett to allow the engineers to have anything to do with the movement, to Alfred Simmons' enthusiastic support on behalf of the Kent and Sussex Labourer's Union. "Thorough" approval also came from the United Trades Council of Belfast. Joseph Arch wrote cautiously that he believed the scheme would succeed, and gave his approval if emigration were restricted to urban labour.

> In the country districts of Great Britain there is, however, now no surplus labour; on the contrary the land needs more and better cultivation . . . . But, from towns and cities throughout the kingdom generally (whither multitudes have been driven, by the operation of bad land laws, from village and hamlet) there is no disputing a large surplus population may be taken away . . . .[38]

4.2 *Birth of a National Association*

In the *Times* of May 30, 1883, a letter from the Rev. John Fenwick Kitto, Rector of Stepney and chairman of the East End Emigration Fund, announced a public meeting to be held at the Great Assembly Hall at Mile End Road on June 6 to discuss steps for promoting state emigration.[39] Out of this and subsequent conclaves was born a national organization to pressure government for a comprehensive program. The intention to function as a lobby, rather than a charity with lobbying activities, was made clear in the clumsy but descriptive title eventually adopted in July—the National Association for Promoting State-directed Emigration and Colonization.

The Great Assembly Hall, with a capacity of 2000, was donated for the occasion by Frederick N. Charrington, a wealthy eccentric who left his father's flourishing brewing business to pursue temperance and social reform in the vicinity of the family works. The meeting was called specifically to advance "Mr. Boyd's scheme" as "a practical method of aiding the poor." It appears to have been organized chiefly by the East End Emigration Fund which had been won over by Boyd and the C.E.S. in April or May. The Duke of Manchester at this time presided over the E.E.E.F., which numbered Charrington and other wealthy men among its benefactors. Meeting in the evening allowed labourers to attend; the audience filled the Hall.[40] The same evening, Rankin tried to introduce a state-emigration resolution in the House of Commons to coincide with the show of public support out-of-doors. His failure to find a quorom indicates the lack of parliamentary interest with which the movement had to contend.[41]

The Mile End meeting was a well-orchestrated affair which gave Boyd a forum to present his scheme in some detail. Friends of the movement remained in control throughout the evening—not always the case when meetings were open to the general public. Some opposition was voiced by members of the Labour Emancipation League who distributed anti-emigration leaflets at the door, but by and large the evening was a success for its organizers. There were letters of support from political notables like C. T. Ritchie, Conservative member for Tower Hamlets. H. W. Rowland of the Amalgamated Cab Drivers moved the resolution

That State-directed emigration and colonization is, for the United Kingdom, a necessity of the time; and that Mr. Boyd's scheme

(dated February 14, 1883) is a practical method of aiding the
unemployed poor, diminishing pauperism, reducing local rates,
and developing our colonial resources—deserving the most careful consideration of Her Majesty's Government.[42]

Though a Mr. Yell of the Hackney Workingmen's Club
interjected that land reform and public works would
remove the necessity of "forcing our wealth producers
into exile," the resolution carried by "an immense majority."[43] The Rev. G. S. Reaney, however, made it clear
that there was room in the movement for those who did
not see in emigration the sole panacea for social ills of the
metropolis. "Many causes were in operation behind the
poverty and distress of thousands of our people, and many
cures would be required."[44]

Thus a new League was born, pledged to use "all
proper means" of bringing pressure to bear on government, Parliament, and the general public to advance
Boyd's proposals. It was the zenith of his personal success.
During the summer and autumn Boyd rapidly lost control
of the movement he created.

Immediately following the Mile End meeting, Boyd set
about recruiting prominent names through letters to the
press and to prominent national figures such as Cardinal
Manning and the Archbishop of Canterbury—both of
whom replied cautiously but not discouragingly.[45] A deputation to Derby at the Colonial Office included Lord
Brabazon, Bishop How, several Anglican clergymen from
East End parishes, two leaders of London Dissent (the
Rev. G. S. Reaney of the Congregationalists and Archibald
Brown of the Baptists), Joseph Arch and four other labour
leaders, a director of the bank of Australia, and three
MPs.[46] Boyd's membership drive slowly built up a sub-
stantial basis of the influential, though his leadership possi-
bly did much to retard growth. He was unknown, and

perhaps distrusted. An effective Victorian lobby required a socially acceptable leader, preferably a peer whose name at the top of subscription lists and on letterheads carried weight among the "gentlemen of influence" Boyd wished to attract. Lord Brabazon, already known in England for his wide-ranging philanthropic interests, eventually assumed this position in the National Association. In the months after its inauguration, he played an increasingly active role in the organization, and managed finally to supplant Boyd in a *"coup de main"* (Boyd's words) in November.

4.3   A Crusading Irish Peer

Reginald Brabazon, twelfth Earl of Meath, is known today, if he is remembered at all, as the founder of "Empire Day", and as a zealous imperial patriot who campaigned at the turn of the century for national military service, compulsory physical education, and Imperialist youth organizations such as the Lads' Drill Association and the Boy Scouts.[47] The image that survives—that of a somewhat crankish proto-fascist—is, however, misleading. Lord Meath, styled Brabazon until 1887, lived a long and active life, dying in 1929 at the age of 88. Before Lord Roberts and the Boer War directed the greater part of his energies toward support for the growing cult of militarism, Meath was known chiefly for his wide-ranging philanthropic activities in London and Ireland. The Earl of Shaftesbury was his model. Lord Brabazon and his wife determined early in their marriage to devote themselves to lives of social service.[47a] In 1888 W. E. Gladstone, commenting on a collection of essays on social problems, used Brabazon's career as a text for a characteristically Gladstonian sermon on the duties of the aristocracy.

Lord Brabazon in costume for a masquerade ball, Berlin, 1869 (Source: Meath, *Memories of the Nineteenth Century*)

Mary, Lady Brabazon, ca. 1869 (Source: Meath, *Memories of the Nineteenth Century*)

Though I think you have been prompted by a higher motive than the interests of your order, yet I must say that you are serving them, as I think, in a most honourable and effectual manner. It is from great instances of persevering devotion to the welfare of the nation and of humanity that the hereditary peerage has thus derived so much of the public estimation it enjoys.

I hope that the on-coming generation may be enabled well and safely to strike the balance, which in my early days was little thought of, between the competing principles of full scope for self-reliance, and of due regard to the obligations of the State towards its people.

Between these large duties and your personal obligations and relations in Ireland you will have your hands full. I warmly wish you all satisfaction in the discharge of your most honourable tasks."[47b]

It is this image of Brabazon as a tireless organizer of civic and private charities and promoter of a variety of urban social reforms which his contemporaries would have recognized.

Lord Brabazon was born in London in 1841, second son of the Earl of Meath.[48] Catherine Gladstone was one of his mother's close friends, and Reginald's godmother. Though the families drifted apart politically—the eleventh Earl opposed Gladstone's Irish policies—relations between Killruddery and Hawarden Castles remained friendly. In 1863, Gladstone offered young Lord Brabazon a position as one of his private secretaries, a job which his father made him refuse.

Reginald's older brother, Norman, died at an early age, leaving him heir to the Irish title and estates—which included considerable property in County Wicklow and in Dublin—and to the English title of Baron Chaworth which gave the Earl a seat at Westminster. Though not spectacular, the family's wealth and position were such as to ensure Lord Brabazon a life of leisure if he wished, and an introduction to the best London Society. He was sent to Eton, but not to University, since his father preferred that he spend a few years in Germany after public school to study German and acquire polish. This was followed in 1863 by his entry into the Foreign Office (by competitive examination) as a junior clerk, again at his father's command. The military career which Lord Brabazon coveted was denied him on the grounds that it would be too dangerous an occupation for the sole heir.

Five years later he exchanged into the diplomatic corps, serving in Berlin during the Franco-Prussian War, at The Hague, and in Paris. But in 1873, his wife's parents (he had married Lady Mary, the only daughter of the eleventh Earl of Lauderdale in 1868) so strongly objected

Killruddery Castle, County Wicklow [Source: Meath, *Potpourri* (London, 1928)]

to his taking a minor post in Athens, that he declined the promotion, and his active work as a diplomat came to an end. Lord and Lady Brabazon consequently returned to London and leisure.

As an admirer of Shaftesbury, Lord Brabazon constructed a personal philosophy which rested on the belief that social position and wealth entailed obligations to bring religion and charity to the less fortunate.[49] This social philosophy of condescension and good works, familiarly Victorian, derived from clearly discernible class distinctions and evangelicalism. Resting on the voluntary efforts of a leisure class, Victorian philanthropy mandated "the healing sympathies of personal ministration and Christian sympathy", a burden eagerly enough borne in many cases because it provided occupation for that mass of unemployed rentiers who populated the clubs and salons of the capital or spun out tiresomely pointless lives in the country. Personal involvement in good works was one of the few legitimate means of escaping from the confining strictures which bound a nonprofessional person of the respectable upper classes. As Lord Brabazon pointed out in 1885 in "An Appeal to Men of Leisure", the man of independent means seeking "useful work" had open to him the almost limitless varieties of charity:

> it would include such unpaid labour as that of poor-law guardians, town councillors, vestrymen, managers of public libraries, baths and washhouses, gymnasia, cricket and football clubs, coffee-taverns, debating and penny-reading societies, sanitary and vigilance associations, Hospital Sunday and Hospital Saturday movements, emigration, temperance, benefit, thrift, charity organization, Kyrle,[50] open spaces, national health, public playground, drinking fountain, ambulance, early closing, people's entertainment, popular ballad concert, workinghouse concert, and country and seaside convalescing societies, &c.[51]

Lord Brabazon himself was faced in 1873 with the problem of leisure. A typically work-oriented Englishman of the nineteenth century, he spent the next 50 years labouring at an exhausting pace for a seemingly endless number of philanthropic projects.

> Prevented by circumstances . . . from following any further the interesting career of diplomacy, my wife and I had to decide how we would spend the future years which might be left us, and we determined that we would devote ourselves, as far as our powers permitted, to the consideration of social problems and the relief of human suffering.[52]

From the beginning, much of his energy went to launch new projects, rather than to carry on day-to-day charity work. This often involved the lobbying of local and na-

tional authorities. Though much of his personal wealth
was poured into these organizations once they were set
going, Brabazon's preference seems to have been for the
aggressive, proselytizing side of good works.

Soon after his arrival in London in 1873, Brabazon
became interested in organizing support for the Hospital
Saturday Fund movement, an effort to raise contributions
from working men to match those of the largely middle-
class Hospital Sunday Fund. This gave him his first experience with public speaking, in the company of national
figures like Cardinal Manning.

> The campaign . . . lasted for nearly a whole year, and during that
> time some seventy public meetings were held in all sorts of queer
> places. I have spoken from a waggon illuminated by torches at

"Hospital Saturday" Meeting in Hyde Park, 1874 (Source: *Ill. London
News,* Oct. 17, 1874)

night, from half-formed engines in factories, from the scaffolding of buildings in erection, and in the company of Cardinal Manning from a wooden platform at the Reformers' Tree in Hyde Park, when *The Times* reported that we had addressed over 20,000 people .... [53]

The Hospital Saturday Fund was also Brabazon's first experience with working class agitation. The greatest problem for one of his caste lay in discovering techniques to bridge the social chasm and to ensure that the men with whom one dealt were truly "representative working men". His first clumsy attempts illustrate the barriers which most upper-class Victorian reformers faced. His first impulse was not to approach trade union organizations, but to try to deal with individuals on a man-to-man, dinner-table basis, as he would approach gentlemen of his own class. The results were disastrous.

It was arranged that [Captain Mercier, Chairman of the Hospital Saturday Fund] should invite to his house near Albert Gate as many of the leading working men as we could get together. I met there Mr. Hamilton Hoare, the banker, and we three discussed the questions, "Who are the leading working men? and how are we to find their addresses?" Ultimately, we decided to search the columns of the newspapers for reports of working-class meetings, and the names of those who attended. Even when we got names it was difficult to obtain addresses. However, after infinite trouble, we collected about one hundred names and addresses of working men, or of so-called working men, who had attended public meetings or in some way made themselves conspicuous. Out of these we hoped to form our contemplated Hospital Saturday Fund Committee ... When the momentous evening arrived ... it was at once apparent to us that we had been guilty of a huge blunder, which it would be very difficult to rectify. As soon as the speaking began, we realized that almost every man we had brought into the room was out for his own purposes, that he had his own pet grievance to air or his axe to grind, and that the genuine welfare of the hospitals was very far removed from the thoughts of the majority. All scented money in the air .... [54]

In the following year, Brabazon and his friends discovered other means for building working-class support.

> The first thing we decided to fight for was publicity, and the second was a genuine election of the Committee by real working men. Both these objects we obtained after months of struggle on the part of the groundlings; and when the genuine election did take place, we three gentlemen and one working man were the only ones elected belonging to the old Committee—all the rest were new men, real workers, and genuinely interested in the welfare of the hospitals.[55]

Brabazon was not squeamish about going into working-class areas to carry his appeals directly to the unemployed, in the case of the emigration agitation, or to try to persuade, through personal appearance, belligerent groups like the Social Democratic Federation (S.D.F.) to abandon opposition. The technique ultimately used to secure labour backing, however, rested less on the power of persuasion than on careful selection. Letters would be sent to T.U.C. delegates, and those replying favourably would be brought within the organization as representatives of their field of labour. For propaganda purposes the line was never drawn too distinctly between the personal support of these individuals and the presumed support of the trade union organizations they "represented."

By 1883, Lord and Lady Brabazon were involved in such diverse projects as the Young Men's Friendly Society (he was its first chairman), the erection of low-rent housing on family property in Dublin and in London, and training schools for nurses (the Brabazon Employment Society was organized by Lady Brabazon). In 1882, he founded and chaired the Metropolitan Public Gardens Association (M.P.G.A.) which was to become a long-lived, popular, and successful activity.[56] In the same year, Brabazon took up the campaign for "early closing". This agitation to limit shop hours brought him into contact with the Shop Hours League and labour leaders like Thomas Sutherst, whom he later recruited for the emigration movement. Brabazon contributed an article on "The Cause of the Overworked Shop Assistant" and chaired a large meeting at the Albert Hall.[57]

After 1883, much of Brabazon's effort was directed to securing parliamentary support for his various projects and organizations: public gardens, early closing, industrial training, and emigration all required pressure on government. Many of these causes were aimed at ameliorating slum conditions. His concern for the "Health and Physique of our City Populations" follows closely the concerns which, we have seen, motivated Froude to advocate state emigration.[58]

4.4 A "Coup de main"

Throughout the summer and autumn of 1883, Brabazon became increasingly involved in the affairs of Boyd's National Association. He and Boyd interviewed Dilke in July. Though Boyd retained direction of the National Association as chairman, Brabazon had become president by August, and this may explain the growth in prominent membership at that time. When formal inauguration took place at Mansion House in late summer, the organization was able to boast an executive committee consisting of a peer (Lord Braye), a Bishop (Bedford, a suffragan of the Bishop of London), 11 MPs, 10 metropolitan clergymen, and "eminent Baptist, Congregationalist, and Methodist ministers, bankers, merchants, gentlemen engaged in legal and other professions, and representative members of the working class."[59] The aging Earl of Shaftesbury, though not a council member, promised to speak at the first public meeting. The subsequent growth of membership in the following year soon made it necessary to create a more elaborate executive structure. The executive committee was limited to about two dozen of the most active workers, while the titles of patron and vice-president were created for those of influence who lent their names and money. There were ultimately about 100 of these. The national council, which grew to a peak of about 250 in 1886, demonstrated, according to Brabazon, the non-partisan nature of the movement, being composed of "Tories, Conservatives, Whigs, Liberals, Radicals, Socialists, Protestants, and Catholics."[60]

The Central Emigration Society and Potter's W.E.L. were following parallel courses of public agitation in the autumn of 1883. The W.E.L. attack reached a climax in September, but then withered away after Brabazon reorganized the National Association to include a large number of trade union representatives. The C.E.S. maintained for several years its separate campaign, retaining its dual function of both agitation for state aid and direct assistance to emigrants. The C.E.S. possessed prestigious leadership—the Archbishop of York, the Bishops of Liverpool and Newcastle, William Torrens, James Stansfeld—but the course of agitation attempted by the society did not run smoothly. A disastrous meeting on November 6, well-reported in the press, did much to discredit them. Members of the Social Democratic Federation (S.D.F.) and radical land reformers took control, negated C.E.S. emigration resolutions, and put up their own. This prompted an unfavourable editorial in the *Times* on "well-meaning gentlemen" and workers who "have no wish to go abroad".[61] Relations between the C.E.S. and the National Association had become somewhat competitive and unfriendly,[62] but the debacle of November 6 effectively removed the C.E.S. from contention for the leadership of the emigration lobby. It was subsequently relegated to a secondary position as one of the National Association's cluster of satellite organizations.

Sir Charles Tupper (Source: *Ill. London News,* July 31, 1886

Meanwhile, Boyd set about contacting colonial representatives in London to try to secure promises of support. He was able to get a sympathetic hearing from the new Canadian High Commissioner, Sir Charles Tupper.[63] Though the Stephen arrangements (see p.83) had fallen through, Tupper continued to lend the support of his office to the emigration lobby throughout the 1880s, occasionally in the face of contrary popular opinion at home. On July 20, he wrote Boyd that he was "quite sure the Canadian Government will be pleased to cooperate, as far as may be possible, in the work in which your association will be engaged." Simultaneously, he made public a statement from the Canadian Ministry of Agriculture that labour was in great demand throughout the Dominion.[64]

With the Archbishop of Canterbury in attendance, the inaugural meeting of the National Association was held at Mansion House on August 18. The Earl of Shaftesbury presided. Since the meeting was open to the general public, there was again some vocal opposition, and S.D.F.

handbills were distributed. Thereafter, the National Association resorted to afternoon meetings and to tickets of admission to prevent embarrassing scenes. On this occasion the emigrationists remained in control and the meeting ended on a note of optimism. Frederick Young, of the 1870 League, rose and rejoiced that the work of thirteen years was "about to bear fruit."[65]

It was clear, however, that the movement had to come to terms with organized labour in some visible, convincing way. This was difficult. While Brabazon was prepared to conciliate potential labour support—from, say, the ranks of the W.E.L.—Boyd was less diplomatic. His attacks on socialists, "professional agitators," and Georgist land reformers, aimed at attracting middle-class support, made amalgamation with labour groups unlikely.

An "Industrial Conference" of delegates from working men's organizations was held August 21 "to consider schemes of state aid to emigration." This was apparently a creation of the National Association, to help it achieve at least the image of labour support. The "representatives" of Leeds, Liverpool, Manchester, and Sheffield labour assembled and passed resolutions favourable to the movement.[66] These men do not appear to have included anyone of importance in trade unionism, and probably were put up by Boyd for window dressing.

One possible reason why Boyd was unable legitimately to attract labour support was his insistence upon the emigration of the urban unemployed, as opposed to agricultural labour.[67] While Joseph Arch approved of this course, the majority of industrial trade union leaders who were sympathetic to state emigration wanted to see it apply chiefly to agricultural workers. Brabazon was later to be sufficiently vague on this issue to attract both urban and agricultural emigrationists. Boyd was too attached to the details of his own scheme to be flexible on this or other issues.

More serious for the future of the movement were the rumors of self-gain which began to be circulated in the press shortly after the Mansion House inauguration.[68] Boyd was forced to answer intimations that he was secretly connected with Canadian land speculators and employers looking for cheap labour. Whether there was any truth to these accusations is now difficult to say. James Rankin was subjected to the same attack by innuendo in the socialist press. Boyd, however, was unknown socially, and suspicions were not easily laid to rest. In any case, the intimation of interested motive was sufficient to make Boyd a great liability. Suspicions voiced publicly or behind club doors almost certainly damaged the Association's autumn membership drive. Boyd's resignation in December was probably demanded by Brabazon, and would seem to bear out the charges leveled against him, though, whether he was in fact "discovered to be a speculator and dismissed" as H. M. Hyndman claimed,[69] or whether he stepped aside for the good of the movement, is impossible to say. In any case, Brabazon's reorganization of the Association in November practically removed Boyd from direction of policy and made his formal resignation inevitable.

By October, Brabazon had become convinced of the need to create some kind of amalgamation with those labour leaders who favoured state emigration, and, at the same time, to separate the fate of the National Association from that of Boyd and his detailed and inflexible program. Boyd was a one-idea man. The National Association needed the flexibility to tack before varying political winds, and above all needed to appeal to the class of men it proposed for emigration.

Brabazon, apparently without Boyd's approval or knowledge, established contacts with interested labour leaders. The first fruits of this were gathered at Maidstone, Kent, on October 13. The 70 "representatives of . . . working class organizations from all parts of England" who assembled there included known and important men in their fields.[70] The conference formed itself into a national committee which invited the National Association to "review and enlarge the scope of that association by accepting such proposals as our sub-committee may make, with a view of promoting a national movement in favour of State-directed emigration."[71]

Brabazon quickly called a special meeting of the National Association on October 23 which he chaired in Boyd's absence, and pushed through an immediate merger with the Workmen's Conference committee. The new organization, which retained the name The National Association for Promoting State-directed Emigration and Colonization, invited "influential men of all classes and all political opinions to join":

> no person who possesses influence with any class of his fellow subjects [will] be excluded from this joint body on account of his political or religious views, or on account of his connexion with any particular class of society.[72]

Brabazon was elected president and chairman, and Boyd, *in absentia,* relegated to "one of the vice-presidents" (there were over 50) and vice-chairman. Alfred Simmons of the Kent and Sussex Farm Labourers became the new secretary. In a letter to the *Times* announcing this move—which Boyd called Lord Brabazon's *coup de main*[73]—the new president-chairman disassociated the movement from Boyd and his scheme.

The Association, it should be understood, is unpledged to the support of any particular scheme of emigration; nor has it (as has been lately stated by Mr. Hyndman, of the Democratic Federation) any connection with any "large and profitable land speculation."[74]

The success of Brabazon's coup was borne out in an increase in prominent support before Christmas. On December 4, the Bishop of Carlisle; the Rev. C. H. Spurgeon, a well-known evangelist; Dr. Oakley, Dean of Manchester; H. N. Hamilton Hoare, a prominent banker; and James Rankin of the C.E.S. took vice-presidencies in the new National Association. By December 11, over 100 labour leaders had been recruited. The time was ripe, Brabazon claimed, for a campaign in provincial centers, but caution had to be exercised against contamination with "land schemes and speculations".[75]

This was a parting shot at Boyd, who had just tendered his resignation the day before. He wished them well, but continued to advance his own scheme throughout the following spring. Boyd's approaches to the Colonial Office, however, now lacked any kind of organized popular movement, while the National Association—remaining for a while aloof from government—proceeded to build a considerable show of support outside Parliament.

Notes on Chapter 4

1. The project had been hanging fire since 1873. It was completed in 1886.
2. P.P. 1889, *Report of the Colonization Committee,* 190–1. In 1882, the Canadian government secured authorization to enter into agreements with chartered companies to colonize the West. There followed a spate of activity by private companies, especially in Saskatchewan. They were not very successful, however, and none

remained in 1891 (G.F.G. Stanley, *The Birth of Western Canada* [Toronto, 1936], 186).

3. Later Lord Mount Stephen. His daughter married H. S. Northcote, son of the Conservative leader of the House of Commons and a vice-president of the National Association for Promoting State Colonization.

4. C.O. 384/146 (nos. 6438, 8019, 7363, and 13241).

5. *Hansard,* Vol. 277 (Commons, 10 April 1883), 2031–2.

6. Lady Gordon Cathcart was the first of the philanthropists to avail themselves of the Dominion Land Act provisions—arranging for the emigration of 10 families in the autumn of 1883 and 56 the following year (Johnson, 73–4).

7. C.O. 384/158 (no. 20418).

8. C.O. 384/153 (7251).

9. Unfortunately, the 1880s were not prosperous years for either Canada or Australia, and the result was a revival, after 1884, of colonial opposition to emigration schemes.

10. P.P. 1890, *Report of the Colonization Committee,* 337ff.

11. The Rev. Andrew Mearns was a member of the executive committee of the Self-Help Emigration Society from 1884.

12. Stedman Jones, Part III, *passim.*

13. Boyd, 20.

14. *Ibid.,* 22. Also see John Bright to Andrew Cumming, 1 Sept. 1858, in H. J. Leech, ed., *The Public Letters of John Bright* (London, 1895, 2nd edn.), 241, and James L. Sturgis, *John Bright and the Empire* (London, 1969), 83, 128, 136.

15. Boyd, 29.

16. *Ibid.,* 30.

17. *Ibid.,* 29.

18. *Ibid.,* 29–30.

19. Training homes to prepare emigrants for colonial life became a reality before the First World War. "General" Booth advocated in 1890 an extensive network of "farm colonies" as part of the Salvation Army's social campaign, and by 1907 the Church Army (Church of England) had established a large training center along these lines at Newdigate, Surrey, for assisted emigrants.

20. Boyd, 25.

21. *Ibid.,* 36. For another example of this theme see Gen. W. H. A. Fielding, "What Shall I do with my Son?" *Nineteenth Century,* Vol. 13 (April, 1883), 578–84.

22. Boyd, 36.

23. See William T. McCullagh Torrens, "Imperial and Colonial Partnership in Emigration," *Proceedings of the Royal Colonial Institute,* Vol. 12 (1880–1881), Frederick Young to the Editor, *Colonies and India,* 11 April 1881, and W. T. M. Torrens, "Transplanting to the Colonies," *Nineteenth Century,* Vol. 9 (March, 1881), 536–46.

24. James Lowther, MP, speaking at Richmond on 29 Jan. 1883, quoted by Boyd, 20n.

25. Sir James Rankin, First Baronet (1842–1915), owned considerable property in Herefordshire, which allowed him to bury his mercantile antecedents in the life of the landed gentry. He represented his home constituency in Parliament, served as Justice of the Peace, and was master of the South Herefordshire Hounds. President of the Central Emigration Society, he also became a member of the Emigrants' Information Office in 1886, and served on the Select Committee on Colonization appointed in 1889.

26. P.P. 1890, *Report of the Colonization Committee,* 91.

27. See, for instance, *Justice,* 12 April 1884.

28. The *Times,* 21 March 1883, 5.

29. P.P. 1890, *Report of the Colonization Committee,* 112.

30. M.H. 19/7 (30243/83, 32771/83, 34413/83, and 450203/83).

31. These were: Protestant and Catholic children to be placed with coreligionists; children to be registered with the Department of Agriculture at Ottawa and with the Poor-Law Board in England, and to have six months training before leaving England; guardians to have evidence of available homes in the colony; girls over the age of 12 not to be sent; and the Poor-Law Board to be limited to 300 child emigrants during the first year (M.H. 19/7 [450203/83]).

32. *Hansard,* Vol. 304 (Commons, 12 April 1886), 1307–8.

33. Argyll Papers, Box 9, letters 262, 268, and 269; Dilke Papers, Add. MSS. 43874, ff. 131, 133; 43896, ff. 65, 67.

34. The *Times,* 16 Feb. 1883, 4.

35. George Potter, "Imperial Furtherance of Emigration," *National Review,* Vol. 1 (1883), 193–207.

36. See the *Times,* 2 Aug. 1883, 4; 10 Aug. 1883, 4; 5 Sept. 1883, 7, for reports of W.E.L. meetings. In late August a W.E.L. deputation had an interview with Dilke, and shortly afterward Potter supported Lord Emly in preparation of a bill to enable the govern-

ment to support the emigration of the unemployed. This was followed by W.E.L. interviews with colonial Agents-General in London.

37. *The Canadian Gazette,* 14 June 1883, 224.
38. *Ibid.*
39. The *Times,* 30 May 1883, 6.
40. The best description is that in the *Canadian Gazette,* 14 June 1883, 224–5, but also see the *Times,* 11 June 1883, 6.
41. *Hansard,* Vol. 279 (Commons, 6 June 1883), 1809.
42. *Canadian Gazette,* 14 June 1883, 225.
43. *Ibid.*
44. *Ibid.*
45. R. T. Davidson to J. H. Boyd, 15 June 1883, and W. A. Johnson to J. H. Boyd, 6 Oct. 1881, in C.O. 384/147 (9779). Boyd had written to Manning in 1881 and had been told that it was impolitic for the Catholic clergy to take a stand on this issue—but later the Cardinal openly supported the lobby.
46. C.O. 384/147 (9779).
47. For a description of Meath's later interests, see John Onslow Springhall, "Lord Meath, Youth, and Empire," *Journal of Contemporary History,* Vol. 5, no. 4 (1970), 97–111.
47a. Brabazon's wife, Lady Mary, only daughter and heiress of the Earl of Lauderdale, had a considerable fortune of her own not legally at Brabazon's disposal. This provided the basis for her many charitable activities, and was kept quite separate from Brabazon's own rather narrower resources.
47b. Gladstone to Meath, March 3, 1888 (Meath Papers, Autograph Vol. II). The Book was Meath's own *Prosperity or Pauperism.*
48. The biographical material which follows is taken from Reginald, Twelfth Earl of Meath, *Memories of the Nineteenth Century* (London, 1923), *passim.*
49. The family motto is *Vota Vita Mea.*
50. The Kyrle Society was founded in 1877 by Octavia Hill and others to "better the lot of working people" by encouraging the establishment of parks and gardens.
51. Lord Brabazon, "An Appeal to Men of Leisure," in *Social Arrows* (London, 1887), 402–4. This originally appeared in the *National Review,* April, 1885.
52. Meath, *Memories of the Nineteenth Century,* 201.

53. *Ibid.,* 206–7.
54. *Ibid.,* 204–5.
55. *Ibid.,* 205.
56. The M.P.G.A. advocated the creation of public parks, especially by turning the many disused burial grounds into gardens and walks.
57. Meath, *Memories,* 224.
58. Reginald Brabazon, "Health and Physique of our City Populations," *Nineteenth Century,* Vol. 8 (July, 1881), 80–89.
59. The *Times,* 8 Aug. 1883, 3. Several members of the Conservative Opposition in the House of Commons took up membership in the National Association at this time: H.S. Northcote, Octavius Coope, E. Ashmead-Bartlett and John H. Puleston.
60. *Ibid.*
61. *Ibid.,* 7 Nov. 1883, 6.
62. Torrens had called for the wealth of the state to be made "answerable to the whole happiness of the people" (the *Times,* 7 Nov. 1883, 6). This language was too strong for Boyd, who attacked him for his radicalism (the *Times,* 8 Nov. 1883, 10).
63. Sir Charles Tupper, Bt. (1821–1915), was a Canadian Conservative and close ally of Sir John Macdonald. Until 1884, he served as the first minister of railways and canals, and was largely responsible for the completion of the C.P.R. He was Canadian High Commissioner from 1883 to 1896.
64. The *Times,* 13 Aug. 1883, 8.
65. *Ibid.*
66. *Ibid.,* 22 Aug. 1883, 11.
67. See for instance his letter to the editor of the *Echo,* 1 Sept. 1883, wherein he states that the southern agricultural labourers did not have as strong a claim on emigration assistance as the unemployed of the East End.
68. In, for example, *Justice,* 12 April 1884, or earlier in the *Echo* in August of 1883.
69. "The Emigration Fraud," *Justice,* 12 April 1884.
70. See the appendix for a list of the men and their organizations.
71. The *Times,* 15 Nov. 1883, 12.
72. *Ibid.*
73. *Ibid.,* 13 Dec. 1883, 7.
74. *Ibid.,* 15 Nov. 1883, 12.
75. *Ibid.,* 11 Dec. 1883, 4.

Chapter 5. The National Association in 1886: An Analysis

The National Association for Promoting State-directed Colonization reached the zenith of its popular appeal about 1886–1887, when it commenced a vigorous lobbying effort at Whitehall and in Parliament. An examination of the national distribution, political orientation, and social and economic interests of its national council and executive makes possible a more exact understanding of the emigration movement. It also, perhaps, illuminates some general characteristics of late-Victorian extra-parliamentary organization. The elites who established themselves in the National Association executive, those "persons of influence" whom Boyd and Brabazon set out to recruit, had many other related lobbying interests. State emigration was only a piece of a large integrated structure of pressure-group activity.

5.1 *The National Council in 1886*

A full listing of the membership of the national council, which was quite large, and of the executive of the National Association was published in the summer of

1886.[1] From this it is possible to reconstruct a geographical and class distribution for the organization. While the precise figures below should be read only as rather rough indicators—in many cases judgments about identity and status were somewhat arbitrary[2]—the overall picture is probably reliable.

The regional distribution of the national council is what one might expect of a pressure group organized in the capital to address what seemed to be a chiefly metropolitan social question (see Table 1a and Appendix D, map 1). More activists joined from London and its environs than from any other area of the country. If we remove labour leaders from the council, this London orientation becomes even more pronounced (see Table 1b). Middle- and upper-class support clearly varied in direct proportion to proximity to the capital. The distribution of labour in the National Association does not, of course, follow this pattern, reflecting the regions where the trades interested in emigration were concentrated. Thirty-six men joined the council from Lancashire, 17 from Yorkshire.

Numerically, labour accounted for the largest occupational block on the national council (see Table 2). The character of this rather diverse group will be treated at some length below. The remaining middle- and upper-class categories reflect a fair cross section of Victorian society—the Church, the State, the Law, the Army and Navy, businessmen, landlords, and a number of leisured rentiers who apparently practiced no profession (designated "none" in Table 2). Included here are many men of national stature in their respective categories. Among the landed proprietors there is the Earl of Fife, fifth largest landowner in the United Kingdom (249,220 acres). Several of the national council owned large estates in Ireland and Scotland, where private emigration assistance for

Table 1a. Geographical distribution of the national council in 1886[a]

	London	North	South	Midlands	West & Wales	East	Scot.	Ire.
Number	106	65	45	24	7	4	10	9
Percentage of known	39	24	17	9	3	1	4	3

Total known: 270 (93% of Total)
Unknown: 19 (7% of Total)
Total: 289

[a] See the appendix for a county-by-county breakdown.

peasant tenants had been a common landlord practice for some time. The military men number four generals, three admirals, and other senior ranks.[3] Sir Garnet Wolseley was probably the most respected military man of his age. The financiers include directors of the Bank of England, Lloyd's, and Barclay's. Other banking institutions represented here did considerable business in the colonies, especially Australia (the London Chartered Bank of Australia and Westgarth and Company). Merchants and manufacturers on the council also had large interests in colonial exports, ranging from textiles and beer to iron and railways.[4]

Of the literary men, scholars, and antiquarians in the movement, the best known, before Tennyson joined in 1887, were probably Froude and H. T. Mackenzie Bell. Froude, who had once nearly emigrated to New Zealand himself,[5] published his popular *Oceana* in 1886. Mackenzie Bell, an associate of the Rossettis and Morris, was a poet and critic closely connected with the imperial federation movement.[6] Similar sympathies can be found in the work of the minor novelist J. S. Little. Perhaps significantly, one also finds among the national council two historians of Roman imperialism, and R. M. Christy, narrator

Table 1b. Geographical distribution of the middle- and upper-class members of the national council in 1886

	London	South	Midlands	North	West & Wales	East	Scot.	Ire.
Number	96	27	18	14	6	4	8	9
Percentage of known	53	15	10	8	3	2	4	5

Total known: 182 (92% of Total)
Unknown: 16 (8% of Total)
Total: 198

of Bristol merchant voyages and seventeenth-century expansion.

There was also a number of women—heiresses and widows—in the Association who spent much of their time and resources in philanthropy.[7] They were accompanied on the national council by wealthy men of similar interests who lived in or near London on income from family or investments, and who had apparently no professional training or who chose not to practice. Many had close connections with the landed aristocracy. Others were simply old men living in retirement, for whom pressure-group work was a form of amusement and recreation.

As in floating joint-stock companies, it was, of course, important to begin with as many titles as possible. By 1886, 20 peers had joined the Association.[8] These included a duke (Manchester) and five earls. The rest varied widely in wealth, family position, and energy, from the very rich Wilbraham Egerton, second Baron of Tatton, to the (later) bankrupt ninth Baron Byron; from 88-year-old George-Henry Roper-Curzon, sixteenth Baron Teynham, to the vigorous circumnavigator Sir Thomas Brassey, created first Baron Brassey in 1886. Robert Curzon,

Table 2. Class and occupation of the national council in 1886

	Number	Percentage of known		Number	Percentage of known
Labour	91	38	Legal	8	3
Church	34	14	Administrative[b]	4	2
None	22	9	Academic	4	2
Land	20	8	Publishing	2	1
Trade and			Medical	1	—
Manufacturing	15	6	Total known:	245 (85% of Total)	
Finance	13	5	Unknown:	44 (15% of Total)	
Military	13	5	Total:	289	
Literary	10	4			
Politics and government[a]	8	3			

[a] Career politicians and office holders without substantial interests outside of government.

[b] Three persons important in administering public charities, and Sir Francis Cunliffe-Owen, Director of the South Kensington Museum.

fifteenth Baron Zouche, was a grandson of Sir Robert Wilmot-Horton, the Tory Under-Secretary for War and the Colonies (1821–28), who had proposed an extensive state-emigration scheme based on the poor-rates.

Considered as a group, some threads of common interest and relation are evident. A number were Irish peers who had particular reason to seek a solution to Irish distress which entailed neither land reform nor Home Rule.[9] The political complexion of the 20 followed the national trend. Ten were Conservatives, eight became Liberal Unionists, and only two remained Gladstonian Liberals. Not many, however, were very active parliamentarians, though Wenlock was whip for the Liberal Unionist peers. Among many there were close family connections—which extended into the non-noble portion of the National Association's membership.

A number of other peers were clearly sympathetic enough to offer their support in print and on deputations, but hesitated to join officially an extra-parliamentary pressure group. Lord Lorne, later Duke of Argyll, preferred to vote freely "on the merits of each Bill," he told his father, with reference to another lobby. "I don't like joining associations."[10] When Brabazon succeeded to the House of Lords on his father's death in 1887, he was able to overcome some of this diffidence. There was a considerable augmentation of peers on the National Association roster. Chief among these were Robert Collier, Baron Monkswell (later Under-Secretary for War in Rosebery's government) and Thomas George Baring, Earl of Northbrook (Governor-General of India 1872 to 1876 and a special commissioner to Egypt, who resigned office in 1886 over Home Rule). Northbrook was a nephew of Sir George Grey who campaigned for the League in 1870.

Turning to the House of Commons, we can identify 32 MPs sitting before the election of July, 1886, as National Association members. But it is difficult to gauge the lobby's strength, organization, and commitment at Westminster from names on a list. Lord Brabazon spoke of the support of over 100 MPs by May of 1888,[11] but there is no evidence that even half this number were dependable on the question. However, there was a dedicated core from both parties which encouraged the lobby to continue its campaign. They were not all back-benchers and political unknowns (see Appendix D).

Of the 32 MPs in 1886, 11 were Liberals. Though the group could claim to be bipartisan, its flavour was clearly Tory, and this was emphasised by the fact that its parliamentary leadership before 1887 was in the hands of two Conservative back-benchers, J. H. Rankin and Henry Seton-Karr. The bias was made more pronounced by recruits to the movement after 1886. In addition many of the Liberal supporters of the movement in both Houses left Gladstone over Home Rule, and became Unionists. Finally, six of the Liberals (five Gladstonians and a Radical Unionist) were not returned in July. Obviously the lobby's parliamentary future lay with the Conservative party and its ability to influence Tory front-benchers. From the autumn of 1886 to the end of 1891 the movement faced a Conservative government. Potentially they had more leverage among Tories than among Liberals, but the Conservative Party was more monolithic in its leadership and perhaps less sensitive to pressure from internal factions. Further, the strong trade union support the movement received did not exercise the same influence among Conservatives which it might have on the other side.

There was, in fact, a number of important Conservative Party workers on the national council of the Association: R. N. Fowler, twice Lord Mayor, helped to re-organize the London Conservative Party in the 1880s; H. H. Gibbs had been (1885), and J. H. Pulestan was (1886), chairman of the Conservative Association of the City of London, while Ellis Ashmead Bartlett chaired (1886–1888) the National Union of Conservative Associations, and was in great demand as a popular speaker. The lobby also claimed C. T. Ritchie, who was given the presidency of the Local Government Board in 1886, and the responsibility for drafting a wide-ranging reform of local government. Emigration clauses appear in the Local Government Act of 1888, and in 1889 Ritchie was made chairman of a select committee to study colonization schemes.

Commitment to the lobby's program, however, appears to have been thin and watery at best among those close to government who were, nominally, members of the National Association. They lent their names, but left it to the back-bench zealots to marshal what troops they could. By late 1886, the lobby badly needed the active parliamentary support of a national political figure. It needed to use and be used by a rising star like Dilke, Chamberlain, or Churchill. Dilke, who might have been willing, was ruined by 1886, while Chamberlain was uninterested and preoccupied. Randolph Churchill, whose brother Alfred was a member of the National Association, had never shown any concern for the emigration question, and in any event was also preoccupied. It was a hard year for young Turks.

The movement did attract the support of relatively new men in the House of Commons, men who were perhaps seeking to establish expertise and a role as spokesmen for certain issues.[12] These relatively junior men included those who were most active in broaching the emigration subject in the House. Reliance on young blood was, however, likely to lead to a certain ineptness in the lobby's approaches to government, and perhaps a reluctance among older hands to treat the movement seriously.

5.2   *The Executive Committee in 1886*

For all practical purposes, the national council was a paper fiction. It apparently was convened only once—for the Colonial Conference in 1886. Direction of the National Association was in the hands of three smaller executive groups: the national officers and London-based executive committee, a finance committee, and the many vice-presidents and patrons.[13] If this executive is subjected to the same analysis applied to the national council, the following patterns emerge.

The London bias is very pronounced for the executive committee, though this is only natural as it was responsible for day-to-day activities, and met rather frequently (see Table 3a). The vice-presidents and patrons are more evenly distributed, the latter being mostly bishops and landed aristocrats. They took little part in running the affairs of the organization. Persons of no particular profession—younger sons of the aristocracy like Reginald Capel, wealthy widows like Lady Strangford or Lady Jane Dundas, and independent gentlemen—made the largest contribution of vice-presidents, followed by the landed gentry and wealthy businessmen.

The executive committee was composed largely of lesser clergymen and labour leaders, representing chiefly London trades, with a scattering of other occupations (see Table 3b). Of these men, a dozen or so were the real activists of the movement. They published articles, wrote letters to the *Times*, corresponded with colonial supporters and officials, organized deputations and public rallies, and kept the emigration question alive, as far as they were able, in Parliament (11 of the vice-presidents were MPs). Brabazon and Simmons, as president-chairman and secretary, did the lion's share of this work, which included finding a place for the movement's spokesmen in such relatively visible affairs as Church Congresses,[14] Trades-Union Congresses,[15] Royal Colonial Institute conclaves, and other well-reported occasions. It also fell to the Central office at Palace Chambers, Westminster, to co-ordinate the lobby's campaign outside Parliament with the progress of its efforts at the Colonial Office and in the House of Commons. Emigration motions in either House,

Table 3a. Geographical distribution of the National Association executive in 1886

Region	Exec. comm. & fin. comm.[a]	V.P.s	Patrons
London	19 (76%)	33 (47%)	7 (29%)
South	2	12	—
Midlands	2	5	4
North	—	6	5
West	—	3	3
East	—	2	—
Scotland	1	7	—
Ireland	1	2	5
Unknown	4	8	—

[a] Three of the vice-presidents were also finance-committee members and are counted among this group rather than as vice-presidents.

and later the deliberations of a select committee, called for a flood of petitions. Supporters out of doors were given precise instructions.

> It is desirable that Petitions in favour of State-directed Colonization should be sent to both Houses of the Legislature. Sympathizers willing to assist in this direction should copy, in writing only, the forms of Petition on the following page. Not less than six signatures should be appended to each Petition, which should be sent to influential members of the House of Lords, and to Representatives in the House of Commons, for the constituency in which the signatories reside. But, if preferred, the signed Petitions may be sent to the Secretary of the Association, 84, Palace Chambers, S.W., who will arrange for their presentation.[16]

By 1886, the lobby's London and provincial activities required a substantial regular expenditure: for office

Table 3b. Class and occupation of the National Association executive in 1886

Occupation	Exec. comm. & fin. comm.	V.P.s	Patrons
Labour	6	—	—
Church	7	4	9
None	2	15	2
Land	1	11	7
Military	2	7	1
Trade	—	10	1
Finance	3	6	1
Literary	3	4	—
Politics	—	5	1
Legal	1	4	—
Academic	—	2	1
Other	—	5	1
Unknown	4	4	—
Total	29	77	24

rental, a small staff, the printing of pamphlets and announcements, and mailing, as well as a variable expenditure for travel, hall rental, and entertainment of colonial representatives. Though many of these services were rendered without charge to the Association, F. D. Mocatta estimated the movement needed a guaranteed minimum income of £ 500.[17]

> Persons interested are invited to communicate with the Secretary, to join the Council, to form local branches, and to subscribe, as FUNDS are greatly needed for defraying expenses of meetings and for spreading information on the subject.[18]

There remains no record of how the Association met its financial needs. If it followed the pattern of the League,

most of its contributions came in the form of small donations from men who had to satisfy many other claims of
a similar nature. Large donations tended not to come
from well-known men, but from eccentrics with fewer
irons in other fires. On occasion, the lobby received direct
contributions from institutions—businesses, labour organizations, and societies of one kind or another. The Skin-
ners and Clothworkers Companies of London contributed 20 guineas each in 1884.

Whatever the source and magnitude of its income, the
National Association managed to sustain a campaign of
provincial tours, public meetings, and publications
through 1886. Its concentration on parliamentary pressure rather than public agitation in 1887 may indicate,
among other things, financial difficulty. It seems probable
that contributions, like the Association's membership,
rose rapidly, from 1885 to 1886, peaked during the worst
of the depression in 1886, and declined with returning
prosperity. Financial support for the emigration lobby
probably followed the general pattern of that for charities, which registered a record jump following the riots of
the unemployed in February of 1886. This would help to
explain the spurt of lobbying activity which occurred in
the spring of that year.

5.3   *Building Blocks: Constituent Groups*

When Brabazon took control of the National Association
in the autumn of 1883, it was a thing of a few dozen
philanthropists, clergymen, and eccentrics serving, perhaps, as a cover for Canadian land speculators. Surprisingly, it prospered. In the next 36 months, it managed not

only to survive, but to achieve respectability—if not political effectiveness. It could boast a national council which
included important labour leaders, 7 Anglican bishops, a
Catholic cardinal, 20 peers, and 36 MPs. A glittering list
of patrons and vice-presidents put the Association into
fancy dress and helped abolish the memory of Boyd and
suspicions of tawdry motives. Beneath all this, however,
the more modest emigration "workers" continued to run
things.

They were drawn by and large from three groups—
middle-class London philanthropy, metropolitan clergy,
and trade union officials. Each of these possessed some
considerable internal organization and communication of
either a formal, as with the clergy and trade unions, or an
informal nature. Philanthropy was bound together by a
large, if elastic, net of evangelical relationships. In one
form or another there was long-standing interest in the
emigration question within each of these three groups,
which together formed something of an infrastructure for
the movement. An area where their interests overlapped,
like the emigration question, was a common platform for
class collaboration and the erection of a national pressure
group.

5.3.1 EMIGRATIONIST CLERGY

And thy seed shall be as the dust of the earth; and thou shalt spread
abroad . . . .   Genesis 28

It is the manifest intention of Providence that when the supply of
labour in one country exceeds the demand, it should be transplanted to where employment is to be had.   John Bate, 1869

The very highest mission upon which a man can be sent is to try
and reproduce wherever it may be possible, all that is noble,
sound, true, excellent, holy, and of good report, to be found in a

fully-developed national life; and surely to a man thus called and chosen it is right to say, "This voice comes to you from God . . . ."
                                                    The Rev. William Panckridge, 1881

Though evangelicals in the late eighteenth century encouraged those with a vocation to go abroad and convert the heathen, there was little interest in encouraging a large "transplantation" of laity. However, the bad times of the Napoleonic war period, the writings of the Rev. Thomas Malthus, and the availability of new lands for settlement persuaded many clergymen that a large emigration was a practical solution to social ills. In 1819, the Rev. J. T. Becher of Southwell helped collect some £ 5000 to aid Nottinghamshire poor to settle in South Africa.[19] As the volume of emigration rose and colonization schemes multiplied in the 1830s and 1840s, another motive was added. The Church needed to preserve its position among the transplanted English, to ensure that emigrants on the frontier kept their religion.

One can see both these motives, social amelioration and Church defense, in the Wakefield settlements in New Zealand. The Canterbury Association, with the Archbishop of Canterbury as its president, sent its "pilgrims" off with a chaplain on each ship and the blessing of the Primate.[20] Among the bishops who supported this experiment in Church-and-community colonization was the active Charles James Blomfield of London. Blomfield saw social distress in London as part of the problem of low Church attendance and disbelief. He helped found the Metropolitan Visiting and Relief Association in 1843, and had earlier been interested in providing labourers with allotments and gardens. His emigration interests may be seen as a logical extension of this—returning the poor to a healthy relationship with the land.[21]

Emigration enthusiasm within the Church, as elsewhere, waned in the palmy days of the late 1850s and
early 1860s. Churchmen at mid-century who continued
to give attention to emigration questions were largely
interested in shepherding the natural outflow of communicants and in creating strong Church communities
abroad. Added to these concerns was the threat, by the
late 1860s, of disunion among the larger Anglican com-
munion itself. Communication between the Mother
Church and the colonial branches took on a paramount
importance due to the growth of synodical government in
the colonies, and the reluctance of the Privy Council to
enforce episcopal authority abroad. The Colenso schism
in Natal seemed a prelude to general fragmentation of the
Church, much as recall of New Zealand troops in 1869
seemed to bode disintegration of the Empire. The
Lambeth Conferences were a response to this undermin-
ing of authority abroad. Not until the Conference of 1887,
however, did emigration receive official attention as a
subject for discussion. At that time it was treated as a part
of the wider problem of communication within the
Church, with an eye to coordinating efforts rather than
increasing the exodus.[22]

By the late 1860s, English clergymen no longer felt
directly concerned with the preservation of the Anglican-
ism of emigrants in the colonies. The colonial churches
were firmly established, by and large, and capable of tend-
ing to the spiritual needs of Anglican immigrants. English
clergymen consequently narrowed their emigration concerns to questions of spiritual care at ports of embarkation
and during passage, and the social portent of emigration
for the home community. In the following decade, pressure mounted within the Church for a regular program of

emigration supervision, if not assistance, by specially appointed clergymen at ports and on shipboard. Though some clergymen did provide letters of introduction, arranged for emigrants' reception by colonial clergy, and on occasion accompanied parties of Anglican emigrants, these efforts were to a large extent informal, unsystematic, and dependent on the time, effort, and resources of the local vicar and his family.[23] In 1878, Archbishop Tait created emigration chaplains to assume some of these responsibilities at the major ports of embarkation.

At the same time there was rising interest, particularly among urban clergymen, in having the Church itself promote emigration as a solution to the social and religious problems of the slum parish. By the 1880s, the encouragement of emigration seemed to many to be as logical a part of the Church's slum mission as churchbuilding, the creation of suffragan bishops, and the appointment of additional curates.

Who in "darkest England" was to be saved? It had long been believed that the rural ingénues who migrated to the cities lost their religion because of gin palaces and the general lack of visibility of their social superiors. Emigration for Hodge would keep him from the pools of urban unbelief, apparent in the growth of secular societies in the capital.[24] It would also help reduce the pressure on housing and jobs. For those already degraded by slum life, there was the possibility of training camps to rehabilitate at least the young and vigorous and give them agricultural skills. Their removal would give those remaining a better chance. Like Andrew Mearns, many clergymen came to believe in environmental change as a precondition to successful soul-saving. And, like Mearns, many of them joined emigration societies and pressure groups. For many social activist clergy who advocated state aid in housing, sanitation, and industrial training, state emigration was a means of paving the way for serious urban rebuilding. It would deprive the slumlord and sweater of some of their labour; the cost of other reforms would be reduced; and those who were assisted would surely feel a debt of gratitude to the Church which led them to a new Canaan.

Growing clerical interest in emigration assistance was inspired in part by Archbishop Tait's expressed concern, after 1878, for some form of emigration program—itself a result of pressure upon Tait from metropolitan clergy and from the Society for Promoting Christian Knowledge (S.P.C.K.) for an "emigration service" organized and funded by the Church. For a while, the subject vied with the perennial questions of temperance and education. Tait, earlier, had supported housing legislation and the efforts of the Earl of Shaftesbury to alleviate overcrowding, but it is unclear whether his emigration interests ever went far beyond a concern for the spiritual supervision of those who left.[25]

It has been shown that a number of clergymen were involved in emigration societies, and in the National Emigration League. Some of the radical clergymen involved in the rural and urban labour movements also advocated emigration as a militant trade tactic. The Rev. E. D. Girdlestone, a pioneer in the agricultural labour movement, helped several hundred Devonshire labourers migrate out of the area in the late 1860s and early 1870s, and thereby improved the position of those who remained. The Rev. John Oakley, "the poor bloke's parson," supported Arch in the 1870s. Later, as Dean of Manchester, he joined the National Association and called for a large program of state colonization. Of course, moderates and reactionaries among the clergy also saw ample reason for supporting state-aided emigration. In 1870, the West of

England Labourers' Improvement Association was organized with an Anglican president and 20 clergymen
among its vice-presidents. Its motto was "Emigration, Migration, but not Strikes". And Oakley was accompanied
into the National Association by Bishop Ellicott, a staunch
enemy of agricultural unionism.[26]

In 1881, the Rev. William Panckridge, Vicar of St.
Mathews (City Road, E. C. London), with the Revs. A. S.
Herring, G. P. Merrick, and Brook Lambert, attempted to
get Tait's support for a Church emigration scheme. Panckridge evidently had become interested in emigration
through the Royal Colonial Institute, where he heard Stephen Bourne deliver a paper on "Extended Colonization
a Necessity to the Mother Country."[27] His own parish in
Clerkenwell suffered from a large unemployment among
watchmakers. He had studied Maria Rye's child-emigration scheme, and believed that the Church

> could approach the question with more chance of a successful
> solution than could any smaller society. She would have on her
> side the enormous advantage of a complete organization, a clear
> line of duty, an immunity from the faintest suspicion of mixed
> motives.[28]

Panckridge had also been in communication with W. M.
Torrens who, in addition to being M.P. for a large working-class district of London and a strong emigrationist,
was also a staunch churchman who vigorously opposed
changing the oath to allow Bradlaugh to take his seat in
the House of Commons. Torrens guaranteed the support
of the Canadian High Commissioner, and Panckridge proceeded to get the Society for the Propagation of the Gospel (S.P.G.) to appoint a subcommittee to "go into the
question."[29]

Though Henry W. Tucker, secretary of the S.P.G., promised hearty cooperation, Panckridge was uneasy that close work with the Evangelicals might "close the chance of getting outsiders, like Lord Dunraven, and others to belong" to the movement. Tucker's offer was left lying for fear that "we lose the help of the Archbishop's name and shut ourselves off for many good people who do care for Emigration but do not care for S.P.G.", and Panckridge made slow progress.[30]

An emigration committee was eventually set up. In the spring of 1881, it was busy writing letters for church newspapers and interviewing visiting colonial bishops.[31] In April, interviews with Tait encouraged Panckridge to draw up a draft resolution to "express the opinion of the heads of the Church upon the necessity for some action." This was a mild suggestion that "a more distinct line of communication" betweeen the home and colonial clergy was needed on emigration matters. "United action" of an unspecified kind was called for, though Panckridge mentioned specifically only the dissemination of emigration information among the parochial clergy, provision of a series of handbooks on the colonies for the laity, and the adoption of a standard form for letters of recommendation.[32] This draft was accepted and issued by Tait under his name, and the next year the S.P.C.K. brought out an official Church of England *Colonization Handbook.* Encouraged, Panckridge wrote a rather more enthusiastic draft preface for this publication, which was refused.[33]

For the present, the official interest of the Church was confined to the protection and guidance of those who wished to leave England, rather than an active encouragement of emigration. A more "commercial" and less "heroic" preface was adopted. The primary intention was to remind the layman that

above all . . . now you are far away from the old parish church . . .
remember you are still a member of the body of Christ; and by all
that is godly and manly in your nature, vindicate and maintain
your Church membership wherever you may be.[34]

At the same time, Tait was under some pressure from
other quarters. The Bishop of Rupert's Land drew his
attention to the opening of the Canadian West by the
railway, and suggested that the Settlers' Society, already
organized in Canada to offer help to members of the
Church of England, should work with an emigrant-aid
society in England under the patronage of the Archbishop.[35] A cousin, Charlotte O'Brien, pressed the Archbishop for his support of a group she had organized to
urge the government to increase protection for female
emigrants. She pled for the creation of special emigration
chaplains in all the major ports.[36] Later in the year, Panckridge echoed the need for a special Church emigration
department,[37] and, in December, Tait responded.

A joint committee was appointed by the S.P.C.K. and
the S.P.G. to work out an emigration program. Its deliberations were guided, one assumes, largely by Panckridge
and the emigration chaplain at Liverpool, the Rev. John
Bridger. Shortly before he died, Tait commended their
proposals to the Anglican clergy in England and in 1885
it was made a permanent institution. Panckridge became
its secretary and Bridger its chaplain.[38]

About this time (1885) Bridger became a member of the
National Association. Like Panckridge, he was interested
in extending the Church's activities beyond mere supervision. In a letter to the Church paper the *Guardian*
(March 11, 1880), he had advocated Church purchase of
colonial land for emigration settlements. At one time a
missionary to British Guiana and the Sandwich Isles for
the S.P.G., he published articles on colonization, and was

a member (1883) of the Royal Colonial Institute. As Vicar of St. Nicholas Church, Liverpool, Honorary Canon of Liverpool, and the S.P.C.K. emigration chaplain, he traveled occasionally to America with the emigrants he assisted. Tait's emigration circular encouraged him to advocate the creation of a Church Emigration Society to assist passages with Church money.[39]

Clearly, it was anticipated that Tait was moving toward support for some kind of direct assistance. Though Panckridge had earlier advocated a voluntary association within the Church, like the Temperance Society, he now proposed a scheme which would have had the Church itself promote "an extended Emigration" to Canada and Australia. He recommended the formation of parish emigration clubs to hold land, select emigrants, and perhaps purchase goods and produce from their settlements. These societies would be formed where congestion required them by rurideaconal action, and would be headed by the parochial clergy.[40]

The next year, however, Tait died, and his successor, E. W. Benson, does not seem to have shared much enthusiasm for the subject. In December of 1883, the Bishop of Carlisle, the Suffragan Bishop of Bedford, and the Dean of Manchester joined the National Association to advocate state aid. Though many now despaired of moving Benson, Bridger and the Bishop of Bedford, William Walsham How, issued a joint statement the following July with the officials of the Waifs and Strays' Society calling for Church emigration homes in Canada.[41] And in 1885 the Central Council of the Church of England Emigration Committee of the S.P.C.K. resolved "That the question of emigration, in its social and religious aspects, is well deserving of consideration by the Diocesan Conference and Churchmen generally . . . ."[42]

Little resulted. When the Rev. Tomlinson organized the Church Emigration Society in 1886, it was chiefly an informal affair among interested clergymen. It raised subscriptions for grants to emigrants if recommended by their vicar.[43] A quarterly, *The Emigrant,* was widely distributed to clergy and laity, and in the 1890s the Church Army set up a training establishment in Surrey to turn slum dwellers into agriculturalists. The numbers the Church assisted in this way were, however, relatively small—averaging 540 a year (1901–1911).[44]

In 1887, the Lambeth Conference passed resolutions recommending better care for Anglican emigrants, but "the wider subject of encouraging and assisting emigration" was "too large a question to be dealt with in the time at their disposal." Recommendations were made, however, for the extension of the office of emigration chaplain to Canadian and American ports, the establishment of Church emigration homes in England and the colonies, better communication between the churches on emigrants' needs, and a revised form of prayer for use at sea.[45]

These measures were chiefly aimed at removing hardships and guaranteeing spiritual care for what emigration there was. Churchmen interested in expanding the flow of emigration could find little encouragement and had already begun to join the state-aid lobby in some force.

Boyd had had close support from a number of metropolitan clergymen at the founding of the National Association in 1883. By 1886, they were a large, perhaps dominant, part of the lobby. Of the total known membership of the national council, 14 percent were clergymen, with Anglicans outnumbering nonconformists nearly three to one. Anglican clergymen counted for about a quarter of the executive committee, and well over a third of the patrons. They were the largest group within the leadership, though the labour representatives possessed a plurality of the general membership (see Tables 2 and 3b, and Appendix C).

By 1886, the emigration lobby could claim the support of the Archbishop of York, William Thomson (a patron of the Central Emigration Society), while 7 bishops, 16 rectors, vicars and deans, 9 nonconformist clergy, and a Roman Catholic Cardinal and priest had become members of the National Association. Benson, however, gave only cautious approval.[46]

The lesser clergy, not the bishops, were the most active of the lobbyists. Most of them were educated in the 1850s when the Christian Socialism of F. D. Maurice was a potent university influence, and, in 1886, were to be found serving East End parishes in Whitechapel, Spitalfields, Bethnal Green, Shoreditch. Typically, the clergymen involved in the movement was a man of modest means, not particularly well-connected, not young, and probably overworked. He was preoccupied with the slum "mission" and the problem of working class nonattendance. Some, like the Rev. R. K. Arbuthnot, who was Vicar of St. James, Ratcliffe, saw in social work among the poor a means of saving the Church by identifying it with those who, since 1885, "have the power of the country in their hands."[47] Most had worked together in philanthropic emigration and shared executive roles in the Central Emigration Society, E.E.E.F., B.C.E.S., and other metropolitan societies before joining the National Association.

Robert Claudius Billing may be fairly representative of the type of clergyman who joined. The son of a provincial school master, he took his B.A. from Worcester College, Oxford, in 1857, and was ordained the following year. Ten years of work as Vicar of Holy Trinity at Louth was fol-

William Boyd Carpenter, the Bishop of Ripon and the Patron of the National Association (Source: *Ill. London News,* May 31, 1884)

The Rev. R. C. Billing, suffragan Bishop of Bedford, member of the National Association (Source: *Ill. London News,* July 14, 1888)

lowed by five years at Holy Trinity, Islington. In 1878, he was made Rector of Spitalfields and Rural Dean. In 1888, after fifteen years' work in the East End, he was chosen to succeed Bishop How as Suffragan Bishop of Bedford. By this time he was 44 years old, and in declining health. He had worked with How and Kitto in East-End emigration for several years, and was a founding member of the Metropolitan Public Gardens Association.

Although there were at least nine nonconformist clergymen in the movement, including the very popular C. H. Spurgeon and his friend and assistant Archibald Brown, the bishops and East-End vicars gave the National Association a strong Establishment character. This was reinforced by the number of prominent Church of England laity who joined—strong defenders of the prerogatives of the Church. Usually they were also strong Conservatives.

Brabazon, who in religion tended to the enthusiastic, evangelical wing of the Church, was, like Shaftesbury, familiar with the leaders of nonconformity. Most Victorian charities depended heavily on the generosity of this remarkable class of endowment-creating rich—Quaker manufacturers and bankers, Congregationalist and Methodist merchants and retailers. Brabazon solicited their support because he needed the resources of men like George Palmer, but also as a gesture toward "balance". As a national lobby, the Association needed to be seen to represent a cross section of society. Further, rousing preachers like Spurgeon, who could draw crowds of thousands, were an obvious asset for an extra-parliamentary pressure group.

Of the eight identifiably nonconformist ministers in the National Association, two were Baptists, four were Congregationalists, and two were Methodists. All but two had congregations in the London area, though they were not concentrated in the East End as were the Anglican clergy. On the whole, they were rather less important in the movement than nonconformist laity like Samuel Smith of Liverpool, an active Liberal politician and Presbyterian philanthropist whose wealth came from cotton brokerage. Smith was closely associated with other members of the National Association in a variety of causes: temperance, child cruelty, and slum philanthropy in general. In the 1860s, he had helped Thomas Barnardo get started, and in the 1880s supported the work of General Booth.[48] There were also Buxtons, Coopes, and Barclays in the emigration movement.

There were not, apparently, many Roman Catholics in the National Association, in spite of Manning's support. The ill feeling which erupted over Maria Rye's militant Protestantism may help explain this. Many Irish-Catholic clergy were known to be strongly opposed to emigration schemes which would undo what success they had had in attracting slum communicants. Working-class Irish and their leaders tended to regard state emigration as a euphemism for transportation and a cover for racial prejudice—not without some justification.

The Catholic hierarchy in England were aware of these views and, if they did not encourage them, were reluctant to fly in their face. Further, the lack of Catholic clergy and laity in the movement may be explained by the tradition of apolitical quietism which marked the English Catholics, and made them rather less accustomed to participate in pressure-group activity. Too, it is doubtful whether the National Association solicited their participation; well into the twentieth century, a strong Catholic presence in an English pressure group was likely to be a liability. Manning himself hesitated to join the National Association because he feared that non-Catholics would interpret his support as an attempt to get special favours for Irish Catholics.[49]

The National Association also contained at least two well-known Jews: Frederick David Mocatta and H. L. W. Levy-Lawson. A Jews' Emigration Society had been active since the 1850s in helping poor Jewish families to the United States. Mocatta and Levy-Lawson were, however, alone on the national council. Other names familiar in Jewish philanthropy are conspicuously absent, and it is possible that, like the Roman Catholics, Jews were sensitive about the racial implications of Jewish emigration. The 1880s saw a large increase in immigration into En-

Cardinal Manning in 1886: A Patron of the National Association (Source: *Ill. London News,* Apr. 3, 1886)

The Most Rev. E. W. Benson, Archbishop of Canterbury: only cautious approval (Source: *Ill. London News,* Jan. 6, 1883)

gland of East European Jews, and a corresponding increase in English antisemitism. At least one member of the National Association, Arnold White, was a rabid foe of Jewish immigration, and saw state emigration as one means of breaking up the East-End sweating industry.[50] Of course, many Sephardic Jews in England were themselves uncomfortable with the large immigration of Ashkenazi and, like Mocatta and Baron Hirsch, advocated their settlement outside of Europe.

Viewed as a whole, these leaders of religion further emphasize the London focus of the movement. With very few exceptions, the clergymen involved came from metropolitan parishes and congregations. The rural clergy do not appear at all in these lists, and there are only a few from the large provincial cities. This is not surprising. London had displaced Manchester as the "shock city" of the time—the focus of social investigation and experimentation by the 1880s. But the absence of rural and provincial men can also be explained by the fact that much of the clerical support the National Association received was funneled into the movement through small permanent philanthropic emigration societies, themselves for the most part based in London and commanding the support of London philanthropy and clergy. These various practical groups, with limited nonpolitical objectives, acted as "feeder" organizations for the lobby by supplying expertise, organization, and money. In the process, it was only natural that the London bias of these eleemosynary institutions should be reflected in the National Association.

The clergymen described here were not guild socialists —the more radically egalitarian clergy of a somewhat younger generation who, inspired by sacramental brotherhood, called for a general social and economic reorganization. They were, however, activists who believed that the religion of the Sermon on the Mount required the amelioration of social ills. Like the Christian Socialists of the 1850s, they emphasized the paternal obligations of the Church, and were prepared to use a variety of means to achieve environmental as well as spiritual reformation. The Social Gospel was a belief that the generality of men could not be improved morally without first being improved physically, and that the vast number in need precluded all but the broadest national program. Those who were unwilling to adopt the egalitarian measures of Headlam and the Guild of St. Matthew, but who did believe that the road away from working-class nonattendance and unbelief lay through dramatic improvement of living conditions in the urban slum, had three alternatives. They could work to expand the activities of the traditional voluntary charities. Charitable donations did, in fact, rise substantially in the 1880s. They could also encourage greater participation in social work by the Church directly. This meant using a greater proportion of Church revenues for social action. The slum missions and the Church Army are evidence of this kind of activity. Finally, late-Victorian clergy could seek to encourage state activity. In England, the union of Church and State meant that this may have been an easier conclusion for Anglicans to arrive at than nonconformists. In the emigration movement, we see churchmen responding in each of these ways. Those who worked in emigration charities also advocated an emigration program within the Church of England, and, ultimately, a large state program financed by the national Exchequer.

5.3.2 PHILANTHROPY AND EMIGRATION

The emigration lobby depended heavily on the support of organized philanthropy. The movement drew many of its activists from the many metropolitan emigration charities, of course, but also recruited from the wide range of environmental reform groups—housing, parks, hospitals, temperance, anti-prostitution, and education organizations. These shared an interlocking membership, drawn together by the unifying thread of Shaftesbury's Christian humanism. Relationships established in any of these fields served to recruit for others. For example, Brabazon's interest in the shop hours, parks, and physical training campaigns is reflected in the National Association where one finds many of his co-workers in these other movements: Thomas Sutherst of the Shop Hours League, E. N. Buxton of the Commons Preservation Society, Bishop Carpenter of the National League for Physical Training, to name only a few. These men shared a regular and frequent intercourse—in correspondence, on executive committees, and on the variety of royal commissions to investigate aspects of the "social problem".[51]

Apart from emigration, perhaps the largest philanthropic interest represented in the National Association was that of child welfare. At the center of this circle were Shaftesbury's Ragged School supporters: Barnardo, Spurgeon, Rye, and Brabazon. Bishop How was president of the Church of England Waifs and Strays Society; Mrs. Ellen Joyce was a leader of the Girls' Friendly Society; Samuel Smith was a member of the Society for the Prevention of Cruelty to Children and a vigorous parliamentary advocate for legislation to suppress child abuse. A conference in 1885 of the managers of children's homes was chaired by J. H. Rankin of the Central Emigration Society, and attended by many members of the National Association.[52]

The middle-class joiner was a common phenomenon of the Victorian age, and the decade of the 1880s saw a proliferation of societies to promote social reforms through philanthropic effort or state action.[53] The depression and unemployment of the mid-1880s acted as a stimulus to this kind of activity, and financial contributions increased correspondingly. By the 1890s, English charities received at least £ 5 million annually, administered with increasing efficiency.[54] Brian Harrison has argued, however, that much of Victorian philanthropy was blind to the interrelation of social ills, and promoted competition rather than cooperation.[55] Though, of course, the briefest glance at the jealousies and idiosyncracies of Victorian charity bear out this view, those who lent their support to the state-emigration lobby are perhaps less culpable than others. In their separate organizations they treated the symptoms of distress, but did apprehend a basic interrelation and found a root cause in overpopulation. Emigration would reduce the grossest distress to a manageable magnitude, facilitating the efforts of philanthropic societies generally and promoting moral regeneration.

These workers in various, sometimes competing, causes were drawn together by the mutual advantages state emigration promised. And it was a partial solution which did not do much damage to the Victorian virtue of self-help. Government aid was sought only to place the recipient in a position to help himself, and it ensured the continuance of the wide range of voluntary charities in England. Social problems, which some argued were approachable only by the state, might after all be manageable without direct state intervention.

Emigration charities themselves were divided over the issue of state aid. There was some concern that the complicated selection procedures involving physical examinations and character references which some societies insisted upon would be discarded. Emigration aid would become a right which anyone might demand. This does not, however, appear to reflect the opinion of the majority within the metropolitan emigration societies. Many of these individuals were active in other charities as well, and may have felt that state aid for emigration would free resources for more valuable direct social work. Some, like the Rev. F. M. Tomlinson of the Church Emigration Society, wanted "the Government of this country to make grants ... to individuals through the existing emigration societies."[56] Finally, it was increasingly apparent that the private societies lacked the kind of leverage needed to negotiate large-scale emigration programs with colonial governments.

There were at least nine emigration societies represented in the National Association. Most of these were based in London, like the Central Emigration Society, which placed most of its executive on the lobby's national council.[57] Beyond the National Association there was little enough cooperation. Organizations were born and died with the turning tide of trade. Large charities took up emigration aid and dropped it according to the whim of their directors. Charity organization in this or that field was often talked about, but never accomplished. Twice in the 1880s, federation of the emigration societies was proposed and defeated. This confusion of private effort prompted many philanthropic emigrationists to see in a broad state program the only hope for rationalization of efforts. They were not, on the whole, loathe to place their own resources at the government's disposal. When the government established an Emigrants' Information Office (E.I.O.) in 1886, many of its unpaid staff were recruited from the private emigration societies.[58]

5.3.3   LABOUR AND EMIGRATION

By the 1880s, many trade unions in England had long histories of assisting their members to emigrate. Like unemployment, sickness, and burial benefits, emigration assistance was frequently provided for by a contributory contingency fund.[59] Emigration overseas was, however, an expensive undertaking and required some knowledge of labour markets abroad, which, before the Emigrants' Information Office was established, could be obtained only through colonial agents and through general or colonial trade unions. Neither was a very objective source.

It is possible to view emigration benefits as a part of the militant industrial strategy of nineteenth-century unions. A thinning of the labour force in a skilled trade where replacements could not easily be found was, in theory, advantageous to those who were left behind. In practice, emigration assistance was rarely extensive enough to push wages upward, or keep them from falling. Too frequently, the bad times or industrial confrontation which made emigration assistance attractive also impoverished the trade unions through payment of unemployment benefits and decreased income, and made emigration aid difficult or impossible.

There was also friction within trade-union leadership regarding the priorities involved. Payment of emigration benefits depleted the strike fund and reduced the number of members to stand behind labour demands. It was easy to castigate emigration aid as defeatism, and as acceptance of the economic doctrines of the employing class. The Social Democratic Federation and some of the socialist leaders of the new unionism took this point of view. But it would be misleading to divide trade-union leaders as passive or militant on the basis of their attitude toward emigration.[60] Emigration assistance had been frequently associated with industrial strife, as a weapon of confrontation. It was not unusual for black-listed men to be helped out of the country.[61] If trade-union emigration was resorted to, all too frequently, in consequence of the failure of strikes, it was nevertheless a demonstration of defiance and solidarity. Employers were, on occasion, strongly opposed to schemes to promote the emigration of workers from depressed areas. Sometimes the threat of emigration was used as a bargaining device, much as the threat of a strike might be used.[62]

The drift away from emigration benefits, not complete by the 1890s,[63] was only partly a result of the new breed of socialist leader who repudiated the liberal wage-fund theory. Partly, it was a result of the more complete integration of the world economy, which meant, by the late-Victorian period, that depression was likely to affect labour's employment in the colonies as well as at home. An increasing number of men who left during bad times, especially those who went to America, returned with stories of unemployment.[64] Cheaper and swifter transportation allowed this sort of reverse migration. Emigration was no longer as final a solution as it had been earlier. The abandonment of emigration assistance by some unions was also partly due to some change in union membership. Skilled men had the money to contribute to their relocation and were relatively sure of finding work in the colonies. When, in the 1880s, unions began to extend their memberships to the semi-skilled and unskilled, the effect was to make emigration benefits on a large scale financially impossible, and even more unpopular with the colonial unions. The strong opposition of trade unions in Canada and Australia to any form of assisted immigration provided a powerful argument against emigration benefits in English unions.[65]

The unions which supported the National Association tended to be those which still retained some form of emigration benefit.[66] Several of these were skilled-craft unions, though some, like the shoemakers, contained increasing numbers of the semi-skilled. The motive for joining the lobby differed from union to union. Those which contained skilled labour might be interested in state emigration for the unskilled in order to relieve the pressure from the lower ranks of labour on their trades. Unskilled men, like the farm labourers, were, on the other hand, interested in aid for themselves, as were some trades which were in decline due to mechanization.

The National Association represented a fair cross-section of organized labour. The unions involved claimed to number some 170,000 to 200,000 men—or about one-fourth of total trade-union membership.[67] While some of these figures, notably those for agricultural unions, are doubtlessly exaggerated, it is clear from the respected leaders who were involved, and from the diversity of the trades and areas represented, that the labour interest in the question was genuine and widespread.

Much of this support came from the North, from Lancashire textile workers, the metal tool trades around Sheffield, and the ironworkers and miners of Northumberland and Durham. Men from the trades councils of ten northern cities were delegates to the National Association.[68] The largest of the northern unions supporting the movement was that of the cotton spinners, led by James Mawdsley, a Conservative who served on the Parliamentary Committee of the Trades Union Congress from 1882 to 1890. It is difficult, of course, to gauge the amount of real rank-and-file interest, though it is improbable that so many of the local executive would have supported emigration so strongly were their men completely indifferent or opposed. At a conference in 1886, Mawdsley credited the spinners' efforts in Manchester with the overcoming of the opposition of the Lord Mayor, who had "come around to our views" and joined the executive committee of an emigration society.[69]

Textile work was well-organized by the 1880s, and strongly led. Although the dramatically bad times of the Cotton Famine were long past, the trade was on the defensive, and there were frequent strikes in the 1880s against the reductions which were the employers' response to increased international competition. In 1885, the Oldham branch, whose secretary (Thomas Ashton) joined the National Association, struck to prevent a 10 percent wage reduction, but after three months acqui-

esced in an immediate 5 percent cut with a further reduction the following year.[70] The spinners were
accompanied in the National Association by scattered
representatives of allied textile trades. In all, the textile
trade accounted for 22 of the 91 trade-union representatives in the lobby.

Drastic, if temporary, decline in the iron and steel shipbuilding industry in the mid-1880s accounts, one assumes,
for the presence in the emigration lobby of the Bolton
Ironfounders' Association and the Boiler Makers and
Iron Shipbuilders' Society of Newcastle. Unemployment in shipbuilding reached a record high of 28 percent
in 1886.[71] Robert Knight, General Secretary of the United
Society of Boiler Makers and Iron Shipbuilders, attended
a conference on colonization that year at the Colonial
Exhibition in London. He officially represented his union
in the National Association, and was accompanied by
practically the entire Newcastle trades council executive.[72] J. C. Laird, president of the council, called for
strong pressure on government in support of state colonization.[73] Other metal-working trades in the North were
also involved in the movement—the Oldham Smiths and
several of the Sheffield tool makers' organizations were
strongly in favour of state aid. The Sheffield File-Cutters'
Society was represented by its secretary, Stuart Uttley,
who was elected to the T.U.C. Parliamentary Committee
in 1890; the Scissor Grinders, by their president, Robert
Holmshaw, and their secretary, J. Whitworth; and the
Edge Tool Grinders, by their secretary, William Styring.
Once a center of early trade-union radicalism, Sheffield
had been the scene of violence at mid-century. By the
1880s, the tool makers' trade, like many other craft trades,
was being threatened by mechanization and increasing
foreign competition. At the Colonial Conference in 1886

Edward Memmott, president of the Sheffield trades council and a member of the National Association, called for
emigration as a solution to the unemployment and low
wages caused by mechanization.[74]

A miscellany of other northern craft trades sent representatives as well, and doubtless for similar reasons. These
small, guild-like unions, dominated by skilled workmen,
were on the defensive due to the threat of new machinery
and the pressure from below by the unskilled. It is not
surprising that they sought a program of state emigration
as a means of stabilization during an agitated period of
change which their own organizations were no longer
able to control. The situation of the boot and shoe makers
is a case in point.[75] Their membership was already much
expanded by new processes, and they fought in this period against the assault of the unskilled who could quickly
learn the simplified trade techniques. Significantly, a chief
concern of theirs was the use of juvenile labour by employers who capitalized on the charity training which organizations like Dr. Barnardo's Homes provided for
orphans. Emigration of orphan children was an alternative to the industrial training which threw them on the
home labour market. The Leeds branch of the National
Union of Boot and Shoe Rivetters joined the London Ladies' Bootmakers in the lobby for state emigration.

The miners of Lancashire and Durham were represented by Sam Woods, president of the Lancashire and
Cheshire Miners' Federation, and W. H. Patterson, financial secretary and later (1890) general secretary of the
Durham Miners' Association. These, however, were the
only miners' representatives in the National Association.[76] The miners constituted a large part of the
unionized labour force—about 150,000 men in 1888
(or 20 percent);[77] but outside the north, their leaders did

not turn to emigration. Only the Northumberland miners were laying out funds for emigration benefits after 1885.[78] In the north, coal mining was shifting away from the open pits to deep mines in south Yorkshire. This migration of the industry precipitated a crisis among the northern men, and may account for their interest in the emigration lobby. A lesser sense of community, feelings of social isolation not known in other mining areas, also contributed to a willingness to leave.[79] Elsewhere, the industry was expanding rapidly and union growth was only momentarily checked by the depression of 1885–1887.

The Midlands contributed rather less to the movement. The Building Trades Council of Nottingham sent their president, W. Baker, and secretary, G. Miller. They were joined by Charles Bloor, secretary of the Ilkeston (Derbyshire) Engineers, Smiths, and Carpenters Association. Leicester labour was represented by the president of the Leicester trades council, D. Merrick of the Leicester Boot and Shoe Finishers, who had presided at the 1877 T.U.C. Absent were men from any of the Birmingham industrial and craft societies.[80] Most of the Midland organizations which did join were the scattered branches of a few craft trades. No important union leader, with the exception of Merrick, helped to promote the National Association in the Midlands, and one assumes that what support there was, derived largely from the whim of a few individuals.

As might be expected, London was a different story. Physically at the heart of the movement, labour in the capital contributed a large part of organized trade-union support. The London shop assistants, who had no national organization until 1891, were brought into the movement by their middle-class leaders, Alderson Morley and Thomas Sutherst. Shop assistants were the lowest class of

white-collar workers who had fought for early closing
from the 1840s, with the support of some leading evangelicals and middle-class friends who brought pressure to
bear on Parliament and local authorities. Brabazon and
Manning were both active in the shop-hours movement
in the 1870s and 1880s.

Sutherst was also involved in an attempt to organize the
London transport workers, and, conceivably, he was responsible for bringing the cabdrivers into the emigration
lobby. Other transport leaders, T. Smith, general secretary of the Amalgamated Cab-Drivers' Association, and
Dyke of the Cab-Drivers' Co-operative, were both members of the National Association. Cabdrivers were well-
organized by the 1880s, and had been occasionally
successful in fighting increases in the rents they paid for
their cabs. But there were powerful reasons for pessimism
—increased omnibus traffic and extension of the under-
ground railway.

London craft trades represented in the movement included tin-plate workers, ladies' bootmakers, paper stainers, and printing compositors.[81] The tin-plate workers
were threatened at this time with American competition,
while the bootmakers and printing trades were troubled
by progressive mechanization. Within the lobby, the London compositors were joined by the Manchester lithogra-
phers and the Bolton and Glasgow Typographical
Associations. A number of the officers of these organizations joined. The most important were G. D. Kelly,
general secretary of the Amalgamated Society of
Lithographic Printers and a Lib-Lab[82] member of the
T.U.C. Parliamentary Committee, and William Coote of
the London Compositors.[83] Unfortunately for the movement, the printing trades, while encompassing about 30,-

000 men, commanded, according to the Webbs, "little influence in the Trades Union Movement as a whole."[84]

A number of the London labour leaders were members of the National Association's executive committee. Their greater voice in the affairs of the pressure group was probably due to their convenient proximity to Parliament and Whitehall, and their availability for daily lobbying activity in the capital. So long as the fight remained one of approach to ministers rather than constituencies, the role of London clergy, philanthropy, and labour was bound to be a conspicuous one.

Finally, there were the Kent and Sussex farm labourers, perhaps 9000 men in 1885, who contributed the largest bloc of labour to the National Association. In all, eleven branches officially affiliated with the movement. Most of the executives of the provincial association, the Kent and Sussex Agricultural Labourers' Union, joined, and their secretary Alfred Simmons, a Maidstone journalist and Gladstonian Liberal, was Brabazon's second in command.

In spite of some Conservative support in Kent for state emigration,[85] Simmons combined emigration with strongly free-trade Radical views. Among the Cobden Club pamphlets of the 1880s is an election piece in which he exhorted the newly-enfranchised farm labourers to beware of "that huge stumbling block in the pathway of the people, Toryism" and "the Conservative landowners and their members of Parliament" who "tried with all their might to keep you down . . . the Tory landlord party is the hereditary enemy of the progress of the people." Organized, Liberal working men, with the secret ballot to protect them, could demand "better Land Laws, better education, and Cheap Food."[86] He was apparently careful, however, not to let this radicalism colour the National Association. Brabazon, though nominally a Gladstonian

Liberal until 1890, was conservative in his attitudes and interests.

Joseph Arch (Source: *Ill. London News*, Apr. 20, 1872)

The involvement of the Kent and Sussex union in the lobby followed logically from its emigration activity in the preceding decade. Under Simmons' leadership, the union had responded to bad times and lock-outs by farmers with emigration assistance for its men throughout the 1870s.[87] In the beginning, the national union led by Arch (with which the Kent and Sussex men were not associated) had done the same. Arch warned that "whether the lands of England were tilled or whether they were barren, [the labourers] should have their freedom and their rights or they should leave the country."[88] In 1874, during a lock-out in the Suffolk area, 400 farm labourers migrated and 440 emigrated rather than submit to the farmers and surrender their union memberships. Arch, like Simmons, approved of union officials functioning as emigration agents, and, about 1888, one of his own sons emigrated to Canada.

But by the 1880s, the permanent depression of agricultural prices had broken the back of Arch's national movement. The Kent and Sussex Union, while it did not suffer the kind of drastic membership decline that Arch experienced,[89] nevertheless shared in the general collapse of morale and acquiesced in the wage reductions which farmers demanded. While some of the labour leaders turned to political solutions—franchise and reform of land laws—the Kent and Sussex men continued to emigrate.

Labour emigrationists from agricultural areas, therefore, wished to see state aid applied to their own men, and their presence in the lobby reinforced a vital part of the movement's propaganda, viz. that there were plenty of men with agricultural skills who wanted to emigrate. Agricultural labour leaders like Simmons argued that their men were the fittest for colonization schemes, and their going would significantly improve the lot of the men left behind. True as this may have been, it could hardly be denied that pursuit of state emigration by the farm unions was largely a policy of despair.

By 1886, there were altogether 91 men on the national council of the lobby who claimed to represent labour— some 33 trade societies and 13 trade councils. The geographic spread was national, reaching from Glasgow to Canterbury, though concentrated in Lancashire, London, and Kent. Most of the major trades were represented: metals, engineering, shipbuilding, mining, textiles, building, transport (though not the railwaymen), printing, and agriculture. Several of the trades which did not affiliate large numbers were represented by their national leaders and by men prominent in trade-union political activity. Executive members of seven national organizations, including three general secretaries (Knight of the Boilermakers, Kelley of the Printers, and Mawdsley of the Spinners) of the amalgamated type of society were members of the National Association. The lobby could also count on the official allegiance of a number of trades councils—especially those of Liverpool, Newcastle-on-Tyne,

Leeds, and Manchester. However, they failed to bring in the trades councils of Birmingham and, importantly, London, which was opposed to emigration as a solution to unemployment.[90] These organizations could provide "a useful means of common action in local politics, approving candidates and organizing campaigns."[91] On a national level, the lobby contained (between 1883 and 1891) four members of the Parliamentary Committee of the T.U.C.[92]

Leaders like Knight and Mawdsley, no revolutionaries certainly, were speaking in the mid-1880s the rhetoric of radical social analysis, of "something wrong in a system which effects such unequal distribution of the wealth created by labour,"[93] and of "no chance of improvement so long as the present state of society continued to exist."[94] The severe trade depression of 1885–87, which gave rise to expressions like these from moderate labour leaders, prompted many of the threatened trades to turn to political pressure for relief. It is not surprising that the peak of the National Association's activity coincided with the nadir (1886) of the trade cycle, or that enthusiasm waned with economic recovery in 1889. Though several unions had been interested before 1885, many, like the housebuilders, the shipbuilders, and the iron workers, were catapulted into the emigration movement by the acute contraction of their trades in the middle years of the decade.

The general unrest of the 1880s, created by a highly erratic trade cycle, had natural consequences in the political pressure activity in which many unions engaged. But most of the trade-union leaders remained tied to a class-alliance approach to politics, in spite of the potential for separate organization inherent in the working-class electorate created in 1885. Labour leaders continued, through "cause lobbies" like the National Association, to pursue the politics of influence within a political system dominated by the traditional social elite, and concentrated on whatever indirect pressure that unions and trade councils could bring to bear. But the mode of approach—grounded in class alliance and cooperation—to some extent defined the kind of programs which labour was likely to advance: better housing and regulation of hours, but also less substantial causes such as bimetallism,[95] anti-prostitution,[96] and international arbitration.[97] In this context a panacea like state emigration was eminently legitimate.

Many of the labour men in the National Association were involved in a variety of other "class collaboration" causes. The same middle- and upper-class clergymen and philanthropists with whom they worked in the emigration fight were their colleagues in the promotion of, for example, temperance,[98] working men's clubs,[99] and education.[100] The National Association was not a random collection of individuals of different classes who happened to have been interested in emigration and were welded together in an unnatural body by the personality of Lord Brabazon. Rather, it was a group of persons with some experience in interclass relationships, who brought to the lobby a network of contacts and expertise in pressure-group activity, and who often shared other promotional interests with a number of their fellow emigrationists.

5.4   *"Interest Group" or "Cause Lobby"?*

Much of the scholarly literature on modern political pressure groups attempts to segregate them into two rough categories: sectional or "interest" lobbies and promotional or "cause" lobbies.[101] To the former would belong such organizations as the Farmers' Alliance or the Country Brewers Society, while the United Kingdom Alliance or the National Association for Promoting State-directed Colonization would logically belong to the latter. While they have their uses, these distinctions are, of course, somewhat misleading. Most causes—temperance and emigration clearly not excepted—provided a cover for at least some form of vested interest.

The National Association promoted itself as a cross section of society motivated by a sincere regard for the health of the nation, but from the first it was forced to deny accusations of selfish interest. What were some of the sectional or class interests which state emigration might serve? Clearly, two large sectional blocs within the membership—labour and landlords—had much to gain. For the trade unions, emigration promised higher wages, relief from the burden of emigration benefits, and some deflection of demands that they reform their restrictive membership policies. For landlords interested in consolidating holdings or reallocating land use from arable to pasture, emigration was a means of reducing the number of dependent tenants and labourers without the opprobrium of large-scale evictions. This was particularly attractive to Scot and Irish landlords, while in England increased mechanization on some large estates meant that a reduction in the supply of farm labour would not necessarily pose much of a threat in the higher wage rates which might result. And, most importantly, it would help undermine radical demand for land reform.

In the colonies, there was a large interest which stood to profit from large-scale emigration and colonization. Speculators and railways possessed large tracts they were anxious to unload. Also there were colonial financiers who looked to supply the capital for new settlements. Any emigration scheme in England invariably incurred suspicions of unscrupulous interests behind the scenes. *Martin Chuzzlewit* (1843–1844) was Dickens' warning to hasty would-be emigrants, while the disastrous experiences of some English settlers in South America, later in the century, provided Thomas Hardy with material for *Tess of the D'Urbervilles* (1891). Colonial employers, of course, also had a reason to promote a large immigration, particularly since the practice of hiring in England for the purpose of undercutting high colonial wage rates became more difficult with the growth of strong colonial unions.[102] But though many of the National Association's supporters can be shown to have had financial interests in the colonies, there is little evidence of direct linkage to colonial speculators and employers.

> The Carthaginians have a constitution which is in practice oligarchical; but they avoid the dangers of oligarchy by encouraging the diffusion of wealth. From time to time a section of the populace is planted out among the dependent cities—a policy which remedies the defects of the constitution and serves to give it stability.[103]

Lastly, to what extent was emigration assistance a social-imperialist device, as Hyndman believed, to reduce pressures for radical reform and working-class political consciousness? There is no simple answer. The Social Democratic Federation was not alone in its assumption that state emigration was a ruse to achieve domestic stability without social change. On January 14, 1885, Joseph Chamberlain, addressing a crowd of agricultural labourers at Ipswich, opposed the application of the rates to emigration assistance on the grounds that radical reform of land law and taxation would enable labour "to find work and employment" in England "without expatriating them against their will."[104]

The lobby was explicitly counter-revolutionary in its public voice; much of its propaganda was devoted to demonstrating the growing threat of violent revolution in England and the need to undercut the appeal of "professional agitators" by reducing unemployment and overcrowding. It is, perhaps, significant that state emigration reached the apogee of its appeal in the periods of uncertainty which followed the extension of the franchise in 1867 and 1885. State emigration was a step "which would at once turn starving and desperate men into contented and loyal subjects, and . . . permanently relieve the State from the sense of impending danger"[105] A few days after riots in London, Birmingham, Sheffield, and Yarmouth in February of 1886, Brabazon wrote to the *Times,*

> the time will assuredly arrive when the last limit of human endurance will have been reached, and it is possible that the larger proportion of these long-suffering masses may then be placed in the terrible dilemma of having either to accept Mr. Hyndman's advice or to starve . . . .
>
> Let us hope that our statesmen will be wise while there is yet time, and turn their eyes across the ocean to those countries under British rule where there are limitless fertile lands waiting to be occupied.[106]

Nevertheless, the National Association did not advertise emigration as a clear alternative to social reform. Instead much of its literature emphasized that emigration was no panacea for social ills, but would help create an atmosphere in which constructive measures would be more likely to succeed. Officially, the lobby proposed emigration first and reform later, and prudently left it to individual supporters to define for themselves precisely the degree or manner of domestic reform which should follow. Obviously, many among the middle- and upper-class emigrationists trusted that emigration would help secure rank, property, and economic freedom.

Gareth Stedman Jones has maintained in his excellent
study of London's casual labour problem that the 1880s
saw the emergence of a new attitude toward poverty.[107]
This was characterized by a separation in many minds of
the problem of the majority of the urban poor from that
of the lowest group, the "residuum". The residuum came
to be regarded as hopelessly beyond reform and dangerous because it contaminated the salvageable classes above
it. The result of these conclusions was strong interest,
reinforced by the disturbances of 1886 and 1887, in containing, isolating, and removing this class—to "labour
colonies" in England or the Empire. It is in this light that
Stedman Jones views the state-emigration movement,
which he believes was clearly an outgrowth of this coer-
cive attitude toward the residuum, a characteristic social
imperialist response by the right wing of the ruling class.

This is a persuasive point of view. Certainly there were
those—not only upper-class imperialists but trade unionists as well—who advocated state emigration for these
reasons. But the National Association did not, in fact, pro-
pose the removal of the residuum. They could never have
hoped to win colonial cooperation if they had. Instead,
they called for the emigration of the respectable industri-
ous poor—those above pauperism, those whom shrewd
selection procedures would identify as the most likely to
succeed, and also agricultural labour—indeed, any but the
residuum. Their assumption was that the removal of any
category above the worst would reduce competition for
better jobs and housing, allowing some degree of "level-
ling up"—an optimistic attitude which was not, as Stedman Jones suggests, quite dead.

One must qualify, then, any judgment that state emigration was simply part of an offensive against the dangerous classes of London. Motivation and objectives were

considerably more complex. No monolithic definition of emigrationist attitude is possible. Different people looked to emigration to accomplish different things. The movement's status as a hybrid group built upon many interests dictated a loosely focused program which allowed wide support and participation, but which also made its ultimate aims rather vague.

Notes on Chapter 5

1. The National Association for Promoting State-directed Colonization, *State-directed Colonization Series, No. I* (London, 1886).
2. Some sources of bias in an analysis of the Association's membership should be mentioned. First, the standard biographical and genealogical reference works used to identify these persons inevitably favour men, the traditional professions, and well-known society figures. This skews the results toward the social and political elite. However, the unidentifiable do not, I believe, constitute a large enough percentage to pose a serious problem: 7 percent could not be identified by residence, 15 percent by occupation. Second, it is difficult to classify many persons of wealth by occupation (in the case, for instance, of an heir of landed estates who is trained in the law, is a director of a commercial firm or bank, and regularly stands for Parliament) or residence (when the family may possess several scattered estates). Decisions have consequently been made rather arbitrarily, based on what is known of an individual's principal interests.
3. Army: Gen. Sir Garnet Wolseley, Maj. Gen. C. E. Cumberland (Royal Engineers, ret. 1887), Lt. Gen. R. L. Lowry, Lt. Gen. W. A. Fyers (ret. 1881), Col. F. W. de Winton (ret. as Major Gen., 1890), Col. E. H. Kennard, Maj. Flood Page. Navy: Admiral Francis Egerton (ret. 1875), Adm. J. C. Dalrymple-Hay, Rear-Adm. E. Field, Capt. E. H. Verney, Comm. F. C. de Lousada, Lt. G. Mansfield Smith. A much larger number held rank in the Territorials, or had served a few years in their youth and retired at an early age.

4. For example, there was G. B. Kent of Kent Brushes; C. T. Ritchie, whose firm traded in the East Indies; J. F. Hutton, with cotton interests in Africa, and George Dixon whose firm traded in Australia. Brewing was represented by O. E. Coope; railways by Thomas Brassey.

5. J. H. Froude, *Oceana* (London, 1886), 241: in 1848, "when the air was full of Socialism and Republican equality."

6. His "In Memoriam, W. E. Forster" (1886) closes with the verse,

    Britain some day—her daughter-lands apart
    No longer—will remember thee whose heart
    Fired hers to win her world-wide heritage.

    Collected Poems (London, 1901), 10.

7. Of the 11 women on the national council, 9 were also vice-presidents: Mrs. E. L. Blanchard (v-p), Lady Gordon Cathcart (v-p), Lady Jane Dundas (v-p), Emily Faithful (v-p), Lady F. Hobart, Anna Swanwick (v-p), the Hon. Mrs. Ellen Joyce (v-p), Maria Susan Rye (v-p), Lady Emily Anne, Viscountess Strangford (v-p), S. Strongi'th'arm, Lady Victoria Wellesley (v-p).

8. A.B.S. Acheson, Earl of Gosford; R. A. S. Adair, Baron Waveney; C. B. Adderley, Baron Norton; W. Pleydell-Bouverie, Viscount Folkestone; William Brabazon, Earl of Meath; Thomas Brassey, Baron Brassey; G. F. W. Byron, Baron Byron; D.-W. Carleton, Baron Dorchester; A. T. T. Verney-Cave, Baron Braye; A.D.R.W. Cochrane-Baillie, Baron Lamington; G.-H. Roper-Curzon, Baron Teynham; R.N.C.G. Curzon, Baron Zouche; A. W. G. Duff, Earl of Fife; Wilbraham Egerton, Baron Egerton of Tatton; Beilby Lawley, Baron Wenlock; W. W. Legge, Earl of Dartmouth; W. D. Montagu, Duke of Manchester; W. L. Pakenham, Earl of Longford; A. de C. Rice, Baron Dynevor; J. R. W. Vessey, Viscount de Vesci

9. Earls Gosford, Meath, and Longford; Viscount de Vesci.

10. Argyll MSS. Box 9, letter no. 284: the Marquess of Lorne to the eighth Duke of Argyll, 21 Oct. 1890.

11. The Earl of Meath, "State Colonization," *Time*, Vol. 18 (May, 1888), 543–55. See the appendix for a listing of National Association MPs and their constituencies.

12. Of the 36 Association MPs in 1886, 14 were returned for the first time in either 1885 or 1886.

13. Late in the Association's campaign, in 1888 or 1889, there was a change in the structure of the executive. The large number of

vice-presidents was reduced to one (Lord Sandhurst), and the executive committee was cut to 12. The new executive was more upper class; all the trade union leaders were relegated to the national council.

14. The Portsmouth Congress (1885) considered emigration questions, as did the Wolverhampton Congress of 1887, at which Lord Meath read a paper on state colonization. From their institution at Cambridge in 1861, these congresses became a national sounding board of Church laity opinion (Owen Chadwick, *The Victorian Church*, Vol. II, 362).

15. Alfred Simmons read a paper on state colonization at the Intercolonial Trade Union Congress of 1888.

16. *State-directed Colonization Series, No. I,* 159.

17. The *Times,* 7 July 1885, 12.

18. *State-directed Colonization Series, No. I,* 150.

19. G. Kitson Clark, *Churchmen and the Condition of England 1832–1885* (London, 1973), 176.

20. Paul Bloomfield, *Edward Gibbon Wakefield* (Edinburgh, 1961), 317–18.

21. Kitson Clark, 170–1, 270; Hugh McLeod, *Class and Religion in the Late Victorian City* (Hampden, Conn.; 1974), 104.

22. William Redmond Curtis, *The Lambeth Conferences* (New York, 1942), 50–1; Lord Davidson of Lambeth, *The Six Lambeth Conferences, 1867–1920* (London, 1920), 29, 141–8.

23. The Church Emigration Society, founded in 1886, relied on the voluntary services of country clergymen and their families (P.P. 1890, *Report of the Colonization Committee,* 162).

24. Chadwick, II, 263.

25. Donald O. Wagner, *The Church of England and Social Reform Since 1854* (New York, 1930), 106–7; the *Times,* 22 Dec. 1881, 6.

26. Wagner, 150–53.

27. See chapter 3.

28. William Panckridge, "The Church and Emigration," *The Clergymen's Magazine,* XII (Jan., 1881), 53.

29. Panckridge to Davidson, 2 Feb 1881 (Tait Papers, Lambeth Palace).

30. *Ibid.,* and 7 March 1881.

31. Panckridge to Davidson, 28 April 1881.

32. *Ibid.* This "Emigration Circular was signed by Tait 20 Dec. 1881, and published in the *Times* on the 22nd.

33. He spoke of the "Divine command to replenish the earth and subdue it", "the very highest mission on which a man can be sent." Panckridge to Davidson, 16 June 1881.
34. *Ibid.*
35. Bishop of Rupert's Land to the Archbishop of Canterbury, 21 April 1881.
36. Charlotte O'Brien to Archbishop Tait, 20 June 1881. The group included William Forster and his wife, Lord and Lady Monteagle, and a number of MPs.
37. Panckridge to Davidson, 6 Dec. 1881.
38. Church of England, *Official Year Book, 1885,* 109.
39. The *Times,* 1 March 1882, 6.
40. Panckridge to Davidson, 27 Dec. 1881.
41. The *Times,* 8 July, 1884, 4.
42. *Official Year Book, 1885,* 129.
43. £ 800 in 1889; £ 4792 in 1911.
44. Johnson, 76, 78, 171. The Church Army worked with the Self-Help Emigration Society in sending its people abroad.
45. Davidson, *The Six Lambeth Conferences,* 146–7.
46. Canterbury to Brabazon, Jan. 5, 1887 (Meath Papers, Autograph Vol. I). By 1889, the Association claimed 12 bishops, including 6 colonial bishops. See the Appendix for a list of the clergymen who were members of the Association in 1886.
47. Robert Keith Arbuthnot, Vicar of St. James, *The Church and the Working Classes: An Address* (London, 1893), 18.
48. *D.N.B.,* and Norman Wymer, *Dr. Barnardo* (London, 1962), 41.
49. W. A. Johnson to J. H. Boyd, 6 Oct. 1881, in C. O. 384/147 (9779). In 1887 Manning wrote an article in *Murray's* (July), "Why are our People unwilling to Emigrate?" which supported the goals of the National Association. He also promised to contribute a pamphlet for the *State-directed Colonization Series.*
50. See Arnold White, *The Problems of a Great City* (London, 1886), and John A. Garrard, *The English and Immigration, 1880–1910* (Oxford, 1971), 18–30. Other members of the National Association interested in the Jewish "problem" included Brabazon, James Lowther, Captain Colomb, and the Rev. G. S. Reaney.
51. Members of the National Association served on the Royal Commission on the Depression of Trade (1885–1886), Accidents in Mines (1881–1886), Housing of the Poor (1884–1885), and City Parochial Charities (1880).

52. Walter B. Paton, *State-Aided Emigration* (London, 1885), 31–2.
53. Herman Ausubel, *In Hard Times: Reformers Among the Late Victorians* (New York, 1960), 74.
54. Brian Harrison, "Philanthropy and the Victorians," *Victorian Studies*, Vol. 9 (June, 1966), 353.
55. *Ibid.*, 367.
56. The Rev. F. M. Tomlinson, evidence before the colonization committee. P.P. 1890, *Report of the Colonization Committee*, 161.
57. The Central Emigration Society, the British and Colonial Emigration Society, the East End Emigration Fund, the Self-Help Emigration Society, Tuke's Committee, the Scottish Emigrants' Aid Association, the East London Colonization Aid Society, the Women's Emigration Society, and the Female Middle-class Emigration Society.
58. Representatives of the metropolitan emigration societies on the executive committee of the E.I.O. included Samuel Smith, J. H. Rankin, Arnold White, Walter Hazel, and Howard Hodgkin. Smith, Rankin and White were also members of the National Association.
59. Charlotte Erickson, "The Encouragement of Emigration by British Trade Unions, 1850–1900," *Population Studies*, Vol. 3 (1949), 248–73. Also see R. V. Clements, "Trade Unions and Emigration, 1840–1880," *Population Studies*, Vol. 9 (1955), 167–80, and Pamela Horn, "Agricultural Trade Unionism and Emigration, 1872–1881," *Historical Journal*, 15 (March, 1972), 87–102.
60. The "new unionist" secretary of the Sheffield File Cutters, Stuart Uttley, was an advocate of state emigration, while John Burnett of the Engineers, Labour Correspondent at the Board of Trade, who was no socialist, was firmly opposed to the emigration of working men. The engineers dropped their emigration benefits in 1885. (P.P. 1889, *Report of the Colonization Committee*, 91–104).
61. Erickson, 263.
62. Clements, 175; H. A. Clegg, A. Fox, and A. F. Thompson, *A History of British Trade Unions Since 1889*, Vol. 1 (Oxford, 1964), 6.
63. Erickson, 265. She lists 15 unions which adopted emigration benefits after 1850; five of these did so after 1880: the Boilermakers; Tin Plate Workers; Journeymen Machine; Engine, and Iron Grinders; and the United Operative Spindle and Flyer Makers.

172   *Emigration in 19th-Century Britain*

64. P.P. 1889, *Report of the Colonization Committee*, 92.
65. Harold A. Logan, *The History of Trade Union Organization in Canada* (Chicago, 1928), 11, 12, 38, 61, 67n; Albert A. Hayden, "New South Wales Immigration Policy, 1856–1900," *Transactions of the American Philosophical Society*, Vol. 61, pt. 5, n.s. (1971).
66. Cotton spinners, iron shipbuilders, flint-glass makers, agricultural labour, London compositors, lithographic printers, Northumberland miners, and probably others.
67. Clegg, et al., estimate trade-union strength at 750,000 in 1888 (p.1).
68. Liverpool, Manchester and Salford, Bolton, Oldham, Burrow-in-Furness, Warrington, Sheffield, Leeds, Hull, and Newcastle-on-Tyne.
69. *State-directed Colonization Series, No. II*, 122.
70. Clegg, et al., 30.
71. *Ibid.*, 12. The Ironfounders spent £ 4712 in emigration benefits from 1877 to 1889 (P.P. 1889, *Report of the Colonization Committee*, 92).
72. President J. C. Laird, Vice President W. Mancur, Secretary T. A. Kidd, and Treasurer J. G. Fewster.
73. *State-directed Colonization Series. No. II*, 121.
74. *Ibid.*, 124.
75. Alan Fox, *A History of the National Union of Boot and Shoe Operatives, 1874–1957* (Oxford, 1958), 18.
76. The Colliery Enginemen's Association (Durham) supported the lobby's campaign but did not join.
77. Clegg, et al., 1.
78. P.P. 1889, *Report of the Colonization Committee*, 92.
79. Christopher Storm-Clark, "The Miners, 1870–1970: A Test Case for Oral History," *Victorian Studies*, XV, No. 1 (Sept., 1971), 52–3.
80. The Journeymen Brassfounders Association signified their approval in 1886.
81. The London Compositors spent £ 5001 from 1867 to 1889 on emigration benefits (P.P. 1889, *Report of the Colonization Committee*, 92).
82. Lib-Lab. A commonly-used label for working-class liberals.
83. Coote was an unsuccessful Lib-Lab candidate for North Camberwell in 1883. Though he later helped to organize the Municipal

Employees Union, by the mid-1880s he was increasingly preoccupied with the largely middle-class movement for the suppression of the white-slave traffic, and was secretary of the National Vigilance Association.

84. Beatrice and Sydney Webb, *The History of Trade Unionism* (London, 1927 edn)., 492.
85. The Conservative MP for Maidstone, and two Conservative MPs in Sussex joined the Association, as did three Kent Justices of the Peace.
86. Alfred Simmons, *Words of Warning to Agricultural Labourers and Other Working Men* (Cobden Club Leaflet No. 26, 1885), 1–2.
87. Rollo Arnold, "The 'Revolt of the Field' in Kent 1872–1879," *Past and Prsent,* No. 64 (August, 1974), 71–95.
88. Pamela Horn, *Joseph Arch* (Kineton, 1971), 104, 109.
89. Clegg et al., 45.
90. Anonymous [George Kenneth Tate], *London Trades Council, 1860–1950. A History* (London, 1950), 58. The London Trades Council voted on Nov. 9, 1883, to oppose emigration of the unemployed.
91. Clegg et al., 40.
92. Robert Knight, 1875–1883; G. D. Kelley, 1871–1872, 1883–1884, 1887–1888, and 1890–1892; Stuart Uttley, 1890–?; and James Mawdsley, 1882–1883, 1884–1890, and 1891–1897.
93. Knight of the Boilermakers in his annual report of 1886 (quoted by Clegg et al, 54).
94. Mawdsley at the International Trade Union Congress at Paris in 1886 (quoted by B. and S. Webb, 379).
95. Allan Gee of the textile workers and G. D. Kelley of the printers were officers of the bimetallist Trade Union Monetary Reform Association, and Mawdsley later (1892) converted to bimetallism. Several of the middle- and upper-class members of the National Association were also advocates of bimetallism.
96. For example William Coote and the National Vigilance Association.
97. There was a Workmen's Peace Association. Within the National Association the most prominent campaigner for international arbitration was Hodgson Pratt.
98. Temperance leaders within the Association included Bishops Ellicott and Wilberforce, Sir William Houldsworth, Sydney Smith, and C. H. Spurgeon.

99. Sir Thomas Brassey (created Lord Brassey, 1886) was President of the Working Men's Clubs and Institute Union; Bishop Webber was a vice-president, and Hodgson Pratt a member of the council.

100. George Dixon, Lord Norton, and H. T. Mackenzie Bell were leading advocates of free public education, while Bishop Goodwin, Sydney Smith, Hodgson Pratt, and Brabazon worked for industrial training for the working classes. Anna Swanwick, Emily Faithful, Maria Rye, J. Boyd-Kinnear, and Lady Strangford were active in promoting female education.

101. See Allen Potter, *Organized Groups in British National Politics* (London, 1961), and S. E. Finer, *Anonymous Empire: A Study of the Lobby in Great Britain* (2nd edn.; London, 1966).

102. Logan, 68–9.

103. Aristotle, *Politics*, Book II, Chapter 9, paragraph 15.

104. Charles W. Boyd (ed)., *Mr. Chamberlain's Speeches* (London, 1914), Vol. 1, 143.

105. Lord Brabazon, "State-directed Colonization: Its Necessity," *Nineteenth Century*, Vol. 16 (Nov., 1884), 766.

106. The *Times*, 17 Feb 1886, 7.

107. Stedman Jones, 289–314.

Chapter 6. Agitation and
Counter-Agitation, 1883–1885

T he National Association made its first approach to
government shortly after its creation in the summer
of 1883. Its target was the Colonial Office, which
had before it at the time a crowd of emigration issues.
Tuke's Committee was at work in Ireland, and colonial
replies to the government's circular on Irish emigration
were still coming in. In May, the chairman of the Royal
Commission on Crofters and Cottars had asked for information on any emigration schemes which might apply to
the Scottish congested districts. The Stephen negotiations
for Canadian immigration dragged on, and a number of
private individuals demanded Colonial Office attention to
other emigration subjects. In early autumn both Potter's
Workmen's Emigration League and the Central Emigration Society asked the government to receive deputations
on the emigration of the unemployed from London.[1] It
was some time before the National Association was identified as the major emigration lobby.

6.1   *Going the Rounds at Whitehall*

The meeting of June 6 had resolved, "amid cheers", upon a deputation to Gladstone and Lord Derby, the Colonial Secretary. A meeting with Derby, but not Gladstone, did take place at the Colonial Office on June 18, and was of a somewhat encouraging nature. The Colonial Secretary explained the major objections to a large scheme, but proclaimed himself favourably inclined toward some sort of government program. He did not, of course, commit himself or the government to Boyd's scheme. "I am only one member of the Cabinet." But he did promise to take the subject up for Cabinet consideration. Meanwhile, the lobby should apply to the Local Government Board, local authorities, and the Treasury, as officials more closely involved than the Colonial Office in setting up a program to relieve domestic distress.[2]

This proved to be the first step in the bureaucratic dance of avoiding responsibility by passing an awkward subject around the various departments. The futility of "going the rounds" at Whitehall was not at first apparent, and the deputation boasted of a success in Derby's stance of "benevolent neutrality". A chief obstacle to effective pressure on government proved to be this problem of identifying departmental responsibility. The Colonial Office ultimately took the emigration issue over, but with bad grace, and only after Chamberlain at the Local Government Board and Childers at the Treasury pushed it upon them. Further confusion followed from the fact that the next three years saw two general elections, four governments, and the breakup of the Liberal Party. The subsequent rapid change of ministers made concerted pressure on them difficult and ineffectual.

Following their "unquestionably encouraging" interview with Derby, the lobby proceeded as instructed to the Local Government Board, and submitted Boyd's scheme to Sir Charles Dilke on July 5.[3] Dilke listened with polite interest to their proposals for a parliamentary grant of £ 1 million to remove 10,000 working class families to Canada, and suggested they approach the Treasury.

Four months passed before the program was dutifully presented to Childers at the Treasury. In the meantime, emigrationist hopes, dampened somewhat by the apparent collapse of the Stephen negotiations, were fanned up by more encouragement from Derby, who told the House of Lords on July 31,

> emigration is the only real remedy for the distress which exists in what we may call the congested districts. All the other plans for the relief of that distress are in comparison very imperfect and temporary expedients. I may go further and say, on behalf of my colleagues, as well as myself, that we have been and are anxious to promote emigration . . . by all reasonable and practicable means . . . .[4]

The Association set about reinforcing its case by launching its first series of public meetings in working-class areas of London. This attracted publicity, the support of some public figures like the Earl of Carnarvon, and the sustained opposition of the Democratic Federation.[5] The lobby also carried out its own survey of the unemployed in the east and south of London. Boyd appointed an agent from Southwark, "the son of an agricultural labourer," to study conditions and write a report. Published in the *Times* on November 21, the investigation concluded that overcrowding was accompanied by a serious lack of employment opportunity in the area. Sixty percent of the men seeking work at the docks were regularly turned away. Of the unemployed, those born in the slums, the "'flotsam and jetsam" of ex-sailors and army pensioners, and broken-down servants and mechanics were unfit for emigration. But healthy Irish and Scots, farm hands drawn to the city, and sweated single women could be rescued. Further, there were, Boyd's agent claimed, many among the poor who wanted to emigrate—though the advocates of "political" solutions were louder.[6]

Though Boyd was removed from the leadership of the lobby in November, his program had already been submitted to the government. The National Association hesitated to put another in its place until its fate had been decided. In the event, Childer's reply proved extremely frustrating. The Treasury held that any initiating action would have to be taken by the Colonial Office. The lobby was, in effect, where it had begun six months earlier. Boyd, apparently without the support of the National Association, continued to lobby the Colonial Office in January of 1884, received some encouragement, but was finally told that the government could not take up colonization unless some intermediary like the C.P.R. would guarantee repayment of settler loans.[7] After February, nothing more was heard of him.

For the lobby as a whole there was, however, a positive side to the disappointments of 1883. The National Association had managed to separate itself from Boyd and the fate of his scheme. Moreover, the Colonial Office appeared to leave the door open to anyone who could "procure substantial backing". There was also some sense in the department that state-emigration appeals ought to be handled differently in the future. Permanent Secretary Herbert agreed that

> It would certainly be well ... to settle some principle on which applications to the Government for the consideration of Emigration proposals should be dealt with, rather than having President LGB, Chancellor of the Exchequer, and Sec of St for colonies passing proposals back and forth without action causing trouble and avoidable correspondence besides irritating those who thus approach the Government in vain.[8]

In the wake of Boyd's defeat, the National Association was not prepared immediately to resubmit proposals to the government. The Colonial Office was not approached again with a detailed program until Alfred Simmons submitted an "official" scheme in 1886. In the intervening two years there were meetings in "all large centers of industry" and, in 1885, an effort was made to federate the London emigration societies in order to give concentrated support to a second approach to ministers. Brabazon does not appear to have been anxious to return to the Colonial Office. Rather, the reorganization of November, 1883, was the beginning of a careful, long-range campaign aimed ultimately at government, but occupied for the time being with demonstrating the depth and permanence of public interest and with exploring methods of attack that were less direct.

6.2 *Indirect Approaches*

Though the National Association itself held aloof from identification with specific proposals, its Executive Committee directly and indirectly encouraged individuals and other organizations to keep emigration issues in the public eye. When Samuel Smith, the Liverpool philanthropist, pressed the Local Government Board for child emigration, he received the assistance of Brabazon and

Lord Norton. All three were National Association members. On March 3, the London Chamber of Commerce
sent a memorial to the Colonial Office calling for state
emigration and imperial federation, and six days later, the
Lewisham Poor Law Union followed with a request that
a decision on emigration be made as soon as possible.[9] The
same month, Carnarvon took up the fate of the Stephen
and Boyd negotiations in the House of Lords, and demanded publication of the correspondence. He received
support from National Association spokesmen on both
sides of the House.[10]

Derby bore the brunt of these criticisms, but, though he
replied to them with the usual Liberal objections to state
emigration, he had in fact done his best behind the scenes
to get Treasury and Canadian Government approval for
colonization.[11] In this, as in other issues, Derby's position
was an increasingly uncomfortable one of having to
mouth platitudes which he did not believe and drawing
criticism for policies he did not support. The exchange in
the Lords drew comment from the *Times* mildly sympathetic to Carnarvon's attack.

> The plan suggested may be viewed as sound or unsound, but
> plausible it most certainly is . . . . What can be more obvious than
> that East London should bring help to the colonies, and the colo-
> nies to East London? . . . The only possible question is as to the
> machinery by which it is to be effected.[12]

It also prompted Brabazon to review Derby's objections
in a long public letter.[13]

Brabazon also called for a National Association conference in London to consider a course of action. The collapse of the negotiations between the Colonial Office, the
Treasury, and the Canadian Government, at a time when
private colonization experiments like that of Lady Gor-

don Cathcart were succeeding, indicated that the Association might best use its resources in improving British-colonial relations. The government should be urged to confer with colonial authorities more regularly on emigration issues. Brabazon meant for the National Association to play the role of go-between if possible, and began to contact colonial authorities on his own. Getting colonial support, however, meant modifying National Association goals. Poor Law emigration was no longer to be advocated: "the less the Poor Law authorities are permitted to have to say to the matter the better." The lobby must be flexible. "If the Government do not see their way to adopting at once a system of adult male emigration, might they not commence by assisting the emigration of women and children?"[14]

The conference which Brabazon convened at Mansion House April 23 was well attended and received the support of Archbishop Benson and T. H. Huxley, among others. Resolutions were passed calling for state emigration. Brabazon felt the Association had now achieved a genuine national stature, and reported to his wife that the meeting was a clear success.[15] At the same time, the Association launched a propaganda campaign in the form of a series of pamphlets—the first "a reply to Lord Derby" written by its secretary Alfred Simmons: "Emigration . . . is a boon to the people who go, a benefit to those who stay at home, and an advantage to the colonies where they are received."[16] But where Boyd had envisioned emigration of the masses of London unemployed, Simmons spoke of sending out men with farming experience.

Brabazon's tactic of circumventing, to some extent, the Colonial Office through direct contact between colonial authorities and the National Association almost immediately bore some fruit. The Emigration Agent for Natal,

Walter Peace, who had a plan for the assisted emigration of young persons to South Africa which was sanctioned by the Natal Land and Immigration Board, came to Brabazon for the National Association's approval before he approached the Colonial Office. With the formal support of the lobby behind him, Peace then submitted his proposals to Derby and asked for an interview.[17]

The plan Peace presented was concerned principally with the emigration of boys and girls under 16 years. It called for training schools in England, recruitment from orphanages and poor-houses, free passage under supervision, and maintenance in the colonies for the adolescents until they could be hired out to farmers on three-year contracts. Derby was, once again, more sympathetic than his permanent staff. The proposals were expanded at his request, and an interview arranged.[18] Meanwhile, Peace got the Girls' Friendly Society to initiate a program of their own along these lines. Again, the National Association played a key role; Lord Brabazon and Ellen Joyce were themselves members of the Council of the Girls' Friendly Society.[19]

Peace was encouraged by his interview with Derby on July 16. His proposals were sent on to the Local Government Board and the Home Office for comment, and, at Derby's request, forwarded to the High Commissioner for Canada and the Agents General for other colonies as well.[20] Though he anticipated at least a commission of inquiry, his plans were ultimately rejected by the Poor Law Board, which sent a lengthy and negative assessment to the Colonial Office in February of 1885. Some umbrage was taken at Peace's implied criticism of Poor Law schools, but their main criticism lay in the cost of the program. Most Poor Law children were supported on a temporary, outdoor basis. Their training and emigration

would require the government to support them at greater
expense and well beyond the age (14 or 15) at which they
were commonly discharged.[21] Though there was some
support among the Colonial Office staff for recommending at least a small experimental program, it was decided
that "we must let Mr. Peace's proposals drop unless they
are taken up and pressed upon this Gov't by the Colonial
Governments."[22]

6.3   *New Prospects: Election, Depression, and Federation*

While the Natal negotiations were in process during the
summer and autumn of 1884, British politics became
highly animated by the Lords' refusal to pass the Liberal
franchise-reform bill without redistribution first. For a
time, a fierce popular agitation against the Lords, led by
Chamberlain and Morley, swamped other questions. In
this charged atmosphere a general election was widely
anticipated.

While a pending general election and the maneuvering
and bidding for support which it entailed offered some
limited opportunity for advancement of the emigration
cause, the atmosphere brought more harm than good.
Ministers were preoccupied with more pressing questions, and less favourable to initiating action on issues that
were perhaps controversial. Furthermore, pressure in
Parliament to advance "bipartisan" objectives like state
emigration was more likely to be read as an unfriendly act
by government, which would feel in time of crisis less
flexible. Thus, in July of 1884, when Eardley-Wilmot, a
Conservative, asked in Commons whether the Liberal
government would consider re-establishing an emigra-

tion department, he was curtly answered that no need existed.[23] Furthermore, the lobby's parliamentary membership tended to fragment on party lines in time of political crisis, and promises of support were unlikely to be honoured if they entailed voting with parliamentary enemies, regardless of the innocuousness of the question. On the other hand, a pressure group which had received a rebuff might be encouraged by the prospect of a ministerial shuffle. Though the Conservatives had done little for the cause before 1880, Carnarvon's return to the Colonial Office was eagerly anticipated, no doubt, by the emigration lobby in 1885.[24]

There is some indication that the National Association had given up hope of persuading the Liberal government to act, and were waiting for a change before launching another assault on the Colonial Office. The lobby's attack on Liberal ministers grew rather more strident. Following Simmons' attack on Derby, Brabazon published an article which criticized the government for refusing to oil "the timepiece of emigration which keeps the balance between the supply and demand for labour, and has been gradually losing ground."[25] He also labeled the government's Irish emigration efforts inadequate, misdirected, and injurious to public opinion in Canada. Brabazon also more clearly identified the emigration movement with the imperialists who criticized Gladstone's foreign policy —with increasing bitterness as the government slid toward disaster at Khartoum.[26]

One cause of public anxiety in 1885 which worked to the clear advantage of the lobby was the dramatic rise in unemployment which saw, in a few months, the number of unemployed trade-union labourers leap from about 2.6 percent to over 8 percent—and in some trades, like shipbuilding, to a much higher figure. This was not only sustained, but continued to worsen over the following year.[27] In February, 1885, Prince Albert Victor, eldest son of the Prince of Wales, spoke in support of emigration as a solution to domestic distress, and there was a Mansion House Committee the following month to investigate "the causes of permanent distress" in London. A number of National Association members were appointed, including Brabazon, Bishop How, and Cardinal Manning. It recommended, among other measures of relief, assisted emigration for the unemployed.[28]

There was a flurry of activity among philanthropic circles. The Central Emigration Society (C.E.S.) sent a questionnaire around the local Boards of Guardians asking their views on emigration assistance. Seventy percent of the Boards which replied (55) claimed never to have made use of the existing legislation which enabled them to emigrate children. Seventy-five percent had never made use of their powers to emigrate adults. But the great majority (48) approved of the objects of the C.E.S.—which included support for state emigration. Armed with these findings and the Report of the Reformatories and Industrial Schools Commission of 1884 (which called for expanded child emigration), the C.E.S. convened a conference in March of the managers of children's homes. This body then asked the Home Office for help.[29]

But the most significant emigrationist activity in 1885 was an attempt led by Arnold White, the Marquess of Lorne, and other members of the philanthropic societies to unite their efforts through federation. Some saw this as a means of focusing attempts to get state aid. Though he led a deputation to Harcourt at the Home Office, White had at this time little hope for state emigration.[30] Rather, he saw in the amalgamation of the 25 or so emigration societies in London the promise of tapping a much

greater portion of the over £ 4,500,000 annually expended on charities in London:

> the diversion of a moderate proportion of this enormous sum from
> the temporary relief of the necessitous to the permanent assis-
> tance of the able and deserving, by means of emigration, would
> be in all senses, a more productive use of the money.[31]

White and his friends made a strong effort in the spring
to form a central council of the emigration societies. A
conference was held at the Westminster Palace Hotel,
and a federated council was proposed by a committee
which included Brabazon, Lorne, W. H. Smith, and W. E.
Forster. The obstacles were, however, great. The many
societies jealously guarded their own objectives, selection
procedures, and religious orientation. Manning, for example, though supporting some kind of loose cooperation,
was concerned that "the separate religious care and provision which we should all alike make for those who belong to our several responsibilities" be guaranteed.[32] A
report, prepared by J. H. Tuke, was defeatist in its tone,
and underestimated the resources available even to the
individual societies.[33]

The *Times* used Tuke's report to make light of the
whole movement. Within the "troop of societies" there
were more officers than rank and file, and resources were
too insignificant to make federation worthwhile. "Coarse
as seems the test, inability to squeeze out of the London
public a tolerable revenue demonstrates a charitable society to be either superfluous or ill-constituted."[34] Though
White maintained that it was precisely the confusion of
small societies with their myriad procedures that kept
subscriptions down, and that a national or at least metropolitan federation would have increased, as well as consol-

idated, revenues, the effort collapsed. State emigrationists saw, of course, in the failure of federation another argument for a state program. The federation committee itself dropped the idea of consolidation and turned to press government for the creation of an emigrants' information bureau.[35]

The agitation for a governmental information service, which culminated in the establishment of the Emigrants' Information Office by the Conservatives a year later, was not overtly a part of the general campaign for state emigration. Lorne claimed that all that was wanted was reliable information about colonial labour markets and wages, colonial assistance programs, and comparative living costs, which would help societies and individuals to plan. Some, however, saw it as the thin edge of the wedge.

Harcourt had already signified some approval, and Lorne now used the federation committee to pressure government further for an "Imperial Labour Exchange." By June, negotiations were under way with the Treasury and between the Colonial and Home Offices. That month, however, the government fell, and in the ensuing confusion the proposals were shelved, pending the expected general election.[36]

The change in governments, the failure of federation, and possibly the rise in public support for metropolitan charities encouraged the National Association to enter the field once again with its own proposals. On July 6, 1885, a Mansion House conference chaired by Brabazon launched a year of energetic campaigning. Present were many of the original founders, and some new men from the recently formed Imperial Federation League. Letters of support were read from the Duke of Argyll, Sir T. F. Buxton, and the Archbishop of Canterbury.[37]

6.4 *Opposition*

State emigration was a pragmatic and limited remedy for many complex social and economic ills. Even if the poor could be persuaded to go, it was limited to whatever underpopulated parts of the Empire might receive them. At best, some critics claimed, it would merely postpone the inevitable Malthusian confrontation between population and resources. Depending on one's point of view, it was a clandestine device of the employing class to prevent social reform or revolution, a panacea promoted by crack-brain philanthropists, or socialist interference with wage rates and the labour pool. State emigration was denounced by Marxists and liberal economists, by trade unions and employers, and by Malthusians and anti-Malthusians. The movement raised up a host of enemies. The virulence and diversity of this opposition indicates not only the ambiguity of the emigrationist program, but the depth of interests threatened in one way or another.

The loudest, if not the most effective, abuse came from the Left—from Marxists like Hyndman, Henry Georgist land reformers, and socialist labour leaders. The Social Democratic Federation followed the lead of Marx himself, who had attacked Wakefield's colonization proposals as an example of class policy aimed at creating in the colonies artificially concentrated labour pools for exploitation by British capital which was no longer able to find profitable returns in England.[38] Wakefield's own arguments were, in fact, cast in these very terms.

Socialist opposition was commonplace at emigration meetings in the 1880s. From its creation in 1881, the Democratic Federation (the Social-Democratic Federation in 1884) was in the vanguard of this counter-agitation. Its leaders delivered anti-emigration lectures, organized public demonstrations, and infiltrated the meetings of the National Association and other societies. The S.D.F. paper, *Justice,* ran a constant barrage of anti-emigration attacks from 1884, written by Hyndman himself, Harry Quelch, and James Blackwell. Until the National Association resorted to afternoon meetings and tickets of entry, its gatherings in London were in constant danger of being broken up with violence and cries of "Emigrate the Landlords and Capitalists."[39]

These attacks were highly irritating to the lobby leaders who were trying to prove emigration had a real appeal for the working class. Boyd lashed out at the S.D.F. as "professional agitators" and artisans who "earn far better wages than the labourers who would only too gladly emigrate, leaving these men to talk Socialism in their clubs."[40] Brabazon tried to turn this dissent into an argument for emigration.

> If there were no starving men and women, and no discontent in England, the persons who support these associations might indeed despair of inducing a practical and naturally conservative people like the English to embrace the wild theories of Professor Wallace, or to throw in their lot with the visionary revolutionists of the type of Mr. Hyndman or Mr. George.[41]

Brabazon himself sympathized with a number of moderately advanced welfare reforms, and was even prepared, if reluctantly, to see England try some kind of peasant proprietorship.[42] In a personal foray to an S.D.F. meeting in Clerkenwell which was much publicized at the time,[43] he attempted to debate emigration before a very unfriendly audience: "It was a most remarkable and exciting meeting."[44] With H. H. Champion rather ineffectually trying to maintain order, Lord Brabazon, amid flying threats and insults, delivered his message that "I was gen-

uinely striving to alleviate suffering, and to advance what
I believed to be their true interest."[45] Afterwards, Cardinal Manning wrote,

> to tell you how wisely & courageously you acted in going into the
> midst of the Socialists. They are what they are because our want
> of human sympathy has left them to fester & to mortify. And I
> must add, I wish all ladies had the courage of Lady Brabazon.[46]

Actually, Champion and Hyndman were somewhat
more ambivalent than the strident anti-Malthusian campaign of the S.D.F. would suggest. Champion was, characteristically, trying to play two rather contradictory roles
at the time: that of leader of the revolutionary vanguard
and, to a different audience, that of a reasonable radical
who might very well be indispensible in leading the working class away from extremism and violence. He ended,
perhaps, by not quite convincing either of his audiences.
After this East End confrontation, he cultivated Brabazon's attention. He supplied him with information about
"the unemployed." He titilated Brabazon's apprehension
of social violence: "I feared that the undoubted misery in
London was going to be 'exploited' by a parcel of men
who have no definite aims beyond making themselves a
nuisance—and perhaps on the 9th something worse than
a nuisance."[46a] And he attempted to use Brabazon to secure an upper class forum for his ideas: "At the Church
Congress last year you told me that you would be willing
to bring up any question in the House of Lords. I shall . . .
bring to your attention a matter of some little importance
which I think you will be willing to ventilate."[46b]

As for Hyndman, he had not always been strongly opposed to emigration. In *England for All* (1881), he had
indicated that land reform alone would not be enough, at
least for Ireland. "Migration and emigration are the only

possible remedies for these people."[47] Also, as a renegade Tory democrat who had looked to Disraeli for dramatic strokes of reform, Hyndman had an enthusiasm for the British Empire which brought him close in spirit to the imperial federation and tariff-reform enthusiasts in the emigration lobby.

> In their temperate climate, and with their unrivalled soil—in Canada, Australia, Tasmania, and New Zealand—millions of our race might find happiness and comfort, which would react upon the welfare of our people at home.[48]

Too much, perhaps, has been made of Hyndman's upper-class background in explaining these views away. More "genuine" working-class men like Potter, Rowland, and Uttley shared them, as we have seen.

In December, 1884, Hyndman assessed the emigrationist case at some length in relatively moderate tones in the *Nineteenth Century.*[49] There was, after all, much of which the socialists could approve in the lobby's rhetoric —its view that the poor had a claim on the state for assistance, and its attack on the low wages, scarcity of jobs, and overcrowded housing that marked the London slum. But, Hyndman argued, there was no proof that overpopulation was itself the root of distress. Wealth appeared to grow faster than population. Unemployment did not rise steadily with the census, but fluctuated cyclically. Until radical social measures had been tried—public works, land reform, the nationalization of industry, and a more equitable distribution of wealth—the emigrationist case could not be proved.

Of course, many emigrationists did not see state emigration as an alternative to all other kinds of social reform. But by identifying the emigration lobby closely with neo-

Malthusians, Hyndman and the socialists of the S.D.F. achieved a propaganda effect—if somewhat unfairly. Most emigrationists were not, in a strict sense, Malthusians, and the Malthusian League, founded in 1877, "waged an unrelenting campaign against emigration as a solution to poverty . . . ."[50] Nevertheless, linking the emigration lobby to the grim birth controllers and social Darwinists of the League proved an irresistible way to lead audiences to the "alternative" of socialism. In 1885, Ramsay MacDonald's first lecture before the Bristol S.D.F. was on "Malthusianism *versus* Socialism."[51]

A characteristic example of the socialist propaganda against the lobby is *Emigration and the Malthusian Craze* by "Justicia", distributed in April of 1886. Emigration was a quack remedy preached by the partisans of *laissez faire*. It was "a snare to entrap the unfortunate," a "wretched tinkering up," and "a mockery."[52] Much of this kind of attack was aimed at supporting the land reform remedies of Henry George, who had, in a lengthy anti-Malthusian section of *Progress and Poverty,* vigorously denied that an overpopulation problem existed[53]. In 1883, the London Trades Council joined a denunciation of emigration with a call for land nationalization.[54] Of course, there were vocal members of the National Association who did argue that emigration was an alternative to land reform. In 1888, Henry Seton-Karr, a Conservative MP, attacked Bradlaugh's resolution for state acquisition of waste and vacant land, maintaining that the measure dealt with 12 million "worn out acres", while state emigration promised 1000 million acres "of foreign soil better than our own . . . in Canada, Australia, New Zealand, and at the Cape."[55]

The first issue of the S.D.F.'s *Justice* advocated land nationalization.[56] In the following years, its pages were

Henry Seton-Karr, MP (Source: *Ill. London News,* Jan. 23, 1886)

full of anti-emigrationist attacks under such banners as *Peers as Emigration Agents, The Emigration Fraud,* and *Transportation for Life.* It claimed that Lords Lorne and Carnarvon, who owned extensive tracts in Canada, were really interested in giving value to their property,[57] and that the National Association was "composed for the most part of speculators with a few well-meaning but incapable philanthropists as figureheads."[58] In the emigration movement, the Church of England had "made common cause with the confiscating classes."[59] The Imperial Federation League was subjected to the same vituperative, though perhaps fairly accurate, analysis. It was

> composed principally of capitalists, landlords, home and colonial politicians of the same classes, professorial prigs, &c., with an odd lord or two thrown in, and with a sprinkling of the clerical element which is indispensible to all associations for the better spoliation of the masses of mankind.[60]

Members of the executive committee of the S.D.F., like John Fielding and C. L. Fitzgerald, gave anti-emigration lectures, upon application, to any who were interested, and Hyndman's pamphlet *The Emigration Fraud* sold well, it was claimed, at a penny a copy in the London East

End.[61] Champion, alone of the S.D.F. leadership, was willing to credit some emigrationists like Arnold White at least with working "to smash up the swindling system of private emigration agencies" by supplanting "the 'private enterprise' of the agents of railway and land companies" with the resources of the state.[62] The predominant view, however, was that expressed in a poem by "H.S.S." entitled *The Blessings of Emigration.*[63]

> The rich, who dearly love the poor,
> Propose to open wide the door
>   Of this o'er-crowded nation;
> To liberate the working-man
> They preach the kind, paternal, plan
>   Of wholesale emigration.
>
> Must it be so? So let it be.
> But which of us shall cross the sea,
>   And who shall stay, my brothers?
> 'Tis clear enough, 'the unemployed'
> Must be the first to make a void,
>   To benefit the others.
>
> 'The unemployed'—and who are they?
> Not those, methinks, who night and day
>   Cry vainly for employment;
> But rather those who feel no shame
> To spend a lifetime on the game
>   Of wealthy self-enjoyment.
>
> Such men the country well can spare,
> Why should each selfish millionaire
>   Not practice what he preaches?
> If some are forced to emigrate,
> 'Tis best that those who drain the state
>   Drop off like full-gorged leeches.
>
> The Prince himself may lead the van,
> With many a lord and gentleman
>   Who lives in idle glory;
> Ay, and amidst the rest I see
> Those philanthropic Samuels three
>   Morley, Smith, and Storey.

So praise to those who teach the poor
Their plan of opening wide the door
    Of this o'er-crowded nation;
For, rightly carried out, I deem
There *is* much merit in the scheme
    Of wholesale emigration.

More serious, because more politically powerful, was
the opposition raised to emigration by colonial labour. In
Australia, where the franchise was broad, labour was a
potent organized force by the 1880s. In Canada, the Conservative Party counted heavily on labour for its electoral
successes. Opposition of the Toronto Labour Council to
assisted immigration in 1883[64] possibly influenced the Canadian government to reject Treasury stipulations, and
thus abort the Stephen negotiations. Circulars requesting
support for emigration schemes sent to colonial governments by the Colonial Office in 1864, 1870, 1887, and
1888 predictably inspired mostly negative replies. Beginning in the 1860s, colonies which had been given control
over their own waste lands greatly reduced assistance
which had been provided from land revenues. During
periods of trade depression and high unemployment, immigration aid was stopped altogether. As early as 1870 the
Colonial Land and Emigration Commission reported,

It can hardly be said ... that the Australian colonies show any
desire for general immigration, or would be likely to cooperate
with the Home Government in paying the expense of passages,
even if the Home Government felt justified in contributing a portion of that expense out of the Imperial Treasury.[65]

In March, 1886, the Toronto Labour Council urged the
abolition of all assisted passages,[66] and two years later the
Toronto City Council adopted a similar stand.[67] When the
Emigrants' Information Office was established in the au-

tumn of 1886, colonial labour leaders strongly objected to
the increase in working-class immigration which, they
feared, would be the result.[68]

Colonial labour was not alone in opposing assisted immigration. There was opposition from many middle- and
upper-class rate-payers who feared English paupers
would be dumped on colonial poor-relief. In spite of the
fact that some employers must have seen cheaper wages
in large-scale immigration, many colonial businessmen
were strongly opposed to state emigration. In 1886, the
Australian Trading World strongly attacked pauper immigration and the National Association.

> We regard the proposals of the National Association for State-
> directed Emigration as quite impracticable, if it [sic] may not be
> denominated actually, if benevolently, Quixotic. For a State to
> interfere in any way with the movement of population is contrary
> to all ideas of economic science. Emigration must wait for a de-
> mand from the Colonies . . . .[69]

Opposition to state emigration on the grounds that it
was offensive to liberal economic orthodoxy was heard in
England as well. But while state aid was clearly wrong to
those who believed absolutely in *laissez faire,* classical
political economy did not present a solid front against
emigration as a solution to domestic ills. The utility of
colonies had been a subject of analysis and debate since
Adam Smith; and Bentham, Malthus, and Mill all admitted the benefits, at least temporary, of systematic emigration.[70] Both Smith and Ricardo were aware of the role
which colonization might play in offsetting declining
profits from capital investment. The framework they be-
queathed "could simultaneously be critical of colonization, yet recognize its great value under extenuating

political conditions."[71] Smith held that increased capital competition lowered prices and interest and raised wages. Acquisition of new territory could arrest this capital glut and the fall in profits it caused. Whether capital accumulation ought to be thus interfered with was another question.

A leading advocate of state emigration in the 1820s and 1830s, Robert Wilmot-Horton, rested his case for Poor-Law aid on a straight-forward interpretation of the wage-fund theory—wages fell because of the greater growth of population relative to capital accumulation. Ricardo himself had doubts, but believed that Horton's scheme would work for a wealthy country like England, so long as the expenses incurred did not significantly reduce home capital. Differences within the classical school on the subject derived from differences over Malthus and the nature of population growth, the determinants of the level of wages and capital accumulation, and the priority of solutions: free trade, emigration, or birth control.

Ricardians opposed E.G. Wakefield's plans for the systematic colonization of Australia in the 1830s and 1840s from a belief that the export of capital which accompanied large-scale colonization (as opposed to simple emigration) was detrimental to the exporting country.[72] Wakefield claimed, on the contrary, that Britain suffered from a shortage of capital investment opportunities, and needed new capital markets abroad. The capital glut controversy was not, however, the central issue in discussions of emigration by economists. Rather, debate focused on whether there would be a positive role for government in economic affairs once protection was dismantled. In a free-trade world might the government not enhance the fluidity of labour by helping it overcome geographical barriers? This provided the grounds for conversion to Wakefield's scheme for some political economists like Robert Torrens and John Stuart Mill.

Though his father opposed state emigration because of its expense, J. S. Mill became a strong advocate of "systematic emigration." Bentham in old age also converted to Wakefield's scheme, as did Nassau Senior, who had earlier been a supporter of Horton's. Wakefield's system, based on the use of colonial land revenues to aid emigration from England, envisaged the creation of labour pools in the colonies—because the relatively high cost of land prevented dispersal—and hence a field for industry and capital investment. This was attractive to utilitarians who saw in it, as in the Workhouse Test, a natural mechanism at once self-regulated, self-contained, and circular. "The sufficient price" of colonial land would regulate, without human tinkering, land sale, capital accumulation, and population growth.

J. S. Mill was converted by Wakefield to the desirability of government action to create circumstances favourable to the development of markets, and this idea was given prominence in his *Principles of Political Economy* (1848). He believed that capital exportation and emigration had become necessary for England's continued prosperity, and required government control and support. In the 1880s, therefore, emigrationists were able to throw quotations from Mill back at their liberal critics.

For many the question of emigration remained one which was cast primarily in Malthusian terms and pivoted on attitudes toward population-growth patterns.[73] Well before mid-century, the pessimistic spirit which Malthus had represented was largely dispersed, though the theoretical assumptions of *The Law of Population* were still powerful. Malthus himself at first refused to believe that emigration posed a real solution to the imbalance of resources and population. He admitted that an artificial reduction of numbers by emigration would temporarily raise living standards but claimed that this would encourage larger families and ultimately an even greater rate of growth. And of course in the end, when colonial lands were filled, the population problem would quickly reassert itself.

Anti-Malthusians, like William Cobbett and G. P. Scrope, denied the assumption that a rise in standards caused by emigration would in fact create an automatic rise in the birth rate, though Cobbett resisted pauper emigration for other reasons. But defenders of Malthus as well occasionally advocated systematic emigration, accompanied by schemes of birth control, as less expensive than other forms of temporary relief like the Poor Law. Francis Place recommended both emigration and contraception, as did J. S. Mill. In 1827, Malthus himself modified his opposition somewhat and testified before a select committee that emigration could be of some use in England if care were taken that the void was not filled by the Irish or Scots.

By the 1860s, Malthusian considerations as obstacles to social change lost some of their force. There had been obvious economic progress in spite of population growth, and some of this prosperity had spread down into the working class. Harriet Martineau credited repeal of the Corn Laws, increased agricultural production and voluntary emigration with extinguishing "all present apprehension and talk of 'surplus population'."[74] In 1852, Herbert Spencer claimed to have found biological evidence for believing that increased comfort bred prudence: species less endangered by extinction appeared to reproduce more slowly.[75] Under the impact of the economic difficulties of the 1870s, this optimism began to show some signs of wear. Faithful dogmatic Malthusians felt confirmed in their views and joined birth controllers and early eugenicists in repudiating all forms of "amelioration".[76] Most people, however, though they might employ bits of Malthusian language from time to time and harbour a suspicion that England was, certainly, too crowded and urban, were not consistent theorists who accepted all the implied logical conclusions of that rhetorical baggage. The National Association emigrationists, with their strong belief in the beneficial social effects of emigration, mostly lay closer to this mainstream than to the true neo-Malthusians of Dr. Drysdale's League.

More powerful obstacles to the lobby than classical theory of the relationship between capital and labour or the refinements of Malthusian prophesying were attacks which derived from the deep and popular Victorian sense of individual responsibility.[77] Many who were quite willing to see workers leave on their own accord, as part of a wholly laudable effort to rise in the world, were adamantly opposed, largely on moral grounds, to government aid. It was a form of "indiscriminant charity" which corrupted the poor and burdened the rate-payer. The argument also took a pragmatic turn. State aid would perhaps result in a stoppage of the very substantial voluntary emigration. Few would choose to pay their own way if a state program were initiated.

John Martineau, chairman of the Emigration Committee of the Charity Organization Society, and an executive committeeman of the Emigrants' Information Office, had been a supporter of the National Emigration League in 1870. By the 1880s, however, he came to oppose state emigration and carried on an active fight against the National Association. He presented the case of those who did not doubt the benefits of an increased emigration but distrusted government interference. The National Association's program was an example of collectivist planning which would tie the emigrant to organized agricultural communities abroad when he ought to be free "to abandon the land and enter the labour market." Moreover, the selection procedures of private societies were far more sophisticated than a large government program could hope to achieve. The establishment of the Emigrants' Information Office had been necessary, but "More than this I cannot see what the Government can or ought to do."

In promoting emigration, as in other matters, money lavishly and indiscriminantly expended discourages the impulses of self- help, and makes ten persons wretched for one whom it relieves.[78]

Many philanthropic emigrationists supported the National Association, but many—those who who made federation impossible and were horrified that the government might emigrate all and sundry who applied—did not. W. H. Smith, for example, supported private emigration assistance but not state aid. J. H. Tuke, who helped coordinate Irish emigration under the Arrears of Rent Act, opposed a national scheme for England. Some, like the chairman of the British and Colonial Emigration Society in 1870, were simply afraid that a state program would "retard subscriptions very materially" for their own organization.[79] Others supported a national program, but wanted it to apply only to certain narrowly restricted categories: Samuel Smith wanted children to emigrate but not adults. John T. Middlemore of the Children's Homes of Birmingham echoed this view: "I feel very strongly that public opinion is drifting in a wrong direction in regard to State interference with adult emigration

.... In my belief ... State aid can only do harm."[80] John Martineau summarized this powerful attitude in 1888.

> What, then, is the moral of all this? Surely that emigration is to be encouraged, in quiet times at any rate, not spasmodically, or by gigantic and costly schemes. Rather is it a matter of sustained painstaking by individuals—painstaking in selecting the right man, the right opportunity, the right destination; in expending money freely, but judiciously, so that its effect may be felt, not only at the moment, but permanently, not only in helping one, but in helping one to help many.[81]

Notes on Chapter 6

1. C.O. 384/146 (7469); C.O. 384/147 (12251); C.O. 384/146 (10662); the *Times*, 5 Sept. 1883, 7.
2. C.O. 384/147 (9779); the *Times*, 20 June 1883, 6.
3. The *Times*, 8 Aug. 1883, 3. Also see C.O. 384/146 (13241) for Dilke's search for precedents for state-aided emigration.
4. *Hansard*, Vol. 282 (Lords, 31 July 1883), 1105–9.
5. The *Times*, 5 Nov. 1883, 8, and 8 Nov. 1883, 10. There were meetings at Stepney, Sept. 17; Haggerston, Sept. 19; and Bethnal Green, Oct. 1. On Nov. 3 Carnarvon wrote Boyd that the time had come for state emigration.
6. The *Times*, 21 Nov. 1883, 4. "Great difficulty was experienced in the effort to collect definite information, as the people were under the impression our inquiry was conducted for purposes of house demolition (a very unpopular operation)."
7. C.O. 384/153 (573); P.P. 1884 (210), No. 7.
8. Herbert minute, 3 Feb. 1884, in C.O. 384/153 (1701).
9. *Hansard*, Vol. 286 (Lords, 28 March 1884), 1000; C.O. 384/152 (3744 and 2423). For Samuel Smith's ideas on child emigration see his "Social Reform," *Nineteenth Century*, Vol. 13 (May, 1883), 896–912.

10. *Hansard,* Vol. 286 (Lords, 28 March 1884), 987.
11. C.O. 384/152 (4785).
12. The *Times,* 31 March 1884, 9.
13. *Ibid.,* 11 April 1884, 5.
14. *Ibid.*
15. *Ibid.,* 24 April 1884, 10; Earl of Meath (ed.), *The Diaries of Mary, Countess of Meath* (London, n.d.), 76.
16. Alfred Simmons, *State Emigration: A Reply to Lord Derby* (London, 1884), as quoted in *The State-directed Colonization Series, No. I,* 55–60.
17. C.O. 384/153 (7251); P.P. 1884 (C. 4751), Nos. 1 and 2.
18. C.O. 384/153 (7251).
19. C.O. 384/153 (4072). Also see E. Joyce, *Emigration* (London, 1884).
20. Peace to Lord Derby, 23 July 1884, in P.P. 1884 (C. 4751), No. 2.
21. M.H. 19/7 (77575A/84); P.P. 1884 (C. 4751). No. 4. Dilke, however, took issue with the analysis: "I can't agree to the memo as representing my views," M.H. 19/7 (26235/84).
22. C.O. 384/157 (2688).
23. *Hansard,* Vol. 290 (Commons, 14 July 1884), 910–11.
24. In the end, F. A. Stanley, Derby's brother, took the Colonial Office.
25. Brabazon, "State-directed Emigration," *Nineteenth Century,* Vol. 16 (Nov., 1884), 765.
26. *Ibid.,* 778.
27. Mitchell and Deane, 64.
28. *Justice,* 24 Feb. 1885; Meath, *Memories of the Nineteenth Century,* 229–30.
29. W. B. Paton, *State-Aided Emigration* (London, 1885), 21–4, 31–2; P.P. 1884 *Report of the Reformatories and Public Schools Commission,* para. 41.
30. The government "was about as much likely to contribute to State emigration as it was to State confectionery." (White, "The Importance of a National Scheme of Emigration," *Journal of the Society of the Arts,* Vol. 34 [April, 1886], 210.)
31. Arnold White, *The Problems of a Great City* (London, 1886), 73.
32. The *Times,* 13 April 1885, 8.
33. As might have been expected, given Tuke's pique at Brabazon's attacks on his Irish operations.
34. The *Times,* 3 July 1885, 9.
35. *Ibid.,* 8.

36. C.O. 384/158 (5388 and 13921). Stanley decided nothing should be done until the election was past.
37. The *Times*, 7 July 1885, 12.
38. Karl Marx, *Capital* (Everyman's, 1930), Vol. 2, Chapter 25, 848–58.
39. The *Times*, 7 Nov. 1883, 6.
40. *Ibid.*, 8 Nov. 1883, 10.
41. *The State-directed Colonization Series, No. I*, 18.
42. Lord Brabazon, *Social Arrows* (2nd edn.: London, 1887), 268–9.
43. The best account I have seen appeared in the *Nottingham Daily Express*, 11 Jan. 1887. Also see the *Times*, 10 Jan.; The *Liverpool Review*, 15 Jan.; and the *City Press*, 12 Jan.
44. Meath, *Memories of the Nineteenth Century*, 231.
45. *Ibid.*, 233.
46. Manning to Brabazon, Jan. 17, 1887 (Meath Papers, Autrograph Vol. I).
46a. Champion to Meath, Nov. 7, 1887 (Autograph Vol. II).
46b. Champion to Meath, Dec. 2, 1888 (Autograph Vol. II).
47. H. M. Hyndman, *England for All* (New York, 1974), 123.
48. *Ibid.*, 161.
49. H. M. Hyndman, "Something better than emigration, a reply," *Nineteenth Century*, Vol. 16 (Dec., 1884), 991–8.
50. Rosanna Ledbetter, *A History of the Malthusian League 1877–1927* (Columbus, Ohio; 1976), 152.
51. David Marquand, *Ramsay MacDonald* (London, 1977), 17.
52. "Justicia", *Emigration and the Malthusian Craze* (London, 1886), 4.
53. Henry George, *Progress and Poverty* (Modern Library, n.d.), Book II.
54. [G. K. Tate], London Trades Council, 58.
55. *Hansard*, Vol. 325 (Commons, 1 May 1888), 1090–7.
56. *Justice*, 19 Jan. 1884.
57. *Ibid.*, 29 March 1884.
58. *Ibid., 12 April 1884.*
59. *Ibid.*, 5 April 1884.
60. *Ibid.*, 13 June 1885.
61. *Ibid.*, 7 Nov. 1885; 16 Jan., 17 April, and 24 April, 1886.
62. *Ibid.*, 12 June 1886.
63. *Ibid.*, 9 May 1885.

64. C.O. 384/151 (5405).
65. The *Times*, 19 Oct. 1870, 7.
66. C.O. 384/163 (5436).
67. C.O. 384/170 (8960).
68. C.O. 384/163 (10964).
69. *The Australian Trading World*, 26 Feb. 1886, 68.
70. See Donald Winch, *Classical Political Economy and Colonies* (Cambridge, Mass.; 1965), Chs. 5, 6, and 9; Edward R. Kittrell, "The Development of the Theory of Colonization in English Classical Political Economy," *The Southern Economic Journal*, Vol. 31 (Jan., 1965), 189–206; and R. N. Ghosh, "The Colonization Controversy: R. J. Wilmot-Horton and the Classical Economists," *Economica*, November, 1964, 385–400.
71. Kittrell, 190.
72. This remained a common point of view for some time. In 1868, T. E. Cliffe-Leslie held that the massive Irish emigration had caused more distress than it cured by depleting capital and preventing the development of resources (*Fraser's Magazine*, Vol. 77 [May, 1868], 611–24).
73. For Malthusianism and emigration see R. N. Ghosh, "Malthus on Emigration and Colonization: Letters to Wilmot-Horton," *Economica*, February, 1963, 44–62. Also see Harold Boner, *Hungry Generations: The Nineteenth Century Case against Malthusianism* (New York, 1955), and Ledbetter.
74. Harriet Martineau, *Autobiography*, Vol. I, 159.
75. Herbert Spencer, "A Theory of Population," *Westminster Review*, 1852, 493, 498–501.
76. For example, Charles Lucas, Secretary of the Emigrants' Information Office, testifying in 1889 before the Select Committee on Colonization, opposed extensive emigration on the grounds that depletion of the population in England would increase the birth rate, and claimed that "the only remedy for overpopulation was, that when the population became excessive the birth rate would be checked," P.P. 1889, *Report of the Colonization Committee*, questions 1439, 1566, 1567.
77. For example, *The Literary World*, 1 Oct. 1886: "Lord Brabazon might, perhaps, more effectively have employed his pen ... by emphasizing the benefits of self-restraint"; or the *Nottinghamshire Daily Guardian*, 3 Jan. 1889: "The only remedies really

worth anything will be . . . greater thrift and prudence, more so-
briety and greater industry."
78. John Martineau, "Natural Emigration," *Blackwood's* (July, 1889),
    36–48.
79. The *Times,* 10 Feb. 1870, 6.
80. *Ibid.,* 4 Jan. 1887, 3.
81. *Ibid.,* 16 Nov. 1888, 14.

Chapter 7. Pushing Forward with Spirit: Government and the Emigration Lobby, 1886–1888

The Association has now become a very powerful one numerically —large bodies of the labouring classes and many well-known philanthropists and other gentlemen having declared their adhesion. The trade, friendly, and other workmen's Societies now officially represented on our National Council number about 170,000 working men, who, with their families, count nearly half-a-million people. We are being urged from all quarters to take energetic steps to press State-directed Colonization upon the attention of the Government. Meetings, conferences, and deputations are being asked for in many parts of England, and there is every indication that the movement will receive public as well as official favour if pushed forward with spirit.[1]

The National Association returned to the Colonial Office in February of 1886. Salisbury had resigned January 28, and it was the Liberals, Granville and his parliamentary Under-Secretary Morgan, with whom Brabazon once again had to deal. The decision to approach government at this time was, most likely, not dictated by the change of ministers—though Stanley had not been inclined to take any action pending elections—but

Riots in the West End, 1886 (Source: *Ill. London News,* Feb. 13, 1886)

by the dramatic outbreak that month of domestic strife in London and elsewhere.

Unemployment was at its severest during the winter of 1885–1886. On February 7, a meeting of unemployed workmen, organized by Hyndman and the S.D.F., led to rioting in Trafalgar Square and the breaking of windows along Pall Mall. A week later, there were demonstrations in Birmingham, a mass meeting at Sheffield, and street disorders in Great Yarmouth. On February 21, police dispersed a mass meeting of 50,000 at Hyde Park. These disturbances had an immediate and dramatic effect on London philanthropy. Within a week of the Trafalgar Square affair, the Lord Mayor's fund for relief of the unemployed leapt from about £ 3000 to £ 32,000. Support for state emigration grew likewise. Brabazon made the

Bloody Sunday, Nov. 10, 1887 (Source: *Ill. London News,* Nov. 13, 1887)

most of the threat of violence, and moved to force his cause on government while public interest was aroused. Gladstone replied February 16 that he could not "but sympathize with the object of the society," and an interview was arranged with Granville at the Colonial Office.[2]

7.1 *The Colonial Office Listens*

The Prime Minister's statement of sympathy was considered a coup by the National Association. Herbert at the Colonial Office predicted, "Lord Brabazon will probably come armed with the above letter from Mr. Gladstone, which gives more encouragement than the advocates of State-directed Emigration have received for a long time."[3] To make ready for their coming, Richard Ebden, Chief Clerk of the General Division, prepared a lengthy resumé tracing the history of state aid from the creation of the Colonial Land and Emigration Commission to the Stephen negotiations. He reiterated the still prevailing view among the staff that "Emigration in so far as it depends upon rates or Parliamentary votes appears to me to be a question not for this office but for the Home Office or Local Government Board." In any event, schemes based on loans were unlikely to recover the money. Herbert agreed, but did not think that this ruled out some sort of program.

> Though I don't think the Government should be deluded into advancing money in expectation of repayment, I am (personally) in favour of a liberal annual grant in aid of the organization of Emigration, or Colonization, as far as expenditure within this country goes.[4]

The deputation, led by Brabazon and Simmons, was received by Granville on February 19. Numbering about 300, it included James Anthony Froude, philanthropists like George Palmer and F. D. Mocatta, a number of MPs, and many labour leaders, who testified to the popularity of state emigration among the working class. Mawdsley claimed that Lancashire was "almost unanimously" in favour of the Association's scheme. Others from Leicester, Sheffield, and Newcastle-on-Tyne echoed these sentiments, and promised that the party which submitted an emigration program "will earn the gratitude of the working classes."[5]

The National Association's scheme which Simmons presented asked for a joint British and Colonial Colonization Board to which colonial governments would donate land.

Eighty-acre grants would be made to settlers, with an unspecified amount held in reserve for future sale. The British government, for its part, would make available to the Board a large fund of perhaps £ 2 million at 2.5 percent. This would be made available in the form of loans to settlers and other emigrants. Labourers who simply emigrated (Class A) would repay their passage loans by having a certain amount recovered from their wages. Settlers (Class B) would repay at 4 percent interest in annual installments, secured by a mortgage on their land. Colonial governments would be responsible for collection. Total administrative expenses, including the new Emigrants' Information Office, were estimated at £ 20,000 a year.[6] The chief distinction between this and the Boyd plan was the removal of commercial companies as intermediaries. All reserved land was to remain at the disposal of the government.

Reaction at the Colonial Office was mixed with regard to the workability of the financial aspects. Herbert advised Granville that the colonies, except Canada, would probably refuse to cooperate, and the recovery of money was "not to be dreamt of." It was agreed, however, that the question required Cabinet decision. The scheme was circulated to the Local Government Board and the Treasury, while a draft was prepared for colonial approval.[7]

Meanwhile, a flurry of other groups over which the Association had some influence lobbied the Colonial Office in support of state emigration. The British and Colonial Emigration Society (B.C.E.S.) submitted *Some Proposals on Emigration,* and offered the society's services as selection board in the event a government program was established. A committee from the S.P.C.K. led by the Rev. John Bridger submitted their views on colonization and arranged an interview. On March 6, the Newcastle

Trades Council petitioned the Colonial Office in favour of the National Association's proposals. All this correspondence was sent to Chamberlain at the Local Government Board, where a memorandum was being prepared on Simmons' scheme, though no decision could be made pending answers to the colonial circular.[8]

The Local Government Board approached the subject with the same ill will which had marked its previous attitude to any suggestion that its burden of work should be increased. Hugh Owen, Secretary to the Board, feared the scheme would involve the state in responsibility for the success of emigrants—"there must invariably be failures, and in such cases the responsibility will be thrown on the Government." The scheme would take a long time to put into operation, and most urban unemployed had no agricultural experience. He did agree, however, that,

> If the depression in trade continues it appears to the Board that it may become necessary for the Government to make exceptional efforts with a view to relieving the distress, and among the various methods of relief which would suggest themselves, emigration naturally occupies a prominent place.[9]

The Treasury was even less forthcoming. The proposals were "not such as they could with propriety assent to." When the colonial circular was dispatched intimating that "satisfactory financial arrangements" might be made, they strongly objected and registered their "complete dissent from any suggestion that H. M. Government are prepared to enter into financial arrangements for State-aided Emigration."[10]

The Treasury's attitude to the £ 2 million loan was hardly surprising. It was famous for a cheese-paring attitude toward public expenditure, and at the same time was obstructing consummation of the Emigrants' Information

Office by offering a ludicrous £ 50 a year for its operation. Treasury admonitions were not infrequent or often accepted as *ultima dicta*. Of more immediate importance to the lobby were the colonial replies to Granville's circular. These took several months to come in. The National Association rightly predicted that they would be discouraging because the Colonial Office circular had made no mention of "colonization" as distinct from the much despised pauper emigration. As of May, South Australia, Victoria, and the Cape refused to have anything to do with state immigration. Natal was less adamant, and New Zealand and Queensland wanted more information. Only Canada replied favourably.[11]

Reacting to what it felt to be the biased wording of the circular, the National Association took its case directly to colonial authorities. In the summer of 1886, colonial agents in London were invited to attend the lobby's Colonization Conference at the Colonial and Indian Exhibition. The following year Brabazon tried to get colonization on the agenda of the first Imperial Conference, and, when his attempt failed, organized an informal gathering of colonial delegates. He personally contacted colonial governments, presented the Association's proposals in a flexible and favourable light, and asked "how far the Government of this Colony would be prepared to accept the principle of the plan."[12] This tactic was disliked at the Colonial Office. When the Governor of Natal, Sir Arthur Elibank Havelock, warmly replied to Brabazon's query, the then Secretary of State, Stanhope, expressed himself "surprised that the Governor should have given so decided an answer" without first referring the question to the department.[13]

In March, Chamberlain resigned and was replaced at the Local Government Board by James Stansfeld. In 1883,

Stansfeld had helped found the Central Emigration Society. Stansfeld hardly had time, however, to reverse policy
substantially, even were he so inclined. The departure of
Chamberlain and Hartington doomed the government,
which lived on only until Gladstone's Home Rule Bill,
introduced April 8, died two months later. Agitation for
state-aided emigration, therefore, reached its apogee during a great political crisis and a general election. Though
a few National Association MPs may have tried to inject
emigration into their constituency campaigns,[14] the question of Home Rule and the future of the Liberal Party
eclipsed for a time all other issues. The National Association's carefully planned summer campaign, culminating
in a Colonization Conference in June (the very day, as it
happened, that Gladstone's government went down to
defeat), was hardly noticed.

Preparations for the summer offensive included a renewed drive for membership and contributions. While
this met with some success, attested by the addition of
fifty-odd new names to the National Council, Brabazon's
correspondence is full of the polite and sympathetic refus-
als of many eminent Victorians to attach their names to
the movement. The explanations they offered reflect the
characteristic misgivings with which many of the Victorian elite viewed state emigration. Archbishop Benson,
for example, felt that the general issue of the relationship
between population and prosperity was far too complex
and unclear and the specific proposals of the Association
too complicated for him to lend the weight and dignity of
his office: "so many problems are rising up, and so many
details, requiring very careful attention . . . ."[14a] Others,
like T. H. Huxley, were more blunt in their disbelief in the
Association's panacea: "A scheme of emigration which
shall relieve the plethora of population without robbing

the mother country of the best elements of its poorer population, has yet to be discovered."[14b] Still others who, like Lord Derby, approved of the principle of state emigration, felt that the movement was doomed from the beginning by the fierce opposition of organized labour in the colonies—though Lady Strangford might continue to dream of a "crown Colony to be established where Trade Unions will be illegal."[14c]

But the Association's appeal did not fall on completely deaf ears. Benson might not accept a patronship or vice-presidency, but he did express publicly his "real interest" and "sympathy". And there were a few quite notable acquisitions, like the national hero, military genius, and Liberal Unionist, General Wolseley. Accepting a vice-presidency, Wolseley wrote Brabazon a letter of warm support, couched in the mixed language of social concern and imperialism characteristic of many right-wing emigrationists.

> I am a great advocate of state assisted emigration as I believe it would help not only to relieve Ireland of hundreds of thousands for whom no occupation can be found there, but that if applied to the Scot crofters and those crowded in our great cities we should all be the richer. I believe that wages are too low all over Great Britain, and until we reduce the population by emigration, the poor man, especially the agricultural labourer, will continue to be underpaid. The Boer difficulty in South Africa is now to be settled most easily by a large amount of emigration from this country.[14d]

Froude also, about this time, overcame enough of his deep pessimism (in March, 1886, he had written Brabazon that there was "no hope of success") to join the National Association. By Christmas he became convinced that "the tone of public feeling has now altered". Winter distress in England was proof that "London, and all our great towns have outgrown their legitimate means of subsistence and nature will have its revenge."[14e]

Preparations for the renewed campaign also included publishing a new series of tracts on state emigration and inducing the government to publish its emigration correspondence in the form of a Blue Book. In answering the Earl of Harrowby, who moved for publication in the House of Lords, Granville paid his respects, somewhat disingenuously, to the Association's three-year campaign and growing membership.[15] "The Government at once thought it their duty to give their careful consideration to the proposal [for state colonization] made with such authority."[16] Together with Gladstone's expression of sympathy in February, this appeared to presage a change in Liberal attitude, and Harrowby was, prematurely, jubilant. The government had "virtually promised to establish a Colonization Department."[17] Privately, however, the Colonial Office displayed something less than an attitude of "careful consideration".

> Lord Harrowby perhaps does not understand that his motion covers every unpractical or inpracticable scheme of inexperienced dreamers. There is hardly any subject on which there is more wilful ignorance committed to writing and print than emigration.[18]

There seems to have been a fairly general sense at this time that the government was moving toward some sort of emigration program. In part, this resulted from a misinterpretation of the purpose of the Emigrants' Information Office, which had received Cabinet approval. Many saw it as a first step toward "systematic emigration", though in fact it was never intended to be more than its name implied. In any event, in the spring of 1886, public interest in the question was unequaled since the campaign of the National Emigration League in 1870. A solicitor of the Supreme Court of Judicature, Henry Herbert Phear, published for the use of philanthropists and lobbyists a summary of legislation already on the statute books for assisting emigration. He traced 50 years of legislative action to prove how far government had accepted "the *principle* of assisted emigration".[19]

On June 8, the Colonization Conference was held at the conference hall of the Colonial and Indian Exhibition. Organized by the National Association, it was well attended by peers, politicians, philanthropists, and labour leaders who were interested in emigration, imperial federation, and colonial relations in general. Shortly before, Brabazon had made an unsuccessful effort to enlist the support of the Colonial Secretary. Granville declined to become a patron of the Association.[20]

Before an audience which included a number of colonial representatives, Simmons explained that the Association's proposals were flexible, would not throw paupers on colonial relief, and were just one step toward closer cooperation between the Mother Country and the colonies. Some progress was made. The Agent General for New Zealand, Sir Francis Bell, warmly approved the proposals and attacked the government's misleading circular. A resolution of support passed unanimously, and it was agreed that the colonial representatives present would send directly to the National Association reports on colonial labour markets.[21]

The conference was followed by a flurry of other activity. Three days later there was a discussion at the Royal Colonial Institute on state emigration. Frederick Young called for a National Colonization Bureau and, to instil an enthusiasm for colonial life, board-school training in colonial history.[22] June 24 and 25, the Central Emigration

Society convened a conference of its own to discuss the best methods of colonization, the duty of the Church toward emigration, and child emigration.[23] Arnold White read a paper on South African colonization to the Geologists' Association, assembled at the Exhibition.[24]

Finally, Alfred Simmons tried to persuade the Trade Union Congress, sitting at Hull in September, to adopt a resolution supporting the National Association. The prospects appeared promising. Not only did the Association have promises of support from a number of labour leaders, but the president of the Congress, Fred Maddison, made favourable mention of the movement in his opening address.[24a] Simmons's resolution, however, encountered both strong opposition and indifference, and a number of labour leaders who had promised support did not attend. While emigrationists narrowly defeated a counter-proposal put up by "nationalizers and socialists", their resolution ultimately foundered amid a number of amendments watering down Simmons's strong appeal for support for the specific program of the National Association. He, nevertheless, saw a bright side to this affair, and indeed it was the closest emigrationists had come to getting a clear statement of support from the T.U.C.

whether the resolution succeeds or not we have fairly set this question in motion, & it must necessarily be discussed by the societies who send men to the Congress. It so happens that seven or eight of our best men are not at the Congress this year . . . . [The President] was a stranger to me until this, but when I heard he was not unfavourable to S[tate] D[irected] C[olonization] I opened with him, & this pointed reference to our Assn. is the result. So that, whatever the fate of my resolution, we shall generally gain ground, by having the question at length before these official bodies of men. Hard work among them from now to next Sept. will very likely secure a substantial majority in our favour.[24b]

The general election held in July had resulted in a Unionist victory. Stanhope and Dunraven went to the Colonial Office, and C. T. Ritchie to the Local Government Board. Dunraven had declared himself in favour of state emigration in 1883, and Ritchie was a member of the National Association. The new government appeared promising indeed, but swelling lobby enthusiasm received its first check on August 26. In reply to a question in the House of Commons, the new Under-Secretary for the Colonies denied any intention of using the Emigrants' Information Office to promote a larger emigration from the British Isles.

7.2 *The Emigrants' Information Office*

The re-establishment of an emigration office in 1886 was a direct result of the pressure mounted by Arnold White and his allies: the Marquis of Lorne, the philanthropic emigration societies, and members of the National Association. Though the Emigrants' Information Office may appear in retrospect a logical step to replace the services of the defunct Colonial Land and Emigration Commission,[25] it is not possible to attribute its creation simply to a process of internal bureaucratic adjustment and growth. No department wanted the office, which was pushed by political chiefs seeking to reduce public and parliamentary pressure. Moreover, once the bureau was established, the departmental staff strongly resisted the idea, widely held outside government, that the new institution would promote still greater governmental involvement in emigration.

In the spring of 1885, White saw Harcourt at the Home Office and got his support for an "imperial labour exchange". A movement for labour exchanges in Britain was under way at the time, inspired by the German registries established in 1883. The chief promoter of this idea, which found widespread support in the bad winter of 1885–86, was Nathan Cohen, a Tory who had established his own labour exchange at Egham. He saw the exchanges as a means of stopping the drift to the great cities, and of redistributing redundant labour from the slums to jobs in provincial towns or the colonies. Cohen hoped to promote emigration as part of the further rationalization of the labour market, and when 25 free registries were set up in 1886, they worked in cooperation with the Central Emigration Society.[26] An Emigrants' Information Office would offer to Cohen's exchanges and to the C.E.S. accurate and systematically organized information.

White, for his part, was mainly motivated by the prospect of a federation of emigration societies, and the role an official information bureau could play in its efforts to organize more efficiently all philanthropic emigration. But after hopes for federation fell through, White and others saw the proposed bureau in a somewhat different light. If only informational at first, it might nevertheless ultimately draw government into a more active role. The lobby was careful to urge only the collection of information in its negotiations with the Treasury and Colonial Office, but its language in public did nothing to dispel the anticipation that creation of the agency meant much more. The government repeatedly denied that the office would function to promote emigration, but those who supported its establishment just as frequently assumed the state would be compelled by the logic of the institution to revive the activities of the old Colonial Land and Emigration Commission. By January, 1886, White was

saying that "the first step in a national scheme of emigration would be to combine these rivulets of knowledge and
to filter and compare them in order that they may be
made of the greatest use . . . ."[27] Brabazon was more specific: "we have got the thin edge of the wedge in, and it
simply requires tact and the weight of public opinion to
insure ultimate success."[28]

Through the autumn of 1885, Stanley at the Colonial
Office put off pressure to move on the issue, but substantial agreement was reached at the Treasury, which had
been won over in part because it was promised the unpaid
services of a number of experienced philanthropic emigrationists in running the proposed office. Among those
seriously considered for these unpaid posts were Brabazon, Simmons, White himself, and James Rankin—all
members of the National Association.[29] Securing positions
on the new governmental agency would have been one
means of making their predictions of expanding government activity self-fulfilling.

The Colonial Office was well aware that the question
was closely intertwined with the general issue of "re-
establishing a great emigration Department."[30] James
Anthony Froude, echoing Carlyle's call for an emigration
service, carried a resolution at Mansion House, January
14, 1886, that the government should establish an Emigration Board.[31] Herbert thought it necessary to emphasize to the Treasury shortly afterwards that "the proposal
now made is wholly unconnected with any scheme for the
promotion of State-aided emigration."[32]

The change of government in February did little to
retard or accelerate the negotiations, though, characteristically, Granville took little personal interest beyond a
desire to see the issue settled as soon as possible. The

Parliamentary Under-Secretary, Osborne Morgan, however, was anxious to get the Office established to relieve the government from increasing pressure in the House of Commons and from the public at large.

> Ever since this ... question was first mooted to the deputation which waited on Ld. Granville on State-aided Emigration, it has grown in popularity with the public, and I am constantly pressed by M.P.'s and other persons to say what is being done towards the establishment of such a Bureau ... the Treasury cannot be too soon or too strongly urged to authorize the expenditure necessary for the purpose.[33]

As late as March, however, the Colonial Office still had hopes of getting the Local Government Board to assume responsibility, though this hope was quickly laid to rest by Chamberlain, who "did not intend, and does not think it desirable, that the collection and distribution [of information] should be undertaken by the L. G. Board."[34] Colonial Office responsibility was grudgingly accepted.

For a while, Treasury parsimony once again threatened to kill the scheme, but the Colonial Office was "callous of Treasury scoldings" and a re-affirmation in Cabinet assured success.[35] Settlement was reached in May, and the following October an Emigrants' Information Office was in operation in its own quarters, with a small full-time paid staff of four and two part-time officers shared with the Colonial Office. It distributed colonial information through post offices and answered inquiries by mail and in person. The E.I.O. executive committee included several persons, important in emigration philanthropy, from the Charity Organization Society and the Central Emigration Society, but not Brabazon or Simmons or White. In fact, Brabazon had written to recommend the secretary of the National Association, but Granville firmly resisted this attempt to infiltrate the new bureau with officials sympathetic to expanding its very tightly circumscribed responsbilities.

> I should have been glad to meet any recommendation of yours and particularly to make use of Mr. Simmons's services, if it had been in my power to do so. But there is, I think, some mistake as to what is being done. When Lord Harrowby spoke of a Colonization Dept., I corrected him, and pointed out that the business of the persons to be employed would be simply to collect and distribute information: and I have already come to a decision as to the appointments to be made.[35a]

These included, beside the representatives of philanthropic emigration societies, a few labour leaders—though none who were known supporters of state emigration. Even so, Granville was suspicious of them: "I should not be in a hurry to name too many of this class."[36] To head the bureau Granville found a man who himself strongly disapproved of going beyond "information pure & simple" and who would obey to the letter his instructions that the office was not to promote emigration.

> It is not intended to promote, directly or indirectly State-aided emigration: the State does not even pretend to guarantee its proper working or the accuracy of the information which it dispenses . . . .[37]

Certainly, however, creation of the E.I.O. was a fillip to state emigrationists who looked forward to the expansion of its responsibilities. Likewise, opponents of state emigration feared the new office would accelerate emigration and serve as a first step to a state program. The Colonial Office hastened to inform colonial labour groups that the bureau, by publicizing unemployment and trade depression in colonial cities, might actually have the effect of discouraging emigration.[38]

7.3 *Jubilee Year: Parliamentary Organization and Public Agitation*

In January, 1887, Henry Holland (later Viscount Knutsford) replaced Stanhope at the Colonial Office, becoming the fifth Secretary of State for that department in less than two years. This was the year of the Queen's Jubilee, and invitations had gone out for the first Imperial Conference. The pending conference offered some scope for lobby agitation, and the National Association moved to demonstrate to the new Colonial Secretary and visiting delegates that there was strong continued interest in state colonization. This first took the familiar form of petition and deputation. On February 4, Brabazon, Manning, and other prominent members of the National Association saw the Prime Minister, Lord Salisbury, at the Foreign Office. Their purpose was to secure a place on the conference agenda for state colonization. On the general question of state aid, Salisbury answered that, while he was personally sympathetic, the Association had "to provide the arguments which would carry the measures through the House of Commons."[39] While nothing was promised regarding the Colonial Conference, this seemed to hold out hope that the Conservative government might, perhaps, allow the spokesmen for state colonization to bring their measure before Parliament under the aegis, if not at the initiative, of the Tory party.

This prompted the National Association radically to change its approach to government. Whitehall was abandoned for Westminster, and in the next two years the lobby concentrated on formal organization within the Houses of Parliament. This activity culminated in the appointment of a Select Committee in 1889—the last resort of the emigration lobby.

On February 18, National Association MPs and peers formed a Colonization Committee of their own, with the object "of formulating and bringing to the notice of the Government and of Parliament a well-considered and practicable scheme" of state colonization. In the Lords, this committee was led by Monkswell, Sandhurst, and Longford, and in the Commons by Seton-Karr and H. L. W. Levi-Lawson. Until May, when Brabazon took his seat as Earl of Meath and Baron Chaworth, the group was chaired by William Henry Houldsworth, Tory MP for North-west Manchester and founder of the National Conservative and Unionist Temperance Association. By March, the committee numbered about 160 (25 peers and 135 MPs). Its first task was the preparation of a colonization bill, though subcommittees were formed to pursue the particular interests of many of the members—child emigration, colonization by army and navy pensioners (in which Rosebery and Sandhurst were particularly interested), and so forth.[40]

In April, 1887, the committee sent out a questionnaire of its own to colonial authorities requesting information on settlement land, whether the colony might guarantee interst on capital invested in settlements, and whether "generally" the colony was "in favour of any form of State-aided or State-directed Colonization." No action was promised without colonial cooperation. By May, they had replies from Canada, Western Australia, Victoria, Queensland, and Tasmania. Victoria and Queensland were firmly opposed, but all the rest declared in favour of state colonization "in principle". Only Canada, however, intimated that a colonial guarantee would be possible. All, except South Australia, claimed to have substantial land suitable for such settlements.[41]

The lobby's proposals were presented to government May 1. Ten days later, the committee met a number of colonial representatives gathered in the capital for the Imperial Conference, and received verbal support from Canada, New Zealand, South Africa, and Western Australia. The meeting concluded with dinner at the House of Commons, Osborn Morgan proposing the toast.[42]

These activities were accompanied by a considerable propaganda assault in the form of articles and letters in the press. Col. Sir Francis de Winton read a paper at the Royal Colonial Institute on "Practical Colonization", and the Rochester Diocesan Conference carried a resolution in favour of "an organized system of colonization."[43] The air was heavy with anticipation. The Colonial Office was approached by an agent from the Minister of Agriculture of Manitoba, who believed "it was the intention of the English Government to make some move with respect to state-aided emigration" and wished to inform the department that Manitoba stood ready "to receive any number of good settlers."[44]

In May, Brabazon's father died. Taking his seat in the House of Lords allowed Brabazon (now Earl of Meath) personally to direct the parliamentary affairs of the lobby. A year earlier he had written,

> no reform has ever yet been obtained in this country without agitation .... Agitation, therefore, is necessary. Agitation for the purpose of enlightening the public ... let every town form ... committees ... organize lectures and educate public opinion ....[45]

Meath now moved to renew the public campaign of the National Association, to bring what pressure he could find to bear on MPs and government. A nationwide series of

lectures and public meetings throughout England and
Scotland was begun. Meath appeared before the Church
Congress at Wolverhampton. On October 24, he spoke
from a platform in Edinburgh, the Lord Mayor in the
chair. There was a disappointing meeting at Birmingham,
a city which had never been very strong for the movement—perhaps because Chamberlain was so clearly opposed. But in Manchester, Meath appeared before a large
audience with A. J. Balfour, the Roman Catholic Bishop
of Salford, and the Rev. John Oakley, Dean of Manchester.[46] Meetings continued to be held throughout the next
year outside London, at Manchester, Bradford, Leeds,
York, and elsewhere.

Early in 1887, Salisbury had told the lobby that it could
expect no parliamentary progress until colonization had
been proven "by experiment" to be successful: "any conspicuous and evident success might very possibly induce
Parliament to risk some money in that direction."[47] In
response, the National Association collected information
on past and going colonization activity, much of which
was the work of members of its own executive. A colony
of East Londoners had been established in South Africa
the year before by Lady Ossington and Arnold White,
under the patronage of the Princess Louise (Marchioness
of Lorne), Lord Wolseley, Cardinal Manning, and Ferdi-
nand de Rothschild.[48] The "Wolseley Settlement" did not
prosper, however, largely due to the attraction of the gold
fields, and another was planned by White with the specific
goal of proving to Salisbury the practicability of colonization for the London unemployed. This new model colony
was named for its chief patron, Lord Tennyson. The Poet
Laureate joined the National Association in 1887, and
wrote to White that

> The advantage of sending thither [South Africa] those who cannot
> gain bread and meat for their children in this country, however
> hard they work, is so great that I shall be glad to know that the
> Government are taking active steps to organize a wide system of
> judicious colonization.[49]

As it turned out, however, the Tennyson settlement was
beset by the same problems which plagued the Wolseley
experiment. In autumn of 1887, an unfavourable report
on the Wolseley settlement by a South African official
appeared. This elicited from White a strong defense of his
efforts and, characteristically, an attack on the official
who, he claimed, had purposely misled for political reasons.[50]

7.4   Scot Crofters

In the spring of 1888, the government itself tried an experiment in settling crofters from the West of Scotland in
Canada. Naturally enough, the lobby claimed some responsibility for this, and considered the settlements an
official trial which might presage a general program.[51] In
fact the Scottish Office had been interested in crofter
colonization since the Irish emigration began under the
Arrears of Rent Act. They moved in 1888 not so much to
placate the National Association but to sooth powerful
Unionist landlords who were fearful of other kinds of reform.

In 1884, the Royal Commission of Inquiry into the Condition of the Crofters and Cottars in the Highlands and
Islands of Scotland reported that "a resort to emigration
is unavoidable." It advocated state loans and direct control of emigration by a government agency.[52] Colonies
which were reluctant to take Londoners or the Irish,
rarely objected to Scots—who were considered industri-

ous and who were protestant. In the wake of the Commission's report, New Zealand and Canada offered free grant lands for Scot colonization.[53]

The Liberal government declined, however, to adopt these proposals, and when G.O. Trevelyan brought in their Scot Crofters' Bill of 1886, it included fixity of tenure and fair rent but left out any provision for assisted emigration. This was attacked on the second reading (March 8) by John Ramsay, a Liberal spokesman for the landlords, and Sir Herbert Maxwell, a National Association vice president. Trevelyan defended exclusion of emigration clauses by pointing to the failure of Irish settlements in Canada (which consistently lost settlers to railway jobs and Irish-American communities south of the border): "my experience in coupling Emigration Clauses with a Land Bill is a very unhappy experience indeed." He claimed that government could not begin a system of emigration while agrarian agitation was rife in Scotland for fear of appearing to want to transport the crofters, and thus "make emigration unpopular." In addition, the Irish precedent had been possible because there was a Church surplus fund in Ireland to finance the effort. No such fund existed in Scotland.[54]

However, when the Conservatives came to power in August, negotiations were begun on a number of schemes to supplement the workings of the Land Act by a systematic emigration of crofters. Initiated by Balfour while he was Secretary for Scotland, these efforts stalled for more than a year. Neither Canada nor New Zealand, while professing their enthusiasm at receiving "so desirable a class of settlers as the Scot Crofters", were willing to assume the responsibility of recovering loans.[55] Discussions were begun again with Sir George Stephen and others, and these were continued by Balfour's successor Lord Lothian.[56] In May, 1887, Lothian took the matter up before the Cabinet, and pressed for "an effective and practical scheme of State-aided emigration." There had been crofter violence in Skye and Tiree, and, he claimed, widespread destitution and starvation. Crofters wanted to emigrate, but did not have the means. No amount of land reform could "sensibly improve the state and condition of the Crofter and Cottar population of the Western Highlands" and other congested districts. Though Lothian drew Salisbury's attention to the fact that he himself had given encouragement to the emigrationists on February 5, the matter was shelved.[57]

Renewed negotiations in the autumn with Canadian land companies and the government of British Columbia

S. H. Kerr, ninth Marquis of Lothian, Secretary of State for Scotland, 1886–1892 (Source: *Ill. London News,* Mar. 19, 1887)

proved unfruitful, but in the spring of 1888, Lothian was finally able to get approval for a trial. The terms were probably less favourable than could have been obtained earlier, and the duty of collecting repayments fell to the British government. Ten thousand pounds were made available for grants of £ 120 per family. Settlements were established at Killarney and Saltcoats in southern Manitoba.[58] It is not clear why the government suddenly decided to try the crofter scheme. Scot landowners and Lothian provided the immediate leverage, but it is likely that years of pressure by the National Association also contributed to the Cabinet's decision to try an experiment in state colonization. Certainly the lobby believed that this was the case, and that the Scot program was

Crofter violence at Lewis in the Hebrides, 1888 (Source: *Ill. London News,* Jan. 21, 1888)

another "thin edge of the wedge". In fact, however, many of those, like Joseph Chamberlain, who sympathized with the Scot crofters, were not at all sympathetic with the general objectives of the National Association.

> I am obliged by your invitation to attend the meeting on May 31, and to move a resolution. I am not, however, prepared to commit myself to any general scheme of state colonization. I have taken interest in the special case of the Crofters, but do not wish to complicate their claims by connecting them with any more general proposals.[58a]

7.5 *The Parliamentary Social Reforms Committee*

The Scot crofter program may have appeared somewhat promising, but in general the lobby's vigorous campaign, launched in 1886, had very little to show for its efforts. Already in January of 1887, Manning was writing in despairing tones that "I feel more than ever the hopeless and helpless confusion in which we are drifting."[58b] Frustration at Westminster helps explain a curious episode in January of 1888 which involved, among others, many of the leaders of the National Association. There was an attempt to create a general organization of back-benchers of both parties who were interested in "social reform". It was, in effect, a revolt of sorts against the increasing party and ministerial control that marked late-Victorian politics. Dominating the parliamentary timetable, the political hierarchy was felt, by those with "causes" to promote, to be increasingly insensitive to the wishes of the rank and file.

On January 1, a letter, signed by 16 members of both houses, was circulated at Westminster requesting support for a non-party organization of "private members".

For some time past it has been the opinion of a number of the
Members of both Houses of Parliament that measures for Social
and Philanthropic Legislative Reform have not received that
share of interest within the walls of Parliament which they considered should be accorded them, seeing that in the main such questions are of much more vital importance to the mass of Electors
than many purely political subjects.

One of the chief hindrances to the progress of such measures is
the inroad which of late years has been made upon the time of the
House of Commons, formerly at the disposal of private Members.
The result of this is not so much a want of interest in Social Reforms, as the devotion of undue attention to purely political subjects. Social Reformers and Philanthropists within the walls of
Parliament are mostly freelances, each fighting for his own hand,
sometimes even in opposition to each other, and unless by some
happy coincidence they can enlist the support of one or more of
the powerful political parties, it is seldom they can obtain a hearing, much less a victory.[59]

By May, 130 members of both houses signed, and a meeting, hosted by the Duke of Westminster, was held to organize a Parliamentary Social Reforms Committee. The
organization was duly created, and a subscription begun.
Meath, at Lord Thring's urging, was elected chairman.

Meath's social reform credentials rested on his activity
in the metropolis and on a collection of essays, *Social
Arrows*, which he published in the autumn of 1886.
Praised by Gladstone, this work was much read and re-
viewed. It covered a variety of causes in which Meath had
been involved—open spaces, early closing of shops, and,
of course, state colonization. Emphasis throughout lay on
the evils of overpopulation and urbanization. The book
was for the most part well-reviewed, as an example of an
aristocrat willing to use his position to do his duty to others. One journalist noted that it appeared "the mantle of
the philanthropic Lord Shaftesbury" (who died the year
before) had fallen on Brabazon's shoulders.[60]

When, the following year, Brabazon became the twelfth Earl of Meath and took his place in the House of Lords, he was already in a state of some ambivalency about where his political loyalties lay. His father had broken with Gladstone over land reform and Ireland, but Brabazon had remained at least nominally loyal to the party led by his godmother's husband. When the Liberal Party split over Home Rule in 1886, Brabazon was still unprepared to follow many of his friends into the Liberal Unionist or Tory camp. He was unimpressed with the Tory record in social reform, and perhaps, in any event, was uncomfortable with the imputations of opportunism which might follow his abandonment of the "out" party for the "in" party. His ascendency to the Lords sharpened this dilemma, and for some time he tried to find a comfortable resting place somewhere between and outside of either the two major parties. Late in 1887 he sounded out a number of Right-Liberal and Left-Tory friends and associates with a draft proposal for a "philanthropic party" at the center of the political spectrum. Lord Rosebery replied with sympathy but no encouragement.

> I heartily hate the trite division of parliament between the "Ins" and the "Outs". I do not despair of some loftier organization taking a preeminent & patriotic part. Indeed some symptoms point to a partial dislocation of party ties which would give an opportunity for such an association. But in the meantime [illegible] it is not for me whom a piteous fate has [illegible] in the fray to hamper himself with new ties, however sensible and sympathetic they may appear.[60a]

But if important rising leaders in either of the parties were predictably uninterested, might not a powerful force be created by organizing men habitually on the periphery of parliamentary politics? The major parties were preoccupied with the violent issue of Ireland. Might not an organization of lesser men be able to promise action in certain narrowly defined areas of social amelioration? On such well-chosen ground Tory philanthropists and Liberal reformers would have much in common, and could leave more divisive issues to the major parties. Such centrist arguments carried enough logic to attract a large number of promises of support—especially after the very wealthy Duke of Westminster gave his blessing. This reflects not only the usual frustrations of the back benches, but also some of the anxiety of those Liberal Unionists, like Westminster, who were groping for some way out of the political wilderness. It is also clear that, since many of these men were already members of the National Association, a social reforms party, if not entirely the creation of the emigration lobby, was intended from the beginning to promote that cause. Only two days previous to the organization of the Parliamentary Social Reforms Committee, Meath and his friends had presented a colonization scheme to the Colonial Office.[61] The first official action taken by the Committee, which held meetings twice a month, was to organize support for state colonization. They pledged themselves "to do their utmost to keep a House and maintain a debate on the subject."[62] Thirty-five other concerns, ranging from industrial education, national insurance, factory legislation and prison reform to public parks, regulation of wages, and restriction of foreign immigration, were suggested for future action.

The Parliamentary Social Reforms Committee attracted mildly sympathetic comment in the press. *The Guardian* believed that it would "do something to raise the tone" of English public life, but distrusted movements which tried to stay outside two-party politics. On the one hand there was "the dangerous tendency of temperance, labour, and other special causes" to develop into parties of their own. On the other, broad nonpartisan movements were doomed to impotence:

> Antagonism, in fact, is the essence of party politics. It is the fatal unanimity with which some of Lord Meath's reforms are acknowledged as desirable that deprives them of their value as party weapons, and thus makes it hard to force them on the attention of the country.[63]

After a brave start—membership rapidly climbed to over 200—little more was heard of the Committee. Meath later reflected that the hopes of its organizers were not matched by a high level of commitment among its membership. The 200 dissolved at the approach of a party whip.[64]

Notes on Chapter 7

1. Leaflet submitted to the Colonial Office, February 1886 (C.O. 384/162 [3719]).
2. The *Times,* 16 Feb. 1886, 6 and 8; 17 Feb. 1886, 7.
3. C.O. 384/162 (2722).
4. *Ibid.*
5. *State-directed Colonization Series, No. I,* 102–27.
6. P.P. 1886 (C. 4751), no. 21.
7. C.O. 384/162 (2722); M.H. 19/8 (LGB 21496/86).
8. C.O. 384/162 (3790 and 3795); M.H. 19/8 (LGB 27373/86).
9. M.H. 19/8 (24235A/86).
10. C.O. 384/162 (3752).
11. P.P. 1886 (C. 4751), nos. 27, 29–31, 33–36, 39; C.O. 384/162 (3872).
12. Brabazon to the Governor of Natal, 11 July 1886, in C.O. 384/159 (18923).
13. The Governor of Natal to Lord Brabazon, 17 Sept. 1886, in *Ibid.*
14. As Admiral Edward Field had done when contesting South Sussex in 1885 (*State-directed Colonization Series, No. I,* 147).

Government and the Lobby, 1886–1888   237

14a. Canterbury to Brabazon, Jan. 5, 1887; also see Canterbury to Brabazon, Dec. 22, 1886 (Meath Papers, Autograph Vol. I).
14b. Huxley to Brabazon, April 5, 1886 (Autograph Vol. I).
14c. Derby to Brabazon, May 30, 1886 (Autograph Vol. I); Strangford to Brabazon, Jan. 4, 1887 (Autograph Vol. III).
14d. Wolseley to Brabazon, Jan. 8, 1887 (Autograph Vol. I).
14e. Froude to Brabazon, March 2, 1886, Nov. 16, 1886?, and Dec. 25, 1886? (Autograph Vol. I).
15. Sixty-one names were added to the Association's national council between February and June of 1886.
16. *Hansard*, Vol. 304 (Lords, 2 April 1886), 592.
17. *Ibid.*, 594.
18. Herbert minute, 9 March 1886, C.O. 384/162 (3752).
19. H. H. Phear, *Emigration: A Summary of the Acts that have been passed for assisting emigration from England, Scotland, & Ireland* (London, 1886), 1–10.
20. Herbert advised Granville that it was "inconvenient and unsound in principle for Sec. St. to join the society, however much he approves their goals." (C.O. 384/162 [9025]).
21. *State-directed Colonization Series, No. II*, 107–64.
22. Frederick Young, "Emigration to the Colonies," *Proc. Royal Colonial Institute*, Vol. 17 (1885–6), 368–89.
23. The *Times*, 30 June 1886, 4.
24. *Ibid.*
24a. Simmons to Brabazon, Sep. 8, 1886 (Autograph Vol. I).
24b. *Ibid.*
25. See Brian L. Blakeley, *The Colonial Office, 1868–1892* (Durham, North Carolina; 1972), 93.
26. P. J. Campling, "Nathaniel Cohen and the Beginnings of the Labour Exchange Movement in Great Britain," *Surrey Archeol. Collect.*, 69 (1973).
27. Arnold White, *The Problems of a Great City*, 77.
28. Brabazon at the Colonization Conference, 8 June 1886, quoted in the *State Directed Colonization Series, No. II*, 153.
29. C.O. 384/158 (13921) and C.O. 384/163 (515).
30. C.O. 384/163 (515).
31. The *Times*, 27 Jan. 1886, 10.
32. C.O. to the Treasury, 26 Jan. 1886, in P.P. 1886 (C. 4751), Appendix No. 8.

33. C.O. 384/162 (4409).
34. *Ibid.*
35. C.O. 384/162 (5540).
35a. Granville to Brabazon, April 6, 1886 (Autograph Vol. I).
36. Herbert, in considering the appointment of Burnett of the Engineers, thought they should ascertain first whether "lately in Paris or elsewhere, he has used Socialist or anti-property language," C.O. 384/163 (12717). Also see P.P. 1886 (C. 4751), Appendix Nos. 25–7.
37. C.O. 384/162 (10718).
38. The *Times,* 9 Oct. 1886, 7.
39. *Hansard,* Vol. 310 (Lords, 1 Feb. 1887), 383–4; the *Times,* 5 Feb. 1887, 8 and 9.
40. The Earl of Meath, "State Colonization," *Time,* Vol. 18 (May, 1888), 543–55; Monkswell, "State Colonization," *Fortnightly Review,* Vol. 43 (Jan.–June, 1888), 391. Trouble was caused when a member of the committee, Henry Kimber, submitted his own ill-conceived plan to the Colonial Office. This was sent to the colonies for their opinion, and added to the confusion. The committee notified the C.O. that Kimber's scheme "did great injustice to their views." (C.O. 384/170 [9802]).
41. P.P. 1891. *Report of the Colonization Committee,* Appendix No. 8.
42. The *Times,* 12 May 1887, 6.
43. Manning, "Why are our People unwilling to Emigrate?"; Meath, "State-directed Colonization," *National Review,* Vol. 9 (June, 1887), and "The Decay of Bodily Strength in Towns," *Nineteenth Century,* Vol. 21 (May, 1887); Monkswell, "State Colonization"; de Winton, "Practical Colonization," *Proc. R.C.I.,* Vol. 18 (1886–7); and Anon., "State-directed Colonization," *Westminster Review,* April 1887. C.O. 384/167 (7876).
44. C.O. 384/167 (11095).
45. Brabazon, *"Social Arrows".*
46. Meath, "Memories of the Nineteenth Century," 243; *Birmingham Daily Gazette,* 5 Dec. 1887; the *Manchester Courier,* 16 Dec. 1887.
47. Salisbury to Arnold White, quoted in White, "The Colonization Report," *Contemporary Review,* Vol. 59 (April, 1891), 617.
48. The *Times,* 9 June 1886, 8.

49. Tennyson to Arnold White, March 1887, quoted in White, "The Colonization Report," 617. "Locksley Hall Sixty Years After" (1886) contained a bleak Malthusian passage: "Earth at last a warless world, a single race, a single tongue—/ . . . /Warless? When her tens are thousands, and her thousands millions, then—/ All her harvest all too narrow—who can fancy warless men?"

50. That is, to appease the Cape Dutch who feared being swamped by English settlers (C.O. 384/167 [23185]).

51. P.P. 1890, *Report of the Colonization Committee,* question 3176. Also see J. H. Rankin, "Duty of the State towards Emigration," *J. Royal Soc. Arts,* Vol. 36 (1888).

52. P.P. 1884, *Report of the Crofters and Cottars Commission,* 97, 108.

53. Cab. 37/19/29 (3).

54. *Hansard,* Vol. 303 (Commons, 8 March 1886), 125–218.

55. Cab. 37/19/29 (1–4).

56. *Ibid.,* Nos. 4–12.

57. *Ibid.* and Cab. 37/20/38.

58. C.O. 384/166 (25663); C.O. 384/170 (7021 and 10778). For the fate of the settlements see Johnson, 240–3; and P.P. 1891, *Report of the Colonization Committee,* 48–9.

58a. Chamberlain to Meath, May 7, 1887 (Autograph Vol. III).

58b. Manning to Brabazon, Jan. 17, 1887 (Autograph Vol. I).

59. *The Reporter,* No. 1 (July, 1888). This was the first issue of what was to have been the official organ of the Parliamentary Social Reforms Committee. The letter was signed by the Duke of Westminster, Lords Aberdeen, Meath, Kinnaird, Dorchester, Egerton of Tatton, Mount Temple, De Vesci, and Monkswell, and MPs James Bryce, Sir Edward Birkbeck, Henry Hobhouse, Sir William Houldsworth, Egerton Hubbard, George Dixon, Sydney Gedge, and Samuel Smith.

60. *The Daily Chronicle,* 18 Sept. 1886; *The Literary World,* 1 Oct. 1886; *Saturday Review,* 27 Nov. 1886; *The Philanthropist,* Nov. 1888; the *Glasgow Herald,* 28 Oct. 1886; and *Modern Truth,* 13 Nov. 1886.

60a. Rosebery to Meath, Oct. 27, 1887 (Autograph Vol. I).

61. C.O. 384/170 (9802).

62. *The Reporter,* No. 1.

63. *The Guardian,* 23 May 1888: "Social Legislation".

64. Meath, *Memories of the Nineteenth Century,* 256.

Chapter 8. The Select Committee on Colonization, 1889–1891

The day the lobby's colonization committee submitted its final scheme to the Colonial Office (1 May 1888), James Rankin addressed an audience at the Society of Arts in London in support of the proposals. These were the distillation of the many previous schemes. The Colonial Office dutifully sent them, *in toto,* by circular dispatch to the colonies. The terms aimed at securing as great a measure of colonial support as possible. The familiar distinction between mere emigration and state colonization was emphasized; colonial governments were to assume no share of responsibility for collecting repayments, and their assent would be required at every step from selection to settlement.[1]

There followed mass meetings in support of the plan in London and Manchester, where the National Association was joined by the Chamber of Commerce. There were also the usual petitions and a deputation. Salisbury, who spoke of the "enormous value of the information that you have got together," told the delegation that the chief obstacles that remained were those of convincing the colonies to take part and of persuading the Treasury of the financial soundness of the scheme. He denied that "my sympathy for your enlightened views and your most beneficent efforts has in any degree grown cold."[2] He may have hoped the lobby would find some solace, if not in the empty charade at Whitehall, at least in the Local Government Bill drafted by C. T. Ritchie. This contained clauses which made it easier for local authorities to assist emigration. The new county councils were empowered to borrow to make advances to persons or companies assisting emigration.[3]

In fact, the Bill was not received enthusiastically by the National Association or its parliamentary organization. The lobby was struggling to overcome colonial fears of pauper emigration, and it was naturally concerned that negative reaction to Ritchie's Bill would affect the reactions to their own circular. On August 8, the Colonial Office received a formal remonstrance from Victoria against the emigration clauses, followed by a similar protest from South Australia.[4] By November, only two colonies had signified even moderate approval of the lobby's proposal.[5]

By that time, however, the situation had been radically transformed. The lobby was given the chance finally to break through the seemingly endless cycle of public meetings, draft proposals, and going the rounds at Whitehall. The government announced its decision to appoint a select committee on colonization.

8.1 *Appointment of a Select Committee of the House of Commons*

On November 22, 1888, W. H. Smith, First Lord of the Treasury and leader of the House of Commons, moved for the appointment of a select committee to investigate "various schemes" for crofter emigration, examine the results of on-going colonization experiments, and report on the best means of carrying out such emigration. It was to advance suggestions for the next parliamentary session.[6]

The decision seems to have come as a surprise to the lobby, which was nevertheless delighted; it hurried to get the terms of investigation expanded as far as possible. For the government's part, the Select Committee appears to have been an effort to deflect some of the blame for the troubles that were plaguing the Scot settlements in Canada, rather than an important gesture of support for the emigration lobby.[7] The Colonial Office, for its part, rejoiced that it could send bothersome promoters to give evidence before the committee rather than dealing with them within the department.

The government accommodated those who wanted the committee's terms of reference expanded, and the Select Committee was ordered

> to report generally whether in their opinion it is desirable that further Facilities should be given to promote Emigration; and, if so, upon the Means and the Conditions under which such Emigration can best be carried out, and the Quarters to which it can most advantageously be directed.[8]

It remained, however, for emigrationists to secure a significant representation on the investigation.

As originally constituted in April, 1889, the committee, chaired by Ritchie, was composed of nine Unionists and six Liberals. The National Association got a substantial representation; four of the fifteen were active members, including James Rankin and Seton-Karr who had drawn up the lobby's most recent colonization scheme. One of the Liberals, William Rathbone, though not a member of the National Association, had been a supporter of the National Emigration League in 1870, and subsequently helped to found Manchester's New Zealand settlement.

The proposed membership, however, met opposition in the House of Commons, and the government altered it somewhat in the weeks to come. Liberals and Parnellites were placated by the addition of two Gladstonians and an Irish nationalist, though two more Conservatives were added at the same time. One of the new Liberals, Osborne Morgan, supported the National Association and had, himself, proposed a colonization scheme.[9] Later another Conservative, Ritchie's private secretary G. W. E. Loder, was added, making a committee of 21.[10]

The Select Committee, which met for the first time 4 June 1889, included a number of prominent men: Sir John Gorst, Gerald Balfour (brother of the Chief Secretary for Ireland and nephew of the Prime Minister), and Campbell-Bannerman. Sir George Baden-Powell was a founder of the Imperial Federation League and had been a special commissioner to the West Indies, Bechuanaland, and Malta, while Sir James Fergusson had been Under-Secretary for India and governor of South Australia, New Zealand, and Bombay. He was also a director of the New Zealand Colonists' Aid Corporation founded by Manchester—a fact that was to have significance when the committee reported.

Smith's announcement was followed by a burst of activity from the lobby. In January, 1889, Meath, who had just accepted the presidency of the Church Army and was standing for a place on the first London County Council (which he won February 5), published an essay on Britain's population problem. *A Thousand More Mouths Every Day* combined support for emigration with a radical-sounding attack on land speculators in the colonies.[11] This was followed by a pamphlet from Meath and two anonymous articles calling for a colonization agitation —these appeared in the *Westminister Review.* The lobby demanded, and was granted, publication of a colonization Blue Book containing replies, some of which were favourable, to the latest colonization circular.[12] And the Marquis of Lorne lent his cautious support:

> judiciously applied, a few thousands spent every year may do a great deal to prevent local trouble which might grow into dangerous disorder, productive of quack agrarian legislation.[13]

In May, a persuasively reasoned article appeared in the *National Review* on the means of increasing Australian immigration relative to that of the United States. The author argued that the American lead would continue to grow in proportion to the existing population (people go where the jobs are) if emigration was allowed to take its natural course. "Heroic measures" aimed at increasing the flow to Britain's colonies were necessary to change this pattern, but only for a short period, after which emigration could be left to take its natural course.

> Possessing a perilous surplus population, super-abundant capital, and marvellous colonies, which are the envy of other nations, our statesmen appear to surrender themselves to the deafening influence of party cries, and party strife, while the best and permanent interests of the Empire are allowed to blindly drift in fancied security .... Meanwhile each winter we have piteous appeals, suppressed turbulence, and a superficial tranquility.[14]

8.2 Making a Case

The select committee met for the first time 4 June 1889, but it did not begin to take evidence until June 23. Sitting much longer than Smith intended, it did not in fact submit its final report until 17 March 1891, by which time employment in the United Kingdom had recovered substantially from the crisis of the mid-1880s.

Evidence was taken the first session from a number of government officials, including Herbert, John Burnett (Labour Correspondent at the Board of Trade), and Sir Hugh Owen (Secretary of the Local Government Board). Herbert reported at length on the probable difficulties of getting repayment, but argued that financial considerations should not predominate.

> I think it would be worth while on all grounds for this Government to make an advance even on the distinct understanding that it would not get it all back ... I think it is desirable to promote colonization even although you may make a loss.[15]

Burnett and Owen, on the other hand, were unsympathetic and self-defensive. Burnett, whose union (the Engineers) opposed state emigration, complained that the labour leaders in the National Association were unrepresentative. Owen cited Local Government Board figures demonstrating a decline in pauperism.[16]

But the official who emerged most aggressively opposed to the lobby was the head of the Emigrants' Information Office, Charles Lucas, a suspicious, narrow-minded man, thoroughly imbued with the cold logic of the Charity Organization Society. An opponent of any government meddling with "natural emigration", he had obviously been chosen for his post to ensure that the E.I.O. stayed in its narrowly circumscribed place. Unfortunately for the lobby, Lucas had taken over from the Colonial Office much of the responsibility of reviewing emigration correspondence. When the Metropolitan Labour Association asked the Colonial Office and Local Government Board in November for assisted emigration and public works to relieve unemployment, Lucas minuted that the expediency of state emigration was questionable, the accounts of suffering and depression were exaggerated, and the request was, in any event, somehow connected with the socialist-inspired Dock Strike of that year.[17]

Meanwhile, petitions from the labour organizations connected with the National Association poured into Parliament. From November 1888 to June 1890, 104 were received at the House of Lords, 112 at the House of Commons.[18] In February, 1890, the Amalgamated Association of Cotton Spinners submitted a statement to the committee signed by their entire executive, asking government to "relieve the congested labour-markets, and the chronic distress existing among the unskilled labour" by means of state colonization.[19] The same month, the Manchester and Salford Trades Council sent a similar statement.[20]

For its part, the National Association circularized the Boards of Guardians and new County Councils asking whether they would avail themselves of the emigration clauses in the Local Government Act of 1888, and offering the lobby's scheme as an alternative to emigration on the local rates. Not surprisingly, the overwhelming majority of those who replied (101 of 102) said they would not use their emigration powers. This information was laid before the select committee as an argument for a national scheme.[21]

When the committee sat again in the spring of 1890, Fergusson (Conservative MP for North-east Manchester), took the chair and retained it for the duration of the committee's life. Evidence was taken from the advocates of emigration schemes and from colonial authorities. An effort led by Campbell-Bannerman, with the support of those most unfriendly to state aid, failed to limit this evidence to the machinery of emigration and to exclude testimony on the "need" for emigration.

This testimony was extensive and, of course, conflicting. The large number of schemes made for long, inconclusive sessions which lacked focus. Among those advocating aid for emigration, there was wide disagreement over the type of assistance and who was to be assisted. On the other hand, the strong and detailed testimony of Meath went far to place the scheme advocated by the National Association in the center of attention.[22] While he talked, some attempt was made to influence the proceedings from out of doors. On April 16, a City of London Labour Association Conference carried a resolution urging a government system of colonization and offering to send delgates to testify. A month later a Metropolitan Labour Association did likewise. These bodies were possibly *ad hoc* creations of the National Association, designed to bring pressure to bear on the select committee. On June 9, the Ven. W. D. Sinclair, Archdeacon of London and Canon of St. Paul's, spoke, in his charge to the clergy of his diocese, of the need for the state to aid emigration and colonization.[23]

The committee rose July 31, 1890, and two of its members, George Baden-Powell and Dr. G. B. Clark, left for Canada to investigate at first hand the crofter settlements. Progress in South Africa was reported by Arnold White in the *Contemporary Review.* He believed that some of the unfortunate experiences at the Wolseley settlement could help save the Tennyson settlement, which aimed at a practical demonstration of the feasibility of colonization—though he warned, quoting Bacon, that "you must make account to lose almost twenty years' profit" to put a colony on its feet.[24] White was obviously making the best of disappointment in South Africa. His troubles were echoed by Lord Brassey, who reported that a scheme of his in Canada had failed in its goal of philanthropy at 5 percent.[25] Meanwhile, reports of the crofter settlements were mixed, though the official report of the Royal Commission on Crofters and Cottars glossed over the difficulties and concluded,

> There is every reason to believe, as the result, that colonization on a much larger scale than has hiterto been attempted is practicable, and that it can be carried out in a satisfactory manner, to the advantage of the settlers, and with the certainty of their attaining a position in a few years which will enable them to return the money advanced to them.[26]

When the committee returned for a final session in February, 1891, a limited amount of further evidence was taken, but the Chairman had already prepared a draft report, written largely by himself and William Rathbone.[27] This document denied that the "present condition" of the country called for "any general scheme of State-organized emigration" but it did recommend further use of the powers of local authorities to emigrate, a permanent colonization board in Scotland and extension of the crofter colonization scheme, cooperation with colonies in colonization when initiated by the colony, grants-in-aid for emigration and colonization societies, and an increase in the annual budget for the E.I.O.[28]

The draft report offered the philanthropic emigration societies much—grants-in-aid and an extension of the valuable services of the E.I.O.—but of course disappointed those favouring state-supported colonization. Without much success, they tried to introduce amendments more favourable to the program of the National Association, though they did succeed in fighting off attempts further to dilute the recommendations. Their final effort was a proposed clause which would have recommended some form of colonization board for the United Kingdom,

> so that if in times of distress a necessity for emigration or colonization should arise, the waste and demoralization which had often accompanied schemes adopted in haste and under pressure be obviated.[29]

This too was defeated, though a weaker proposal that such a board might be created when need arose was adopted.

8.3 *Failure and Blame*

The final report of the Select Committee on Colonization was a disappointment to most emigrationists. The positive recommendations the committee did make were so mildly set forth and so obviously lacking in consensus or enthusiasm that government action of any kind appeared unlikely. A copy of the report, before it had been completely amended, was leaked to the *Times* and, on March 18, a nearly complete version appeared, occupying six prominently placed columns.[30]

In the main, the lobby reacted with hopeful resignation, grasping at the straws offered in the recommendations. Meath even claimed in the House of Lords that the committee had shown themselves "distinctly in favour of State colonization", by which he apparently meant that they had approved, in principle at least, a possible recourse in the future to a state program, if the economy seemed to require it. The economic recovery, which dramatically reduced the rate of unemployment while the committee had been sitting, effectively knocked the legs from under the state-colonization argument. Though it left the door open for future action, the report reflected the optimism engendered by the recovery.

Some, however, saw other reasons behind the commit-tee's judgments. The day after publication of the report, Sydney Holland, son of the Colonial Secretary, wrote to Arnold White expressing his extreme irritation at the re-fusal of the committee to take much evidence on South Africa, and in particular on the now prospering settle-ment he and White had helped Lady Ossington establish there. The fact that many of the philanthropists on the committee had special interests of their own in Canadian emigration accounted, he thought, for their bias.

> It is, I suppose, impertinent of me to criticise the Report of a Parliamentary Committee, but . . . I can understand from the com-position of the Committee that their eyes should naturally have been directed towards Canada . . . . I can understand such a bias, but I cannot understand it having led them totally to ignore in their Report any mention of South Africa . . . .[31]

This theme was taken up by White and amplified with intimation of personal gain in a vitriolic article the follow-ing month in the *Contemporary Review.* Speaking for the frustrated lobbyist in general, he attacked the whole sys-tem of select committees and royal commissions which tended "to drug the national conscience with the idea that the thing really is being done which ought to be done, whereas it is only being talked about." The Coloniza-tion Committee followed the example of the Commis-sion on Housing which was the government's response to *The Bitter Cry,* the Sweating Committee, and the Commission on Foreign Immigration. They all "lulled the sense of individual responsibility that alone can end the evils . . . ."[32]

White was smarting from rejection. The committee had refused to hear evidence from him on his return from Africa in February. He was obsessed that his evidence was "pointedly excluded". The report demonstrated, he claimed, a lack "of any serious intellectual effort to grasp the subject matter remitted to the Committee for consideration," and he noted darkly that the one scheme to receive favourable mention, the Fielding Settlement in New Zealand, was established by a corporation which had as its director the chairman of the committee, Sir James Fergusson. Another member (Rathbone), White revealed, also had "pecuniary interest" in this private company.

Turning from the personal interests of the committee members, White pointed his accusing finger at the Foreign Office which, he claimed, had exerted pressure to keep the committee from examining South African problems out of a desire to do nothing to upset Cecil Rhodes. Rhodes owed his political position to the Cape Dutch, and was therefore opposed to a greater imperial presence.

> Mr. Rhodes' power of bending peoples' will to his own purposes savours of hypnotic suggestion . . . he has apparently persuaded [the government] to enter into partnership with him with the view of preventing any competition in the territories he has occupied rather than acquired, and of deterring immigration into a Colony where he reigns rather than rules.[33]

These South African allegations were perhaps somewhat far-fetched, but White's accusation of Fergusson's vested interest was well-founded. The draft report he submitted did in fact single out his company as the only example of an entirely successful colonization. In addition, while ignoring the National Association's call for a program completely directed by the state, he had recommended grants-in-aid to such societies as he himself ran. On the other hand, members of the National Association on the committee did not contest the point at the time. The New Zealand settlement had, after all, been a success. And the fact that White was not allowed to testify in 1891 probably owes more to his already having testified once before than to the interest Fergusson or the Foreign Office may have had in muzzling him.

Though Meath and Argyll in the House of Lords and Rankin and Seton-Karr in the House of Commons continued to speak of the need for action on the limited suggestions of the select committee—with mild encouragement from Knutsford at the Colonial Office and Lothian at the Scottish Office—it soon became obvious that government was not going to move. On July 6, W. H. Smith replied to a query that since the committee had been "unable to recommend any large scheme" the government did not feel justified in trying any further experiment in Scotland or elsewhere.[34]

The National Association apparently did not survive long enough to see the return of bad times in the mid-1890s which might have forced the question back into public attention. Though systematic emigration remained an occasional subject for debate, no significant government action was taken until the creation of the Overseas Settlement Office in 1918 and the free-passage scheme for veterans of the First World War. In the 1890s, much of the enthusiasm for state emigration was directed toward the similar panacea of home labour colonies—already tried on the continent, and recommended by both Charles Booth and William Booth of the Salvation Army.[35]

The National Association exhausted itself in the final campaign before the select committee. After its report appeared, there is no record of further meetings, demonstrations, or deputations. One assumes that financial as well as spiritual resources were drained, and disappointment was too great to allow the lobby to rebound from defeat. The movement had been sustained for eight years on very meagre encouragement from government. It died of starvation, like scores of other causes which came and went with the seasons, and were, like gentlemen's clubs, friendly societies, and evangelical charities, hallmarks of the Victorian world.

Notes on Chapter 8

1. James H. Rankin, "Duty of the State towards Emigration," *Journal of the Royal Society of Arts*, Vol. 36 (1888); C.O. 384/170 (9802).
2. The Times, 12 July 1888, 12.
3. Henry Matthews' Industrial Schools and Reformatories Bill also contained, perhaps in response to pressure from the C.E.S., clauses for the emigration of children.
4. C.O. 384/170 (17975).
5. *Ibid.*, 9802.
6. *Hansard*, Vol. 330 (Commons, 22 Nov. 1888), 1933, 1940–2.
7. The program cost more than intended and a supplementary estimate had to be voted. The settlements were begun late in the year and in the wrong area.
8. P.P. 1891, *Report of the Colonization Committee*, iii.
9. *Ibid.*, 88–9.
10. The Committee when it reported in 1891: Sir James Fergusson (chairman), Sir George Baden-Powell, Gerald Balfour, Henry Campbell-Bannerman, Gavin Brown Clark, Sir John Colomb, Ronald Munro-Ferguson, Henry Hobhouse, G. W. E. Loder, James Maclean, William M'Arthur, Pierce Mahoney, Col. John W. Malcolm, Osborne Morgan, James Rankin, William Rathbone, William Redmond, C. T. Ritchie, Charles E. Schwann, Henry Seton-Karr, and E. R. Wodehouse.
11. Meath, "A Thousand More Mouths Every Day," *Nineteenth Century*, Vol. 25 (Jan., 1889), 57–72.
12. Meath, *State Colonization* (London, 1889); "Colonies and Colonization," *Westminster Review*, Vol. 131 (Feb., 1889), 13–25; "The Future of Emigration," *Ibid.*, 167–76; C.O. 384/175 (5259); and P.P. 1889 (106 and 232). Also see the *Times*, 22 Jan. 1889, 5; 9 Feb. 1889, 5.

13. The Marquis of Lorne, "Suggestions on Local Mortgage-Companies to Assist Emigration," *Nineteenth Century,* Vol. 15 (1889), 610.
14. Stephen Thompson, "The Lessons of Emigration," *National Review,* May, 1889, 376.
15. P.P. 1889, *Report of the Colonization Committee,* question 1088.
16. *Ibid.,* questions 1796, 3012–4. But Owen himself admitted "There is a less liberal administration of outdoor relief."
17. *Ibid.,* 1438, and C.O. 384/174 (22842).
18. P.P. 1890, *Report of the Colonization Committee,* question 3168. The farm labourers apparently did not petition. After Simmons resigned from the leadership of the Kent and Sussex Union in 1887, they fell away from political activities.
19. *Ibid.,* Appendix No. 8, 489.
20. *Ibid.,* question 3172.
21. *Ibid.*
22. *Ibid.,* 3166–316.
23. *Ibid.,* 3168.
24. White, "Recent Experiments in Colonization," *Contemporary Review,* Vol. 58 (Nov., 1890), 655.
25. The *Times,* 23 Jan. 1891, 14.
26. P.P. 1890–1 (C. 6287), 6.
27. The *Times,* 18 March 1891, 3.
28. P.P. 1890–1, *Report of the Colonization Committee,* xix-xxix.
29. *Ibid.,* xxxix.
30. The *Times,* 18 March 1891, 3.
31. Holland to White, 19 March 1891, quoted by White in "The Colonization Report," *Contemporary Review,* Vol. 59 (April, 1891), 612–3.
32. White, "The Colonization Report," 609–10.
33. *Ibid.,* 615.
34. *Hansard,* Vol. 352 (Lords, 24 April 1891), 1302–13; Vol. 353 (Commons, 1 June 1891), 1391; Vol. 354 (Lords, 12 June 1891), 247–75; and Vol. 355 (Commons, 6 July 1891), 438.
35. Charles Booth (ed.), *Life and Labour,* Vol. 1 (1902 edn.), 154ff.; William Booth, *In Darkest England and the Way Out* (London, 1890), Part II, Chapters 2–4. See John Brown, "Charles Booth and Labour Colonies, 1889–1905," *Econom. Hist. Rev.,* Vol. 21 (1968), 349–60.

Chapter 9.   Epilogue

Unemployment is baffling us. The simple fact is that our population is too great for our trade . . . .   Ramsay MacDonald, 1930[1]

"Overpopulation" has provided a simple and en-
duringly persuasive argument to explain the in-
tractable nature of social ills in times of acute
distress and apprehension. The late-Victorian movement
for state emigration fed upon the agricultural and industrial crises of the "great depression" of that period, and it
eventually collapsed in the face of a seeming return to
prosperity. For more than 20 years, a wide variety of
individuals, organizations, and interests exerted pressure
on government with the hope of influencing public policy
toward an emigration solution to distress. In 1869, the task
facing the movement had been to animate a government,
enervated by *laissez faire* doctrine, to interfere in natural
processes. By the 1880s, their task had to some extent
changed. They increasingly had to defend the priority of
emigration from other demands for public action.

The campaign of the National Association was the last
time the emigration lobby in England was able to find
relatively broad popular support for large-scale migration
as a solution to economic distress.[2] It was an attempt to

257

apply an ancient remedy to the problems of a highly ur-
banized industrial society. As such, it is illustrative of the
Victorian quandry over the causes of unemployment.
From time out of mind, where local distress had existed,
migration had seemed an effective remedy. Irish experience at mid-century reaffirmed this opinion. But Victorian England, as is evident today in a country of twice the
number, was not overpopulated. Clearly, economic
growth in the nineteenth century more than kept pace
with population growth—indeed in some sense depended
on it. The economic crises of the second half of the century were sectional, cyclical, and of relatively short duration. They reflect a "dialogue" between changing and
expanding markets and increasing productivity which
could probably have been affected only marginally—and
not always in a predictable direction—by population controls. Political economists had good reason to question the
long-term results of state emigration for the nation as a
whole. But "overpopulation" remained a powerful and
beguiling explanation of economic distress for many who
were concerned to find at least short-term solutions: to
ameliorate pockets of distress, and to better the lives of
those who had to bear the brunt of economic change. In
1885 Sir Henry Main, for example, pointed to the United
States, with its moving frontier, to reinforce this point of
view that

> there has never been a country in which, on the whole, the per-
> sons distanced in the race have suffered so little from their ill-
> success. All this beneficent prosperity is the fruit of recognising the
> principle of population, and the one remedy for its excess in per-
> petual emigration.[3]

Economic analysis based on overpopulation provided
the argument that held the very diverse elements of the

movement together. As a whole, they had little else in common; the confusing variety of proposals for state action reflects the diversity of interests involved. The government was able to placate some of the constituent interests of the movement by yielding on a number of small points, without adopting the central objective.

In assessing the results of two decades of agitation, it may be useful, however, to consider the lobby not solely as a "cause" group pursuing a single objective but as an amalgamation of interests operating much of the time in a "spokesman" capacity, maintaining a constant pressure on officials in a broad area of emigration concerns. Viewed in this way, the lobby was effective in getting government cooperation on a number of levels. Emigration under the Arrears of Rent Act in Ireland and the Scot crofter scheme of 1887–1888 appeased elements of the landed interest. The establishment of the Emigrants' Information Office in 1886 pleased many of the philanthropic emigrationists within the movement, as did renewal of the Local Government Board's sanction of child emigration, the inclusion of child-emigration clauses in Matthew's Industrial Schools and Reformatories Act, and elaboration of local authorities' power to assist in the emigration of paupers in Ritchie's Local Government Act of 1888. But having made these gestures toward the most socially significant interests within the lobby—land and philanthropy—the government moved no farther.

Why was the lobby unable to secure serious consideration of systematic emigration or colonization? In 1887 the *Birmingham Daily Gazette* offered this analysis.

> Promoted by the chiefs of all political parties, the Association has supplied to no one a "cry", and has had its aims recorded on no election banner. Half a dozen bishops, with Cardinal Newman

[sic] and Mr. Spurgeon, are counted amongst its patrons, yet it has not been able materially to influence the charity of the Churches. How is it that an Association, so catholic in its programme as to secure the services of Professor Seeley and the late Earl of Idde-sleigh, Mr. Moreton Frewen and the Earl of Carnarvon, Lady Gordon Cathcart and the Rev. Newman Hall, and of philanthro-pists of every school, has during a whole decade made so small a stir and accomplished so very little? . . . It is not because their hopes are Utopian and impossible of realization. . . . State coloniza-tion, as enunciated by Lord Brabazon on Saturday, is recom-mended simply as a means of curing an unnatural congestion by perfectly natural transference . . . .

Two obvious objections have been raised against the Associa-tion. In the first place the idea of the wholesale exportation of the able-bodied labour of the United Kingdom does not commend itself; and in the second place, farmers and farm labourers are not only (unfortunately) a decreasing quantity, but they form but a proportion of the three million who are in receipt of parish and private relief, and of the other million or two who "just manage to hobble on." . . . The chief trouble is that it would be of little use to assist our own poor to better quarters if the paupers of the Continent are to be allowed to keep our workhouses and slums crowded. . . . All that the Earl of Meath and his coadjutors can do for the present is to hasten the sometimes tedious process known as "educating public opinion."[4]

Failure to persuade either of the two major political parties to adopt their program, the "benevolent neutral-ity" of ministers like Derby, and the "tepid attention" of much of the public suggest a general apathy, reflected in the usually light turnout at Westminster for emigration debate. Indifference, according to one political analyst, is "almost a greater handicap than opposition."[5] Beneath this difficulty in generating interest—the movement only came close to sparking a serious public agitation for a few months in 1870 and 1886—lay widely spread *laissez faire* attitudes and a strong prejudice against the relief of the able-bodied, fears that emigration would create a vacuum to draw pauper immigrants from Europe, and the opposition of some of organized labour. Also working against the lobby's chances was lack of agreement within the movement itself. Consensus on a specific program is vital to most lobbying organizations, and its lack is a chief cause of loss of influence.[6] Philanthropists, labour, and landlords proposed different emigration solutions. This lack of unity, probably an inherent weakness in most "mixed promotional groups", was turned to advantage by the government.

The chief strength of Brabazon's Association, the support given him by a large part of organized labour, was somewhat illusory. The high unemployment which prompted this support was not general. Many industries, especially those producing for domestic consumption, were in fact thriving and not at all amenable to talk of state emigration.[7] Though the National Association legitimately claimed the support of many influential labour leaders, such support was not indicative of a general receptivity among the working class, and trades-union congresses did not adopt emigration resolutions. Further, labour opposition was strongest where it hurt the lobby most, in London. The London Trades Council refused its support, and the Social Democratic Federation actively campaigned against the lobby. This opposition is important in explaining the reluctance of the otherwise favourably inclined Conservative government to take up an emigration program after 1886. The desertion of London labour from the Liberal Party in 1885 was an important factor in the Conservative electoral success after that year.[8] Party managers were naturally reluctant to do anything which might encourage a Liberal revival among working-class electors in London.

Further, that traditional element of strong influence within the Conservative Party which did support with some unanimity the Association's proposals—the landed

gentry—by the 1880s had lost much of the electoral control it once claimed. There was, in any event, no other
party to which the landed interest could turn. The Irish
and Scot experiments, and promises of no drastic land
reform, had to satisfy them.

A chief obstacle to Conservative adoption of an emigration program was the threat which such action posed for
amicable colonial relations. The second Salisbury government carefully pursued an imperial defense arrangement
with the colonies, and was unlikely to endanger those
negotiations.[9] That there was considerable colonial opposition to systematic immigration was demonstrated time
and again. For example, organized labour in New South
Wales reacted to the increased flow of immigrants following the depression of 1878–1879 by organizing a campaign to terminate all government assistance. Labour in
the colony effectively counter-lobbied through trade
councils, workmen's defense associations, and intercolonial trades-union congresses.[10]

The emigrationists were also faced with a number of
entrenched ministerial attitudes, regardless of party,
which militated against expansion of state responsibility.
As W. L. Burn has emphasized, the Achilles' heel of Victorian governmental policy, reflected in so many Treasury
minutes, was a "cheese-paring reluctance to spend public
money without an immediate, tangible return, even
though its spending might save far more money in the
course of time."[11] Also typical was the opposition to cen-
tralisation. Causes before state emigration had perished in
the conflict between local and central authorities. Thus,
the government demonstrated time and again that, while
it was anxious to encourage local guardians to assume a
wider emigration role, it was reluctant to supersede them.
This same reluctance to add to the responsibilities of the

central government is seen in the often expressed fear of public officials that an emigration program would burden them with responsibility for individual success or failure and involve the state in a creditor-debtor relationship with the emigrants. Gladstone was seriously concerned that land reform would lead to a "Creditor state" and impose upon government the uncomfortable task of having to evict tenants.[12]

To many politicians the emigration remedy must have seemed singularly unattractive simply because it removed from the electorate those whom it benefited most. Typically, men like Chamberlain, who built their careers on constituency organization and control, were opposed to the campaign of the National Association. The popular arguments of reform of the House of Lords, inheritance taxation, and land law provided more promising material for the manipulation of the new electorate.

Finally, one must try to view the emigration lobby in the general context of the late-Victorian political system. At some point it is necessary to consider the environment in which any extra-parliamentary movement had to struggle. Clearly, the climate for such causes worsened considerably after mid-century, when the new political structure, implicit in the Reform Act of 1867, began to evolve. Certainly, the difficulty state emigrationists faced in getting politicians to listen to their deputations, to consider their petitions, and to hear their evidence reflects the weaknesses of their argument, organization, and leadership. But also at work to narrow their chances of success were some general trends over which they had little control. Theirs was a steeper climb than similar activists faced a generation earlier. It was in the 1870s and 1880s that

English politics had to adapt to a relatively democratic franchise. The structure of parliamentary politics, in particular the way in which government responded to non-ministerial sources of policy, changed due to the development of stronger party controls and the growth of the Civil Service. This had serious implications for public access to government. The emigration movement of the 1870s and 1880s was an attempt to work through an altered and still-changing system with techniques fashioned a generation earlier.

The victory of the Anti-Corn-Law League gave rise to a number of causes after 1846 which imitated its style of campaign. But the parliamentary executive, after the political chaos of the 1840s and 1850s, was re-established on a firmer footing. It, rather than the private MP, increasingly became the source of legislative innovation. Party programs emerged in the Queen's Address. In some instances, the agitations of the earlier period had resulted in the creation of a bureaucracy which itself took over the formulation of new policy. By the late 1860s, forced resignation due to votes of no-confidence were no longer much of a threat to ministers, while the departments they led were undergoing a creative change in structure and personnel.

No doubt these trends can be exaggerated, but it does seem clear that public opinion generally was turning against "the busy-bodies and crotchet-makers of the House and country"[13] and toward an executive which spoke authoritatively and exercised greater political control. Consequently, many of the extra-parliamentary agitations which marked the "quickening of interest in politics" in the 1860s either identified with one of the major parties or were doomed to growing impotency. At the same time, the parties themselves appear to have become more sensitive to constituency opinion and to co-opt serious constituency causes. The success with which political parties channeled and, by implication, controlled public opinion after the 1860s had mixed consequences for pressure-group action. On the one hand, institutions were being elaborated for the expression of opinion within the parties themselves. On the other, general nonpartisan movements which approached government from the outside, in the style of the movements of the 1840s, were less likely to secure a ministerial ear. This was the world into which the emigration movement was reborn in 1869.

The emigration front of 1869–71 derived largely from the parallel activities of a number of previously established pressure-groups and philanthropic organizations. When the movement came to the fore again a dozen years later, this was still true, though the development of the Canadian West had added a considerable commercial and colonial vested interest. These organizations were characteristic of nineteenth-century society. The Victorian world, in which traditional pre-industrial relationships were disintegrating, was one in which voluntary associations—friendly societies, fraternal orders, clubs, philanthropic societies—became a dominant form of social organization. Such bodies, "maintained by the contributions of the wealthier classes, staffed mostly by unpaid workers, and self-governing,"[14] formed the layered base for many pressure movements.

What kind of response could a pressure group like the National Association have expected from ministers and civil servants in the 1870s and 1880s? What uses could it serve? Nineteenth century government was cautious about recognizing groups claiming to represent in some formal way large sections of the population. Receiving deputations and some consultation about legislation and administration were acts of recognition, and might be interpreted as giving a particular section of the public a "right" to have its wishes consulted in the future. Certainly, grants entailed future obligation and created interest groups which were difficult to suppress. Ministers were also likely to refuse deputations from groups employing extreme tactics and those whose concerns were already being lobbied by an established faction.[15]

It took, as we have seen, a considerable time and effort for the emigration lobby to secure serious attention and recognition from Whitehall. The unstable political situation in the 1880s, frequent change of ministers, refusal of departments to accept the issue as lying within their proper field of responsibility, and, finally, the appointment of the select committee all worked to prevent the lobby from establishing a close working relationship with government.

If, as seems likely, the chance an extra-parliamentary group had of initiating legislation was seriously diminished in the second half of the nineteenth century, nevertheless the increasing complexity of legislation and regulation called for sources of technical and specialist information at Whitehall, and this created a favourable climate for the "consultative" lobbying of special interests. Increasingly, a lobby's chances of establishing a close relationship with government were improved if it could provide information and, in some cases, people to advise and help administer new excursions into regulation and public service. Thus, the emigration movement provided several members of the Emigrants' Information Office committee. The National Association assembled detailed information on colonization schemes, on the use of emigration statutes by Poor-Law authorities, and on unemployment in London. Had a large colonization scheme been initiated, it would quite possibly have been directed, at least in part, by the executive of the National Association.

But while government was increasingly responsive to lobby groups in the actual machinery of administration, there is ample evidence that the ability to initiate such programs was receding beyond the reach of most nonpartisan general agitations. The hearing an extra-parliamentary group received was dependent, of course, on the immediacy of the issue—expressed in manifestations of general public support, in the degree of commitment of the spokesmen, and in the pace of other political events —but party organization and increased parliamentary control enabled government more easily to ignore nonministerial voices. In the long run, the anonymous, professional, "special interest" replaced in the corridors of power the rentier amateur, the clubman philosopher, and the Tory philanthropist.

State emigration was, in a sense, a victim of this process of "modernization". Perhaps, in any event, it was an issue doomed from the beginning. But born into the new world of the tight parliamentary timetable, the three-line whip, and the Closure Act, it carried an extra burden which made success highly unlikely.

The emigration movement, however, is of historical interest, precisely because it failed so completely. It thereby assumes a typicality. For every group that achieved its goals, dozens, perhaps hundreds, failed. State emigration is a characteristic example of the decline of faddism and the waning potency of the social groups which habitually engaged in pressure from without.

Notes on Chapter 9

1. Marquand, 537.
2. The issue of "empire settlement", it is true, re-emerged with some force after the First World War (see Ian M. Drummond, *Imperial Economic Policy 1917–1939* [Toronto, 1974], 43–144) but this was, in spite of a loud press campaign, clearly a thing of the imperialist faction of the Tory party. It lacked working-class support, and was, in any event, less concerned with finding a solution to domestic ills than with imperial unity and defense.
3. Sir Henry Maine, *Popular Government: Four Essays* (New York, 1886), 51.
4. The *Birmingham Daily Gazette,* 5 Dec. 1887.
5. Richard Rose, *Politics in England* (London, 1965), 131.
6. Allen Potter, *Organized Groups in British National Politics* (London, 1961), 112.
7. Charles Wilson, "Economy and Society in Late Victorian Britain," *Econom. Hist. Rev.,* Vol. 18 (1965), 186.
8. Paul Thompson, "Liberals, Radicals and Labour in London 1880–1900," *Past and Present,* No. 27 (1964), 27.
9. Tyler, 121–2.
10. Hayden, 28–35.
11. W. L. Burn, *The Age of Equipoise* (London, 1964), 151.
12. John Morley to Harcourt, 24 Dec. 1886, quoted by Michael Hurst, *Joseph Chamberlain and Liberal Reunion* (Newton Abbot, 1970), 129.
13. Walter Bagehot, *The English Constitution* (London, Dolphin Books), 220.
14. Potter, 38.
15. Potter (p. 204) and others see much of this as characteristic of 20th century politics, but clearly "modernization" in this respect must be pushed back to the germinal period of the generation following the Second Reform Act.

Appendix A

The National Colonial and Emigration League: Officers, Council, and Vice-Presidents, 1870[1]

Officers

> President: the Duke of Manchester
> Secretary: Edward Jenkins
>   (Rev. Horrocks Cocks, after May 19, 1870)
> Chairman of the Committee: Frederick Young
> Treasurer: G. Duddell

Council[2]

Robert Applegarth (E)	A. Houlder (E)
Rev. J. A. Aston	George Howell
William Baglehole	James Jackson
John Bate (E)	Edward Jenkins (E)
Edmund Beales (E)	Blanchard Jerrold
J. Bergtheil	John F. King
George Brooke	F. P. Labilliere (E)
James Bryen	J. H. Lamprey (E)
William Carter	R. Marsden Latham (E)
David Chinery	Alexander McArthur
B. F. Bing Clarke	James Madden
E. Clarke	John Martineau (E)
Rev. Horrocks Cocks (E)	Col. F. C. Maude, C. B., V. C. (E)
W. Hinks Cox	Dr. Milligan
Henry Cridland	Rev. F. J. C. Moran
George Druitt (E)	George Odger
George Duddell	E. L. O'Malley
T. J. Dunning	Rev. G. P. Ottey (E)
Francis Fuller	F. J. Partridge
Robert Flemming	Thomas Plummer
R. H. Gamlen	Capt. Bedford Pim, R.N.

---

[1]From the *Prospectus of the National Colonial and Emigration League,* in the Manchester Papers, Box 20A (not dated; from the context, it was drawn up sometime after April 26, 1870 and before the end of May, 1870).
[2]E signifies member of the Executive Committee.

Appendix A (*continued*)

William Gladstone[3]
J. E. Gorst
Sir George Grey, K.C.B.(E)
D. Guile (E)
H. Hardcastle
Rev. A. Styleman Herring (E)
E. T. Holland

George Potter (E)
Daniel Pratt (E)
Rev. J. G. Rogers
George Shipton (E)
J. R. Taylor
Frederick Young (E)

Vice-Presidents[4]

Rev. Dr. Hugh Allen
Rev. Dr. Bayley
Sir John Bowring, L.L.D., F.R.S. (L)
Edgar A. Bowring, M.P.
Thomas Brassey, Sen.
Henry Brassey, M.P. (L)
Donald Cameron, M.P. (C)
Lord Colchester
Thomas Chambers, Q.C., M.P. (L)
W. T. Charley, D.C.L., M.P. (C)
Col. Andrew Clarke, R. E.
Sir Daniel Cooper, Bt.
Maj. Gen. Sir W. Denison, K.C.B.
R. Dimsdale, M.P. (C)
Lord Dunsany
E.B. Eastwick, M.P., C.B. (C)
J. Elphinstone, M.P. (C)
C. W. W. Fitzwilliam, M.P. (L)
Viscount Garlies, M.P. (C)
Dr. J. H. Gladstone
Edward T. Gourley, M.P. (R)
Lord Claude J. Hamilton, M.P. (C)
Lord George Hamilton, M.P. (C)
J. Steward Hardy, M.P. (C)
J. Holms, M.P. (L)
E. K. Hornby, M.P. (C)

Sir Edward Hulse, Bt.
John Huton, M.P (C)
J. C. Lawrence, Bt., M.P. (L)
Lord William Pitt Lennox
Sir F. Lycett
Arthur Stanhope, Lord Mahon, M.P.
Charles McGarel
William McArthur, M.P. (L)
R. A. Macfie, M.P. (L)
M. H. Marsh
Viscount Milton, M.P. (L)
Rev. George Murphy
Sir Charles Nocholson, Bt.
Col. Pitt Kennedy
Charles Reed, M.P. (L)
Rev. William Rogers
Dr. Richardson, F.R.S.
Lord H. J. M. D. Scott, M.P (C)
Lt. Col. J. F. D. Crichton Stuart, M.P. (L)
R. R. Torrens, M.P. (L)
W. T. M. Torrens, M.P. (L)
Edward Wilson
Charles Waring
G. H. Whalley, M.P. (L)
Sir H. Drummond Wolff, K.C.M.G.

---

[3]Not the Prime Minister.
[4]L indicates Liberal; C, Conservative; R, Radical.

Appendix B

Labour leaders reported as supporting emigration resolutions at the "workmen's conference," 1883[1]

1. J. Ambler, T.U.C. delegate, Hull Trades Council
2. Thomas Ashton, Sec., Oldham Cotton Spinners' Assn.[2]
3. W. Beech, Oldham Trades Council
4. W. A. Coote, T.U.C. delegate, London Compositor's Soc.
5. W. R. Cornell, "of Dulwich"
6. Mr. Dyke, Cab-Drivers' Co-operative Assn.
7. John Fox, Sec., Bristol West of England, and South Wales Providence Soc.[2]
8. Allen Gee, Huddersfield Weavers' and Spinners' Assn.[2](became Gen'l. Sec., Textile Workers Union, 1888)
9. J. Judge, Leeds Trade Council; rep., Leeds branch, National Union of Boot and Shoe Rivetters.
10. J. C. Laird, Pres., Newcastle Trades Council
11. Mr. Luke, Paper Stainers' Assn., London
12. James Mawdsley, Manchester and Salford Trades Council; rep., Manchester Cotton Spinners[2]; member, parliamentary committee, T.U.C.
13. Edward Memmott, Pres., Sheffield Trades Council[2]
14. D. Merrick, Pres., Leicester Trades Council (became Pres., T.U.C., 1878)
15. Mr. Noon, Member, London Trades Council; member, Ladies' Bootmakers' Soc.
16. W. H. Patterson, Financial Sec., Durham Miners' Assn.
17. Mr. Pilcher, Chairman, Kent and Sussex Labourers' Union

---

[1]From the *Times,* Nov. 15, 1883, p. 12. Conference held Oct. 13, 1883, at Maidstone, Kent.
[2]Labour organization sent the individual as an "official representative" to the conference.

Appendix B (*continued*)

18. John Potter, Pres., Maidstone Trades Council
19. William Roberts, Sec., Erith and Belvedere Liberal Assn.
20. W. H. Rowland, Gen. Sec., London Cab Drivers' Assn.
21. Alfred Simmons, Sec., Kent and Sussex Labourers' Union
22. T. Smith, London Trades Council; Gen. Sec., Cab Drivers' Assn.
23. Thomas Strange, Birmingham School Board Inspector
24. Edward Woods, Sec., Friendly Soc. of Ironworkers of England, Ireland, and Wales[2]

Appendix C

National Association Membership, 1886

Officers
    Chairman: Lord Brabazon
    Treasurer: Sir R. N. Fowler, M.P.
    Secretary: Alfred Simmons, Kent and Sussex Labourers' Union

Executive Committee
    H. T. Mackenzie Bell
    Hon. Reginald Capel
    Frederick Cleeve
    W. A. Coote, London Compositors' Soc.
    T. Dyer Edwards
    E. Fulcher,Cromwell Workmen's Club
    R. H. Gamlen
    John Grieg, Justice of the Peace and Sec., Scot. Emigrants' Aid
        Soc.
    Capt. A. Hamilton, Sec. East London Emigration Fund
    E. Hepple Hall
    T. J. Hester, Chairman, United Friendly Socs.
    Rev. Hugh Huleatt, St. John's Bethnal Green
    Rev. F. Fox Lambert, Clothall

Appendix C (*continued*)

Edward R. Meade
Rev. G. P. Merrick, Chaplain, Millbank Prison
Rev. H. W. Robinson, Shoreditch
Lt. Mansfield Smith, R.N.
Thomas Smith, Sec., Amalg. Cab Drivers
Thomas Sutherst, Pres., Shop Assistants' Assn.
H. Seymour Trower
Rev. H. G. Watkins, Sec., East London Colonization Aid Soc.
B. Wishaw
Rev. E. Wyatt-Edgell

Interests Represented	Labour	Clergy	Emigration Socs.
National Association Executive Committee (1886), out of 26	6	6	3
National Emigration League Executive Committee (1870), out of 20	5	3	5

Church of England Bishops[1]
William Walsham How, Suffragan Bishop of Bedford (V)
Henry Goodwin, Bishop of Carlisle (P)
William Boyd Carpenter, Bishop of Ripon (P)
George Howard Wilkinson, Bishop of Truro (P)
Ernest Roland Wilberforce, Bishop of Newcastle (P)
Charles John Ellicott, Bishop of Gloucester and Bristol (P)
William Thomas Thornhill Webber, Bishop of Brisbane (Australia) (V)

Church of England Clergy
R. K. Arbuthnot, Vicar of St. James, Ratcliffe (East London)
R. C. Billing, Rector and Rural Dean, Spitalfields (East London)

---

[1]P indicates Patron; V, Vice-President and, *ex officio*, Exec. Com.; E, Executive Comm.; F, Finance Committee.

Appendix C (*continued*)

Edward Bray, Rector of Shadwell (St. Paul's) (East London)

Septimus Buss, Vicar and Rural Dean at St. Leonard's, Shoreditch (East London)

E. P. Green, Vicar of St. Simon Zelotes, Bethnal Green (East London)

Hugh Huleatt, Vicar of St. John's, Bethnal Green (East London) (E)

W. P. Insley, Rector of Bow (St. Mary Stratford) (East London) (V, F)

J. F. Kitto, Rector of Stepney and Rural Dean; 1886—Vicar of St. Martin's-in-the-Fields (West-central London)

F. F. Lambert, Rector of Clothall (Herts.) (E)

G. P. Merrick, Chaplain at Wormwood Scrubbs Prison; 1886—Chaplain at Millbank Prison (E)

John Oakley, Dean of Manchester (Manchester) (P)

F. D. Perrott, Priest (London)

A. J. Robinson, Rector of Whitechapel (East London)

H. W. Robinson, at St. Leonard's, Shoreditch (East London) (E)

H. G. Watkins, Priest in Wimbledon Park (West London) (E)

E. Wyatt-Edgell, Rector (retired) of North Cray, Kent (E)

Nonconformist Clergy

A. B. Brown, Baptist, East London Tabernacle (East London)

C. Newman Hall, Congregationalist, Christ Church (Lambeth—S. London) (P)

J. Oates, Congr. (?), Reading (Reading)

G. S. Reaney, Congr., Stepney Meeting House (East London)

W. Spensley, Congr., Abney Church (Stoke) (V, F)

C. H. Spurgeon, Baptist, Metropolitan Tabernacle (South-East London) (P)

C. Worboys, Methodist, Central Methodist Free Church (?)

J. Jackson Wray, Methodist (Wes.), Whitfield's Church (Central London)

Appendix D

Geographical Distribution of National Association Membership by County[1]

London (106)	East (4)	North (65)	Midlands (24)
Scotland (10)	Lincoln (1)	Lancs. (36)	Bucks. (1)
Ireland (9)	Essex (3)	Liverpool (4)	Herts. (2)
		Manchester (17)	Salop. (1)
	West (7)	Yorks. (17)	Hunt. (1)
South (45)		Westm. (1)	Leics. (2)
Sussex (5)	Somer. (1)	Cumb. (1)	Staffs. (2)
Kent (32)	Devon. (1)	Durham. (3)	Chesh. (5)
Surrey (1)	Cornw. (1)	Northumb. (7)	Notts. (3)
Hants. (2)	Glos. (2)		Derby. (3)
Wilts. (1)	Here. (1)		Warwick.
Berks. (3)	Wales (1)		(Birm.) (4)
I. of W. (1)			

National Association Members of Parliament, 1886[2]

James W. Barclay (LU), Forfarshire, 1885–?
Ellis Ashmead Bartlett (C), Sheffield, 1880–4; 1885–1902
Thomas Brassey (L), Hastings, 1868–86[3]
Edward North Buxton (L), Walthamstow, 1885–86[3]

---

[1]See Map 1.
[2]See Map 2. The constituencies named were those represented in 1886; the dates apply to the member's entire parliamentary career. L indicates Liberal; C, Conservative; R, Radical; U, Unionist.
[3]Members who sat in the previous Parliament, but were not returned in July of 1886.

Appendix D (*continued*)

William Pleydell-Bouverie, Viscount Folkestone (C), Middlesex, 1874–89

J. C. R. Colomb (C), Tower Hamlets, 1886–92[4]

Octavius Coope (C), Middlesex, 1847–48; 1874–86[3]

George Dixon (RU), Birmingham, 1867–76; 1885–98

Francis Egerton (L), Derbyshire, N-E, 1868–86[3]

John Whittaker Ellis (C), Kingston, 1884–92

Edward Field (C), Sussex, S., 1885–1900

Robert U.-P. Fitzgerald (C), Cambridge, 1885–1906

Robert N. Fowler (C), City of London, 1880–91

Edward T. Gourley (R), Durham, 1868–1900

George B. Gregory (C), Sussex, E., 1868–86[3]

Charles E. Hamilton (C), Southwark, 1886–92[4]

James F. Hutton (C), Manchester, N., 1885–86[3]

Henry Seton-Karr (C), St. Helens, 1885–?

Henry Kimber (C), Wandsworth, 1885–1913

John Boyd-Kinnear (RU), Fife, E., 1885–86[3]

Harry Levy-Lawson (LU), St. Pancras, 1885–92

Stanley Leighton (C), Oswestry, 1876–1901

J. William Lowther (C), Westmorl., N., 1867–92

Herbert E. Maxwell (C), Wigtowns., 1877–1906

Henry Stafford Northcote (C), Exeter, 1880–99

John Henry Puleston (C), Devonport, 1874–92

James H. Rankin (C), Leominster, 1880–85; 1886–1906

Charles T. Ritchie (C), St. George's, 1874–85; 1886–92; 1895–1905

Alexander H. Ross (C), Maidstone, 1880–88

Thomas Salt (C), Stafford, 1869–85; 1886–92

Samuel Smith (L), Flintshire, 1882–85; 1886–1906

Edmund H. Verney (L), Bucks., 1885–86; 1889–91[3]

C. E. Howard Vincent (C), Sheffield, 1885–?

John Wilson (L), Edinburgh U., 1886–?[4]

Samuel Wilson (C), Portsmouth, 1886–92[4]

Newton Wallop, Lord Lymington (LU), Devonshire, N., 1880–91

---

[4]Members who were returned for the first time by the election of 1886.

Map 1   County distribution of the National Council of the National Association in 1886

277

Map 2 Location of constituencies of National Association Members of Parliament in 1886

278

Appendix D (*continued*)

The National Association for Promoting State-directed Colonization: General Membership, 1886

John Abrahams
A. B. S. Acheson, Earl of
  Gosford
R. A. S. Adair, Baron Waveney
E. Adams
Sir. C. B. Adderley, Baron
  Norton
Morley Alderson
J. Ambler
Rev. R. K. Arbuthnot
G. Armitage
William Ashby
Thomas Ashton
W. Baker
Thomas Banks
James W. Barclay
Dr. Thomas John Barnardo
Ellis Ashmead Bartlett
John S. Bath
John Battersby
Mr. Beaumont
W. Beech
Henry Thomas Mackenzie Bell
Rev. Robert Claudius Billing
Mrs. E. L. Blanchard
Charles Bloor
W. Pleydell-Bouverie, Viscount
  Folkestone
William Brabazon, Earl of
  Meath
Reginald, Lord Brabazon

Sir Thomas, Lord Brassey
Rev. Edward Bray
Rev. John Bridger
W. Bright
Sir Richard Brooke
Rev. Archibald Geikie Brown
Rev. Septimus Buss
James Butler
W. Buttress
Edward North Buxton
T. H. Bryant
G. F. W. Byron, Baron Byron
J. T. Campbell
William Cape
Reginald Algernon Capel
D.-W. Carleton, Baron
  Dorchester
C. Carpenter
W. B. Carpenter, Bishop of
  Ripon
Lady Gordon Cathcart
A. T. T. Verney-Cave, Baron
  Braye
F. Chalmers
Alexander Macomb Chance
Robert Miller Christy
Lord Alfred Spencer Churchill
A. Clark
Frederick Cleeve
David Clegg
R. Cocking

Appendix D (*continued*)

A. D. R. W. Cochrane-Baillie,
  Baron Lamington
Sir John Charles Ready Colomb
Octavius Edward Coope
William Alexander Coote
W. R. Cornell
Jessee Coulter
Francis Burdett Money-Coutts
James Cowan
J. D. Cowper
G.-H. Roper-Curzon, Baron
  Teynham
Charles Edward Cumberland
R. N. C. G. Curzon, Baron
  Zouche
W. Davey
R. Davis
W. Archibald E. Delf
Commander Francis Clif-
  ford de Lousada
James Herman De Ricci
George Dixon
D. H. Drummond
A. W. G. Duff, Earl of Fife
Lady Jane Dundas
Mr. Dyke
Rev. Edgell Wyatt-Edgell
T. Dyer Edwards
Admiral Francis Egerton
Wilbraham Egerton, Baron
  Egerton of Tatton
C. J. Ellicott, Bishop of
  Gloucester and Bristol
Sir John Whittaker Ellis
William Ellison
G. E. Evans
Emily Faithful

F. Fenton
F. G. Fewster
Admiral Edward Field
John Fielding
S. Fildes
Sir Robert Uniake-Penrose
  Fitzgerald
E. Fleming
W. Flood
Sir Robert Nicholas Fowler
Francis W. Fox
John Fox
William A. Freston
James Anthony Froude
E. Fulcher
Lt. Gen. William Augustus
  Fyers
R. H. Gamlen
Allen Gee
Thomas Gent
Henry Hucks Gibbs
E. Gibson
J. R. Gill
J. Glyde
Harvey Goodwin, Bishop of
  Carlisle
N. Gorrie
Sir Edward Temperley Gourley
Rev. Edward Peter Green
William Saunders Sebright
  Green
George Burrow Gregory
John Grieg
J. E. Griffin
Simeon Charles Hadley
Rev. Christopher Newman Hall
Edward Hepple-Hall
T. Hallett

Appendix D (*continued*)

Sir Everard Alexander Hambro
Captain Andrew Hamilton
Col. Charles Edward Hamilton
J. Hargreaves
Capt. J. W. Harrel
T. B. Harris
Harold Heneage Finch-Hatton
Admiral Sir John Charles
　Dalrymple-Hay
T. J. Hester
H. Higson
H. N. Hamilton Hoare
Sydney Hoare
Lady F. Hobart
John Hobbs
J. Hocking
Robert Holmshaw
W. W. How, Bishop of Bedford
E. Howarth
Rev. Hugh Hulcatt
James Frederick Hutton
Rev. William Pimblatt Insley
Mr. Jenkins
W. Johncock
Jasper Wilson Johns
D. Johnson
John J. Jones
Samuel Jones
The Hon. Mrs. Ellen Joyce
J. G. Judge
J. Judge
Henry Seton-Karr
G. D. Kelley
Col. Edmund Hegan Kennard
Stephen P. Kennard
George Barton Kent
T. A. Kidd
Henry Kimber

John Boyd-Kinnear
Rev. John Fenwick Kitto
Robert Knight
J. F. Ladd
J. C. Laird
Rev. Frederick Fox Lambert
Beilby Lawley, Baron Wenlock
Sir H. L. W. Levy-Lawson
W. W. Legge, Earl of
　Dartmouth
Stanley Leighton
H. Leppard
James Stanley Little
S. Schofield Lord
Lt. Gen. Robert William Lowry
J. W. Lowther
Mr. Luke
George Macan
Colin Mackenzie
Sir Alexander Malet
Joseph Mallinson
W. Mancur
W. E. Mann
Henry Edward, Cardinal
　Manning
S. H. Marke
George Martin
James Mawdsley
Sir Herbert Eustace Maxwell
Edward R. Meade
Edward Mellor
Edward Memmott
D. Merrick
Rev. George Purnell Merrick
G. Miller
Frederick Mitchell
George Mitchell
Frederick David Mocatta

Appendix D (*continued*)

W. D. Montagu, Duke of
Manchester
H. Moore
H. Mortley
Henry William Newton
Patteson Nickalls
Mr. Noon
John Norris
Henry Stafford Northcote
Rev. John Oakley
Rev. J. Oates
Sir Francis Philip Cunliffe-Owen
Major Flood Page
W. L. Pakenham, Earl of
Longford
George Palmer
E. H. Parry
W. H. Patterson
H. J. Pattison
Rev. Frank Duerdin Perrott
James Philpot
Col. William Pinney
George Pointer
John Potter
Hodgson Pratt
John Henry Puleston
M. Randall
James H. Rankin
Rev. George Sale Reaney
A. de C. Rice, Baron Dynevor
Robert Richardson
Charles Thomas Ritchie
William Roberts
Rev. Arthur J. Robinson
Rev. H. W. Robinson
James Robinson (of the
Spinners)

James Robinson, F.R.H.S.
James Robinson (of West
Hartlepool)
Charles Day Rose
Major Alexander Henry Ross
George William Rusden
Marie Susan Rye
Thomas Salt
Albert Shaw
J. Simmonds
Alfred Simmons
Sir John G. T. Sinclair
Lt. G. Mansfield Smith
Samuel Smith
T. Smith
Walter Smith
George Somes
Rev. William Spensley
Rev. Charles Haddon Spurgeon
J. Stanley
Sydney James Stern
Thomas Strange
Lady Emily Ann, Viscountess
Strangford
Miss S. Strongi'th'arm
William Styring
Thomas Sutherst
Edward J. Swain
Anna Swanwick
S. Thompson
W. Thurston
W. Tippen
James Tootil
H. Seymour Trower
Alexander Turnbull
Prof. John Tyndall
Stuart Uttley
Rev. J. Vaughan

Appendix D (*continued*)

Capt. Edmond Hope Verney
J. R. W. Vessey, Viscount de
Vesci
Sir Charles Edward Howard
Vincent
J. A. Wade
Henry Wagner
Rev. Henry George Watkins
J. W. L. Webb
W. T. T. Webber, Bishop of
Brisbane
Lady Victoria L. Wellesley
William Westgarth
Arnold White
J. Whitworth

E. R. Wilberforce, Bishop of
Newcastle
G. H. Wilkinson, Bishop of
Truro
C. A. Wills
John Wilson
Sir Samuel Wilson
B. Wishaw
Garnet J., Viscount Wolseley
William Wood
Edward Woods
Sam Woods
Rev. Charles Worboys
Rev. James Jackson Wray
Frederick Young

Bibliography

Manuscript Collections

A. Public Record Office, London:

Cabinet Papers (Cab. 37/19–22 [1887–8]).
Colonial Office, Series 384 (Emigration Correspondence, 1883–91).
Ministry of Health, Series 19 (Poor-Law Board Correspondence 1883–91).

B. Private:

Aldenham (Henry Hucks Gibbs) Papers (Guildhall, London):
  Family Letters, First Baron Aldenham.
Argyll Papers (Castle Argyll, Inverary, Scotland):
  Letter books of the Marquis of Lorne, 1878–1883.
  Ninth Duke, Misc., 1877–1913.
  Transcripts of family letters, 1807–1940.
Sir John C. R. Colomb's Papers (National Maritime Museum, Greenwich).
Dilke Papers (British Museum), 1883–5.
Gladstone Papers (British Museum).
Granville Papers (Public Record Office 30/29).
Manchester Papers (County Record Office, Huntingdon, Huntingdonshire): Sixth Duke, letters (1869–86).
Meath Papers (Killruddery Castle, County Wicklow, Ireland):
  Autograph (Letters Received) Volumes I–III.
  Newspaper clippings and miscellaneous papers collected by the Twelfth Earl, 1872–1896.
Charles Haddon Spurgeon's Papers (Spurgeon's College, London).
Archibald Tait (Archbishop of Canterbury, 1868–1882) Papers (Lambeth Palace, London):
    Official letters.
Sir Frederick Young's Speeches and Notices, 1870–1872 (Royal Commonwealth Library).

Official Papers

A. *Hansard's Parliamentary Debates,* Third Series, vols. 195–354.

B. Parliamentary Papers:

1864, XVI, 477. Twenty-fourth General Report of the Emigration Commissioners.

1870, XVII, 111. Thirtieth General Report of the Emigration Commissioners.

1870, XLIX, 595. Circular to Governors of different Colonies.

1875, LII, 105. First Report of the Select Committee of the Parliament of Canada on Immigration and Colonization.

1875, LXIII, 255. Report to the President of the Local Government Board by Andrew Doyle of the Emigration of Pauper Children to Canada. (Also LXXI, 1)

1881, LXV, 39. Report of the Privy Council of Canada on Irish Immigration.

1882, LV, 133. Local Government Board Report on Emigration under the Arrears of Rent (Ireland) Act of 1882.

1883, XXIX, 1. Annual Report of the Local Government Board (Ireland).

1884, XXXII–XXXVI. Report from the Royal Commission on Crofters and Cottars.

1884, XLV, 1. Report from the Royal Commission on Reformatory and Industrial Schools.

1884, LIV, 619. Correspondence on State Emigration to Canada; Mr. Boyd's scheme.

1886, XXI–XXXIII. Reports from the Royal Commission on the Depression of Trade and Industry.

1886, XLV, 525. Correspondence on the Proposed Formation of an Emigrants' Information Office.

1888, LXXII, 1. Correspondence on Colonization Schemes.

1888, LXXX, 293. Memorandum of Arrangements for a Colonization Scheme for Cottars and Crofters, with correspondence.

1889, X, 1. Report from the Select Committee on Colonization.

1889, LV, 27. Correspondence from Colonial Governments in answer to the Memorandum by the Parliamentary Colonization Committee of May, 1888.

1890, XII, 1. Report from the Select Committee on Colonization.
1890, XXVII, 237. First Report of the Crofter Colonization Commissioners.
1890–1, XI, 571. Report from the Select Committee on Colonization.
1890–1, XXVI, 1. Second Report of the Crofter Colonization Commissioners.

Newspapers

The Australian Trading World (London).
The Behive (London).
Bells Weekly Messenger (London).
The Birmingham Daily Gazette (Birmingham).
The Blackburn Times (Blackburn).
The Canadian Gazette (London).
The Capitalist (London).
City Press (London).
Colonies and India [London (home edition of *The European Mail*)].
The Daily Chronicle (London).
The Daily Telegraph (London).
The Echo (London).
The Evening Standard (London).
The Guardian (London).
The Glasgow Herald (Glasgow).
Justice (London).
Land and Water (London).
The Literary World (London?).
The Liverpool Review (Liverpool).
Lloyds Weekly Newspaper (London).
The Manchester Courier (Manchester).
Modern Truth (London).
The Nottingham Daily Express (Nottingham).
The Nottinghamshire Guardian (Nottingham).
The Philanthropist (London).
The Sheffield Weekly Telegraph (Sheffield).
The Times (London).

Other Series

The Annual Register (London).
The Church of England Yearbook (London).
The Constitutional Yearbook (London).
Low's Handbook of London Charities (London).
State-Directed Colonization Series (London).
Dod's Parliamentary Companion (London).

Emigration Tracts

Aspdin, J. *"Our Boys": What shall we do with them?* Manchester, 1890.

Bate, John. *Emigration. Free, Assisted, and Full-Paying Passages.* London, n.d. [1869?].

Boyd, J. H. *State-directed Emigration.* Manchester, 1883.

Buckler, Charles Dugald. *Imperial Colonization a profit to the State.* London, 1886.

Forster, Joseph. *Stay and starve: or, go and thrive.* London, 1884.

Freston, William. *Report of the Conference Presided over by the Duke of Manchester on the Question whether Colonization and Emigration may be made Self-supporting or even Profitable for those investing capital therein.* London, 1869.

Hastings, H. L. *Hints on Emigration.* London, 1882.

Herring, Rev. A. Styleman. *Emigration for Poor Folkes.* London, 1869.

Herring, Rev. A. Styleman. *Letters from Abroad, with Hints to Emigrants.* London, 1871.

Joyce, Ellen. *Emigration.* London, 1884.

Meath, Reginald Brabazon, Twelfth Earl of. *State-directed Colonization: Its Necessity.* London, 1886.

Monkswell, Robert Collier, First Baron. *State Colonization.* London, n.d.

Paton, Walter B. *State-Aided Emigration.* London, 1885.

Ross, Adelaide. *Emigration for Women.* London, 1886.

Rye, Maria Susan. *Emigration of Educated Women.* London, n.d.

Seward, Henry. *Capital-aided Colonization.* London, 1887.

Simmons, Alfred. *Old England and New Zealand.* London, 1879.

Simmons, Alfred. *State Emigration. A Reply to Lord Derby.* London, 1884.

Tait, J. S. *Emigration by Colony for Middle Classes.* Edinburgh, 1885.

Torrens, W. T. M. *Imperial and Colonial Partnership in Emigration.* London, 1881.

Wakefield, Edward Thomas. *State-aided Emigration made Self-Supporting.* London, 1883.

Whellams, C. J. *Emigration a commercial enterprise.* London, 1886.

White, Edward. *Land Reform and Emigration, the Two Remedies for Overcrowding.* London, 1884.

Wilson, Edward. *A Scheme of emigration on a National Scale.* London, 1870.

Young, Frederick. *Transplantation, the true System of Emigration.* London, 1869.

Books and Articles

A. Primary:

Arbuthnot, Rev. R. K. *The Church and the Working Classes: An Address.* London, 1893.

Argyll, John D. S. Campbell, Ninth Duke of (the Marquis of Lorne). "Suggestions on Local Mortgage-Companies to Assist Emigration," *Nineteenth Century,* Vol. 25 (1889).

Arnold, R. Arthur. *The History of the Cotton Famine.* London, 1864.

Bagehot, Walter. *The English Constitution.* London: Dolphin Books, n.d. (2nd ed., 1872).

Bell, H. T. Mackenzie. *Collected Poems.* London, 1901.

Booth, Charles. *Life and Labour of the People.* 3 vols., London, 1891.

Booth, William. *In Darkest England and the Way Out.* London, 1890.

Bourne, Stephen. "Extended Colonization a Necessity to the Mother Country," *Proceedings of the Royal Colonial Institute,* Vol. 11 (1879–80).

Boyd, Charles W., ed. *Mr. Chamberlain's Speeches.* 2 vols., London, 1914.

Brassey, Sir Thomas, First Baron. *Papers and Addresses, Imperial Federation and Colonization from 1880 to 1894.* London, 1895.

Cliffe-Leslie, T. E. "Political Economy and Emigration," *Fraser's Magazine* Vol. 77 (1868).

de Winton, Col. Sir Francis. "Practical Colonization," *Proc. Royal Colonial Institute*, Vol. 18 (1886–87).

Dicey, A. V. *Introduction to the Study of the Law of the Constitution.* London, 1889 (2nd ed.).

Discussions on Colonial Questions. London, 1872.

Fielden, J. C. "State-directed Colonization and Emigration," *Manchester Geographical Society*, Vol. 4 (1888).

Fielding, Gen. W. H. A. "What shall I do with my Son?" *Nineteenth Century*, Vol. 9 (1883).

Fielding, William S. "Imperial Migration and Settlement," *National Review*, Feb., 1887.

Foster, B. W. *The Political Powerlessness of the Medical Profession.* London, 1883.

Froude, James Anthony. "England and her Colonies," *Fraser's Magazine*, Vol. 1, n.s. (1870).

Froude, James Anthony. *Oceana.* New York, 1887.

George, Henry. *Progress and Poverty.* Modern Library, n.d. (orig. pub. 1879).

Gisborne, W. "Colonization," *Proc. Royal Colonial Institute*, Vol. 20 (1888–89).

Greswell, William H. P. "Colonization and the Friendly Societies," *National Review*, July, 1888.

Hamilton, A. "On the Colonies (Part V, Emigration)," *Journal of the Royal Statistical Society*, Vol. 35 (1872).

Hazell, Walter. "Practical Means of Extending Emigration," *Proc. Royal Colonial Institute*, Vol. 19 (1887–88).

Hazell, Walter, and Howard Hodgkin. *The Australasian Colonies: Emigration and Colonization.* London, 1887.

Hetherington, F. W. *Handbook for Emigrants.* London, 1884.

Hyndman, H. M. "Something better than emigration, a reply," *Nineteenth Century*, Vol. 11 (1884).

Hyndman, H. M. *Socialism versus Smithism.* London, n.d. (1883).

"Justitia." *Emigration and the Malthusian Craze.* London, 1886.

Leech, H. J., ed. *The Public Letters of John Bright.* London, 1895 (2nd ed.).

Maine, Sir Henry. *Popular Government: Four Essays.* New York, 1886 (orig. pub. 1885).

Manning, H. E., Cardinal. "Why are our People unwilling to emigrate?" *Murray*, July, 1887.

Martineau, John. "Natural Emigration," *Blackwood's*, July, 1889.

Marx, Karl. *Capital.* 2 vols., Everyman's, 1930.

Mearns, Rev. Andrew. *The Bitter Cry of Outcast London* (ed. by A. S. Wohl). Leicester, 1970 (orig. pub. 1883).

Meath, Reginald Brabazon, Twelfth Earl of. "A Thousand More Mouths Every Day," *Nineteenth Century*, Vol. 25 (1889).

Meath, Reginald Brabazon, Twelfth Earl of. "The Decay of Bodily Strength in Towns," *Nineteenth Century*, Vol. 21 (1887).

Meath, Reginald Brabazon, Twelfth Earl of. *Memories of the Nineteenth Century.* London, 1923.

Meath, Reginald Brabazon, Twelfth Earl of. *The Prevention of the Degradation of Women and Children.* London, 1883.

Meath, Reginald Brabazon, Twelfth Earl of. *Social Aims.* London, 1893.

Meath, Reginald Brabazon, Twelfth Earl of. *Social Arrows.* London, 1887 (2nd ed.).

Meath, Reginald Brabazon, Twelfth Earl of. "State Colonization," *Time*, Vol. 18 (1888).

Meath, Reginald Brabazon, Twelfth Earl of. "State-directed Colonization," *National Review*, May, 1887.

Meath, Reginald Brabazon, Twelfth Earl of. "State-directed Colonization: Its Necessity," *Nineteenth Century*, Vol. 12 (1884).

Meath, Reginald Brabazon, Twelfth Earl of, ed. *The Diaries of Mary, Countess of Meath.* London, n.d.

Meath, Reginald Brabazon, Twelfth Earl of, ed. *Some National and Board School Reforms.* London, 1887.

Monkswell, Robert Collier, First Baron. "State Colonization," *Fortnightly Review*, Vol. 43 (1888).

Morgan, G. Osborne. "On Well-meant Nonsense about Emigration," *Nineteenth Century*, Vol. 21 (1887).

Norton, Sir Charles Adderley, First Baron. *Socialism.* London, 1895.

Panckridge, Rev. William. "The Church and Emigration," *The Clergyman's Magazine*, Vol. 12 (1881).

Paton, W. B. *The Handy Guide to Emigration to the British Colonies.* London (?), 1885.

Phear, H. H. *Emigration: A Summary of the Acts that have been passed for assisting emigration from England, Scotland, & Ireland.* London, 1886.

Potter, George. "Imperial Furtherance of Emigration," *National Review*, Vol. 1 (1883).

Ramm, Agatha, ed. *The Political Correspondence of Mr. Gladstone and Lord Granville, 1868–1876.* 2 vols., 1952.

Ramm, Agatha, ed. *The Political Correspondence of Mr. Gladstone and Lord Granville, 1876–1886.* 2 vols., Oxford, 1962.

Rankin, James H. "Duty of the State towards Emigration," *Journal of the Royal Society of Arts,* Vol. 36 (1888).

Rawson, Sir R. W. *British and Foreign Colonies.* London, 1884.

Seebohm, F. "The Historical Claims of Tenant Right," *Nineteenth Century,* Vol. 9 ((1881).

Seeley, J. R. "Georgian and Victorian Expansion," *Fortnightly Review,* Vol. 42 (1887).

Simmons, Alfred. *Words of Warning to Agricultural Labourers and Other Working-Men.* Cobden Club Leaflet No. 26, 1885.

Smith, Goldwin. "Why send more Irish to America?" *Nineteenth Century,* Vol. 13 (1883).

Smith, Richmond Mayo. *Emigration and Immigration, A Study in Social Science.* London, 1890.

Smith, Samuel. *My Life Work.* London, 1902.

Smith, Samuel. "The Industrial Training of Destitute Children," *Contemporary Review,* Vol. 47 (1885).

Smith, Samuel. "Social Reform," *Nineteenth Century,* Vol. 13 (1883).

Spencer, Herbert. "A Theory of Population," *Westminster Review,* (1852).

Swanwick, Anna. *An Utopian Dream and How it may be Realized.* London, 1888.

Thompson, Stephen. "The Lessons of Emigration," *National Review,* May, 1889.

Todd, Alpheus. *On Parliamentary Government in England.* 2 vols., London, 1887 (2nd ed.; orig. pub. 1867).

Torrens, Robert. *Self-Supporting Colonization. Ireland Saved, without Cost to the Imperial Treasury.* London, 1847.

Torrens, W. T. M. "Imperial and Colonial Partnership in Emigration," *Proc. Royal Colonial Institute,* Vol. 12 (1880–81).

Torrens, W. T. M. "Transplanting to the Colonies," *Nineteenth Century,* Vol. 9 (1881).

Tuke, James H. "Irish Emigration," *Nineteenth Century,* Vol. 9 (1881).

Tuke, James H. "State Aid to Emigrants: A Reply to Lord Brabazon," *Nineteenth Century,* Vol. 17 (1885).

Tuke, James H. "With the Emigrants," *Nineteenth Century*, Vol. 12 (1882).

Wakefield, Edward Gibbon. *A Letter from Sydney and other writings.* (With an Introduction by R. C. Mills.) Everyman's, 1929.

Wakefield, Edward Thomas. *Irish Disaffection, Its Cause and Cure.* London, 1881.

Webb, Beatrice. *My Apprenticeship.* London: Penguin, 1971 (orig. pub. 1926).

White, Arnold. "The Colonization Report," *Contemporary Review*, Vol. 59 (1891).

White, Arnold. "The Importance of a National Scheme of Emigration," *Journal of the Royal Society of Arts*, Vol. 34 (1886).

White, Arnold. *The Problems of a Great City.* London, 1886.

White, Arnold. "Recent Experiments in Colonization," *Contemporary Review*, Vol. 58 (1890).

Young, Frederick. "Emigration to the Colonies," *Proc. Royal Colonial Institute*, Vol. 17 (1885–86).

Anonymous. "Colonies and Colonization," *Westminster Review*, Vol. 131 (1889).

Anonymous. "The Economy of Emigration," *Westminster Review*, Vol. 125 (1886).

Anonymous. "Emigration and its Effects on the British Isles," *North Britain*, Vol. 18 (1852–53).

Anonymous. "The Future of Emigration," *Westminster Review*, Vol. 131 (1889).

Anonymous. "State-directed Colonization," *Westminster Review*, Vol. 127.

Anonymous. "The Training for Emigration among the Middle and Upper Classes," *Bankers' Magazine*, Vol. 43 (1883).

Anonymous. "Work for Willing Hands: a practical plan for state-aided emigration," *Blackwood's*, Feb., 1888.

B. Secondary:

Appleyard, R. T. *British Emigration to Australia.* Toronto, 1964.

Arnold, Rollo. "The 'Revolt of the Field' in Kent 1872–1879," *Past and Present*, No. 64 (1974).

Atlay, J. B. *The Life ... of Ernest Roland Wilberforce.* London, 1912.

Ausubel, Herman. *In Hard Times: Reformers among the late Victorians.* New York, 1960.

Barnardo, S. L., and Sir J. Marchant. *Memoirs of the Late Dr. Barnardo.* London, 1907.

Barrington, Emiline. *Servant of All.* London, 1927.

Best, Geoffrey. *Mid-Victorian Britain, 1851–1865.* London, 1971.

Blakeley, Brian L. *The Colonial Office, 1868–1892.* Durham, N.C.; 1972.

Bloomfield, Paul. *Edward Gibbon Wakefield.* Edinburgh, 1961.

Bodelsen, C. A. *Studies in Mid-Victorian Imperialism.* Copenhagen, 1924.

Boner, Harold. *Hungry Generations: The Nineteenth Century Case against Malthusianism.* New York, 1955.

Brown, John. "Charles Booth and Labour Colonies, 1889–1905," *Economic History Review,* Vol. 21 (1968).

Burns, A. F., and W. C. Mitchell. *Measuring Business Cycles.* New York, 1946.

Calkins, W. N. "A Victorian Free Trade Lobby," *Econom. Hist. Rev.,* Vol. 13 (1960).

Carrier, N. H., and J. R. Jeffrey. *External Migration, A Study of the Available Statistics, 1815–1950.* London, 1953.

Carrothers, W. A. *Emigration from the British Isles.* London, 1929.

Chadwick, Owen. *The Victorian Church.* 2 vols., London, 1966, 1970.

Chilston, E. A. A.-D., Third Viscount. *W. H. Smith.* London, 1965.

Clapham, J. H. *An Economic History of Modern Britain.* 3 vols., Cambridge, 1926–38.

Clark, George S. R. Kitson. *The Making of Victorian England.* Cambridge, Mass., 1962.

Clegg, H. A. C., Alan Fox and A. F. Thompson. *A History of British Trade Unions Since 1889,* Vol. I, Oxford, 1964.

Clements, R. V. "Trade Unions and Emigration, 1840–1880," *Population Studies,* Vol. 9 (1955).

Cowan, Helen I. *British Emigration to British North America.* Toronto, 1961 (orig. pub. 1928).

Curtis, William Redmond. *The Lambeth Conferences, 1867–1920.* New York, 1942.

Lord Davidson of Lambeth. *The Six Lambeth Conferences, 1867–1920.* London, 1920.

Drummond, Ian M. *Imperial Economic Policy 1917–1939.* Toronto, 1974.

Duncan, Ross. "Case Studies in Emigration: Cornwall, Gloucester-shire and New South Wales, 1877–1886," *Econom. Hist. Rev.,* Vol. 16 (1963).

Erickson, Charlotte. "The Encouragement of Emigration by British Trade Unions, 1850–1900," *Population Studies,* Vol. 3 (1949).

Farr, David M. L. *The Colonial Office and Canada, 1867–1887.* Toronto, 1955.

Finer, S. E. *Anonymous Empire: A Study of the Lobby in Great Britain.* London, 1966 (2nd ed.).

Fox, Alan. *A History of the National Union of Boot and Shoe Opera-tives, 1874–1957.* Oxford, 1958.

Garrard, John A. *The English and Immigration, 1880–1910.* Oxford, 1971.

Ghosh, R. N. "Malthus on Emigration and Colonization: Letters to Wilmot-Horton," *Economica,* Feb., 1963.

Ghosh, R. N. "The Colonization Controversy: R. J. Wilmot-Horton and the Classical Economists," *Economica,* Nov., 1964.

Guttsman, W. L. *The British Political Elite.* London, 1963.

Gwynn, Stephen, and Gertrude M. Tuckwell. *Life of the Right Hon. Sir Charles W. Dilke.* 2 vols., London, 1917.

Hamburger, Joseph. *James Mill and the Art of Revolution.* New Haven, 1963.

Hammerston, A. J. "A Study of Middle-Class Female Emigration from Great Britain, 1830–1914." Unpub. Ph.D. thesis, Univ. of British Columbia, 1969.

Hanham, H. J. *The Nineteenth Century Constitution.* Cambridge, 1969.

Harrison, Brian. "Philanthropy and the Victorians," *Victorian Studies,* Vol. 9 (1966).

Harrison, Royden. *Before the Socialists.* London, 1965.

Hayden, Albert A. "New South Wales Immigration Policy, 1856–1900," *Transactions of the American Philosophical Society,* Vol. 61, pt. 5, n.s. (1971).

Henderson, William O. *The Lancashire Cotton Famine, 1861–1865.* Manchester, 1934.

Hitchins, Fred H. *The Colonial Land and Emigration Commission.* Philadelphia, 1931.

Hodder, Edwin. *The Life and Work of the Seventh Earl of Shaftes-bury.* 3 vols., London, 1888.

Horn, Pamela. "Agricultural Trade Unionism and Emigration, 1872–1881," *Historical Journal,* Vol. 15 (1972).

Horn, Pamela. *Joseph Arch (1826–1919). The Farm Workers' Leader.* Kineton, 1971.

How, Frederick Douglas. *Bishop Walsham How, A Memoir.* London, 1889.

Johnson, Stanley C. *A History of Emigration.* London, 1914.

Jones, Peter d'A. *The Christian Socialist Revival, 1877–1914.* Princeton, 1968.

Kittrell, Edward R. "The Development of the Theory of Colonization in English Classical Political Economy," *The Southern Economic Journal,* Vol. 31 (1965).

Logan, Harold A. *The History of Trade-Union Organization in Canada.* Chicago, 1928.

Lynd, Helen. *England in the Eighteen Eighties.* Oxford, 1945.

McCord, Norman. *The Anti-Corn Law League, 1838–1846.* London, 1968 (2nd ed.).

MacDonagh, Oliver. *A Pattern of Government Growth, 1800–60.* London, 1961.

MacDonagh, Oliver. "The Nineteenth Century Revolution in Government," *Hist. Jour.,* Vol. 1 (1958).

Madgwick, R. B. *Immigrants into Eastern Australia, 1788–1851.* London, 1937.

Major, H. D. A. *The Life and Letters of William Boyd Carpenter.* London, 1925.

Mason, A. J. *Memoirs of George Howard Wilkinson.* 2 vols., London, 1909.

Mills, R. C. *The Colonization of Australia (1829–1842): The Wakefield Experiment in Empire Building.* London, 1915.

Mitchell, B. R., and Phyllis Deane. *Abstract of British Historical Statistics.* Cambridge, 1962.

Mocatta, Ada, ed. *F. D. Mocatta, A Brief Memoir, Lectures, and Extracts from Letters.* London, 1911.

O'Connor, Sir James. *History of Ireland, 1798–1924.* New York, 1926.

Page, G. E. A[rchibald] G[eikie] B[rown]. London, 1944.

Parris, Henry. *Constitutional Bureaucracy.* London, 1969.

Patterson, Clara Burdett. *Angela Burdett-Coutts and the Victorians.* London, 1953.

Pike, Godfrey Holden. *The Life and Work of Archibald G. Brown, Preacher and Philanthropist.* London, 1892.

Plant, G. F. *Overseas Settlement. Migration from the United Kingdom to the Dominions.* Oxford, 1951.

Potter, Allen. *Organized Groups in British National Politics.* London, 1961.

Price, Richard N. "The Working Men's Club Movement and Victorian Social Reform Ideology," *Victorian Studies,* Vol. 15, No. 2 (1971).

Rawnsley, H. D. *Harvey Goodwin, Bishop of Carlisle. A Biographical Memoir.* London, 1896.

Reese, Trevor R. *The History of the Royal Commonwealth Society, 1869–1968.* London, 1968.

Reid, T. W. *Life of Forster.* London, 1888.

Roberts, B. C. *The Trades Union Congress, 1868–1921.* London, 1958.

Roberts, Geoffrey K. *Political Parties and Pressure Groups in Britain.* London, 1970.

Rose, Richard. *Politics in England.* London, 1965.

Rostow, W. W. *The British Economy of the Nineteenth Century.* Oxford, 1948.

Saul, S. B. *The Myth of the Great Depression, 1873–1896.* London, 1969.

Scholes, Alex G. *Education for Empire Settlement.* London, 1932.

Shepperson, W. S. *British Emigration to North America.* Minneapolis, 1957.

Soldon, Norbert C. "Laissez Faire on the Defensive: the Story of the Liberty and Property Defense League, 1882–1914." Unpub. Ph.D. thesis, Univ. of Delaware, 1969.

Southgate, Donald. *The Passing of the Whigs.* London, 1962.

Springhall, John Onslow. "Lord Meath, Youth and Empire," *Journal of Contemporary History,* Vol. 5, No. 4 (1970).

Stanley, George F. G. *The Birth of Western Canada.* Toronto, 1961.

Stedman Jones, Gareth. *Outcast London.* Oxford, 1971.

Stewart, J. D. *British Pressure Groups.* Oxford, 1958.

Storm-Clark, Christopher, "The Miners, 1870–1970: A Test Case for Oral History," *Victorian Studies,* Vol. 15, No. 1 (1971).

Sturgis, James L. *John Bright and the Empire.* London, 1969.

[George Kenneth Tate]. *London Trades Council, 1860–1950.* London, 1950.

Thompson, Paul. "Liberals, Radicals and Labour in London 1880–1900," *Past and Present,* No. 27 (1964).

Tyler, J. E. *The Struggle for Imperial Unity (1868–1895).* London, 1938.

Wagner, Donald O. *The Church of England and Social Reform since 1854.* New York, 1930.

Walpole, Spencer. *The Life of Lord John Russell.* London, 1891.

Webb, Sydney and Beatrice. *The History of Trade Unionism.* London, 1926 (rev. ed.).

Wilson, Charles. "Economy and Society in Late Victorian Britain," *Econom. Hist. Rev.,* Vol. 18, ser. 2 (1965).

Winch, Donald. *Classical Political Economy and Colonies.* Cambridge, Mass., 1965.

Wymer, Norman. *Dr. Barnardo.* London, 1962.

Young, G. M. *Portrait of an Age.* Oxford, 1960 (orig. pub. 1936).

INDEX *

*(n = note, e.g. 239n69 means note 69 on page 239)

Brian Harrison on, 148
middle-class, and the
National Association,
131
in the Victorian era,
102–03
Pim, Captain Bedford, R. N.,
48n36
Place, Francis, 199
Political economy, and
emigration, 26, 196–98,
258
Political system, late
Victorian, 232, 263–67
Poor Law, as a precedent for
state emigration, 35, 36
Poor Law Amendment Act
of 1834, 5
Poor law authorities, local
and the Central
Emigration Society,
185
emigration by, 17, 25,
55–57, 181, 185
circularized by the
National Association,
247
of London
National Emigration Aid
Society attempts to
mobilize, 23, 28
request a metropolitan
rating for
emigration
assistance, 28–29
mentioned, 103, 180
see also Poor Law Board;
Local Government
Board
Poor Law Board
and child emigration, 57,
61, 78n15
circulates warning on
emigration, 50n59
National Emigration Aid
Society deputation to,
28
National Emigration
League deputation to,
34
see also Emigration, of
children; Poor law
authorities, local;
Local Government
Board

Poor rates
colonial fears of increase
in, 17
emigration and
colonization to reduce,
27, 29, 89, 98
used to finance
emigration, 5, 22, 35
Poplar
poor law authorities in call
for an emigration tax,
29
unemployed shipbuilders
in assisted by the East
End Emigration Fund,
23
Population
growth of, 46n4
seen as source of wealth,
68
see also Overpopulation:
Birth rate; Birth
control; Malthusianism
Portsmouth, Church
Congress at (1885),
169n14
Potter, George
campaigns in the
provinces, 32, 35, 37
gets emigration on agenda
of 1869 TUC, 21
"Imperial Furtherance of
Emigration", 95
increasingly isolated, 45
leads deputation to
Gladstone, 20
and the London Working
Men's Association, 20
and Lord Emly, 116n36
and the National
Emigration League,
51n62
and the Reform League,
14
state emigration ideas of,
16, 44, 95
revives campaign for state
emigration, 95
and the Workmen's
Emigration League,
20, 175
mentioned, 30, 191
Pratt, Daniel, 51n62
Pratt, Hodgson, 173n97,
174n99, 174n100

Presbyterians, in the
National Association, 143
Pressure groups, 119, 162–63
see also Cause lobby;
Interest lobby
Printing compositors, of
London, 157
Printing trades, weak
influence of, 157–58
Prison reform, 235
Public works
better than emigration, 98
Hyndman on, 191
Pulestan, John H., 117n59,
125

Q

Queensland, government of
asks for British loan in
exchange for taking
immigrants, 39
negative reply to Irish
emigration circular, 72
offers emigration
assistance during
cotton famine, 14, 15
opposed to state
colonization, 225
Quelch, Harry, 189

R

Ramsay, John, 229
biography, 115n25
attacked by socialists as a
land speculator, 92,
111
and J. H. Boyd, 92
and the Central
Emigration Society,
92, 93, 115n25
chairs conference of
managers of children's
homes, 148
chief emigration
spokesman in House
of Commons, 91
on colonization, 241
urges Dilke to restore
child emigration
sanction, 94